READING EPIC

Individual epics have been catered for by many fine scholarly books. But few of these are easily accessible to the student of ancient literature in translation or to the general reader. Such readers usually do not know the languages, nor are they familiar with the major intellectual and historical trends of antiquity. This book addresses their needs. Peter Toohey surveys all of the major Greek and Roman epics: he begins with Homer and concludes with an overview of the development of late ancient epic and of the interface between epic and the novel.

Reading Epic aims to show what these poems might have meant within the likely intellectual constraints of their era. It does not simply retell the stories. In most cases its readings are provided within the format of interpretative paraphrase. The intention is to help new readers with the story and, at the same time, with its ideas.

Peter Toohey's readings provide clear and stimulating introductions to the central Greek and Latin epics – and to the genre as a whole. Students and teachers of classics and of literature in general will find this a valuable overview of ancient epic. They should also find it a suggestive and often provocative starting point.

Peter Toohey is Senior Lecturer in the Department of Classics and Ancient History at the University of Armidale, New South Wales.

READING EPIC

An introduction to the ancient narratives

Peter Toohey

London and New York

First published 1992
by Routledge
11 New Fetter Lane, London EC4P 4EE

Simultaneously published in the USA and Canada
by Routledge
a division of Routledge, Chapman and Hall, Inc.
29 West 35th Street, New York, NY 10001

© 1992 Peter Toohey

Typeset in 10 on 12 point Bembo by
Redwood Press Ltd, Wiltshire
Printed in Great Britain by
Redwood Press Ltd

British Library Cataloguing in Publication Data
Toohey, Peter
Reading Epic: Introduction to the Ancient Narratives
I. Title
883.0109

Library of Congress Cataloging in Publication Data
Toohey, Peter
Reading epic : an introduction to the ancient narratives / Peter Toohey.
p. cm.
Includes bibliographical references.
1. Epic poetry, Classical—History and criticism—Theory, etc.
2. Epic poetry, Classical—History and criticism. 3. Mythology,
Classical, in literature. 4. History, Ancient, in literature.
5. Literature and history—Greece. 6. Literature and history—Rome.
7. Narration (Rhetoric) 8. Rhetoric, Ancient.
PA3022.E6T66 1992
883'.0109—dc20 92–7032

ISBN 0–415–04227–5   ISBN 0–415–04228–3 (pbk)

To Phyl

CONTENTS

CONTENTS

INTRODUCTION

Thirty years ago this book would have been aimed at sixth formers and first year undergraduates. Perhaps it is a good thing that this is no longer possible. *Reading Epic*, instead, has four targets: senior undergraduate students who are reading ancient epic for the first time in classical or modern literature courses; scholarly tyros and graduate students requiring something with which to orientate themselves in the field of ancient epic; and even hard-pressed university teachers (especially those outside the trade) who need a ready guide to authors beyond their normal range. I hope these groups will find some help in my critical overview. But I would hope too that there is something here for the more patient general reader. For these sorts of readers my book is intended as a suggestive and, I hope, provocative starting point. I must stress, however, that this survey could never hope, nor does it try, to make definitive or critically 'truthful' statements. It represents just one attempt at a reading of the body of ancient epic.

The individual discussions may seem crabbed. There is such an amount of ground to be covered in such a short space that I thought it best to compress as much as possible. Quotation, therefore, has been all but excluded. (The few translations are mine.) The discussions of the individual epics presuppose a fair knowledge of the narrative. Where this fails, a text handy with proper line numbers for easy reference should make the course of events clear.

Compression has also meant getting rid of footnotes. The bibliography exists in their place. Citations are keyed into this. The citations are included not always to indicate my source, but as often to provide a starting place for further reading. These references have been weighted towards later epic. It is easy to find books about

Homer. Try finding something on Valerius Flaccus. What about my sources? Space has hindered proper acknowledgement. My apologies to the many authors whom I have pillaged but left unthanked. I must also point out that two very important books, Feeney (1991) and Van Nortwick (1991), have not been taken into account. These arrived, unfortunately, too late for inclusion.

For the beginning reader – the target of this book – I have provided as full an interpretative paraphrase for each of the epics as space allowed. To 'read' these poems in any real way requires some form of full-scale interpretation. In some places, however, paraphrase was unnecessary. There are a number of studies of this kind for Virgil and Ovid. That is not the case for Apollonius or Lucan. Nor, strangely, for Homer: he is the subject of many books – which, despite their scholarly worth, are often hard tack for the inexperienced.

Spelling Greek in English is always a problem. I have, in the main, followed the traditional transliterations favoured in English circles. Because my epics come from both the Greek and Latin languages, the Latinate transliteration minimizes confusion when shifting between cultures. Here is a typical problem. Achilles is what Lattimore calls Achilleus – that is fairly close to the Greek. But Catullus calls him Achilles and so does the original Penguin translator of the *Iliad*. Whom should we follow? Some names resist resolution: Apollonius' Heracles becomes Valerius Flaccus' Hercules. Such confusions may be solved by consulting the index.

A number of people have helped by reading and listening to my discussions. A book of this type would be impossible without their generous assistance. I would like to thank Mr Peter Dale, Mr Charles Martindale and Professor K. F. Quinn. Mr Michael Dyson and Mr Garth Barker tested the argument, checked references, provided many corrections, and offered many suggestions of their own. Some of my material has appeared or been heard elsewhere. Parts of Chapter 4 were read to a friendly audience of students in May 1991 at Melbourne University. My thanks to Dr Chris Mackie for arranging this. Parts of Chapter 6 were read to a seminar on Latin literature held in Armidale in July 1990. A part of Chapter 1 is a reworking of material first published in *Past, Present and Future: Ancient World Studies in Australia* (the 1990 commemorative volume of *Antichthon*). Mr Richard Stoneman, who arranged it all, has been extraordinarily forbearing and encouraging. I would also like to acknowledge the patient assistance given me by Ms Virginia Myers and Ms Heather

McCallum. Last of all comes my family: Phyl, Katy, Matthew, and Paddy. Their patience matches my gratitude. The main debt is last: it is in the dedication.

Peter Toohey
Armidale, Christmas 1991

1

EPIC: THE GENRE, ITS CHARACTERISTICS

WHAT IS EPIC?

For Greece and Rome this is the simplest explanation: it is a long narrative written in hexameters (or a comparable vernacular measure) which concentrates either on the fortunes of a great hero or perhaps a great civilization and the interactions of this hero and his civilization with the gods (Merchant 1971: vii). A little more thought suggests a contrast between the type of epic which was passed from generation to generation by word of mouth ('oral' or 'primary' epic such as Homer's *Odyssey*) and the epic which was composed with a pen ('secondary' or 'written' or 'literate' epic such as Virgil's *Aeneid*). But such distinctions are very crude. Lucan (AD 39–65) wrote an epic poem entitled *The Civil War*. It is long, it is narrative, and it is in hexameters, but it has no hero, no gods, and its regard for 'civilization' is scant. Hesiod (*c.* 700 BC) may have written an epic poem entitled *The Shield of Heracles*. It certainly has a hero, gods, and a narrative, and it is, in its way, about civilization. Yet it is extremely short.

Are there surviving ancient discussions of epic? Koster (1970; compare Thraede 1962) attempts to reconstruct some. The most influential was by Aristotle. Aristotle, in *Poetics* chapters 23 and 24, specifies some of the characteristics which an epic ought to show. Here are some (I am following Halliwell 1986: 257f.; compare Heath 1989: 38–55): it must have a plot structure which is 'dramatically' put together; the plot should present a single action 'with beginning, middle and end'; epic should have a unity that is not merely temporal or sequential, nor produced simply by concentrating on a single hero (compare Heath 1989: 38); an epic plot ought to be 'compact enough to be grasped as a whole unit'; an epic, like tragedy, should contain

1

reversal, recognition, and calamity; and finally an 'epic should conform mostly to the criterion' of what is probable. But such an account, however sensible, does not provide definitions capable of embracing the full range of ancient epic literature. How useful are these edicts when applied to later historical epic, such as that of Silver Latin or late antiquity?

Rome's Quintilian (*c.* AD 30–100) and Manilius (*fl.* AD 14) provide a less subtle, if more generous, classification (compare Plato, *Ion* 531c). Quintilian (*Institutio Oratoria* 10.1.46ff., 10.1.85ff.) includes, alongside mythological epic, didactic and pastoral poetry, and even the miniature epic. Manilius, at the beginning of the second book of his *Astronomica*, is no less open-handed. Quintilian and Manilius provide us with what may be the most useful way to think of ancient epic. Within the culture of classical antiquity there were a variety of elastic, ill-defined, but nonetheless recognizable subspecies or subgenres (on which notion see Fowler 1982) of epic: mythological epic is one; but so too is didactic epic (which can deal with subjects as varied as science, philosophy, religion, and agriculture); another form was the small-scale epic practised by the Alexandrian writers in the third century BC (which could include pastoral); there was even a comic or parodic epic. Some (Hardie 1986: 22ff. and Pöhlmann 1973: 820ff.) have argued that to distinguish didactic, for example, from mythological epic is misleading. In Homer the technical and the didactic are imperceptibly blended with a heroic, mythological narrative.

In the paragraphs to follow I will examine briefly some of the major subgenres. Mythological and historical epic (the focus of this book) will receive the main stress. A brief caution: my discussion 'essentializes' epic subgenres. This makes for simpler apprehension. But it must be borne in mind that, in real life, genres and subgenres are constantly evolving and transforming. My picture, therefore, is over-schematic.

Mythological epic

Sometimes subsumed under the lemma of 'heroic epic', mythological epic represents the classical epic at its finest (Bowra 1952, Chadwick 1912, or Chadwick 1932 are helpful). Homer's *Iliad* and Virgil's *Aeneid* are the canonical examples. A definition of mythological epic might emphasize these qualities: narratives concerning the heroic actions of mythological heroes; a concern with the relation between these heroes and divine powers; length matched with an elevation of style; the use of the hexameter metre; an ostensible glorification of the past – often achieved by repetition of description, by catalogues, and by fixed descriptive formulas. There are, too, shared technical features such as similes, battles, set speeches, invocations of the Muses, councils of the gods and of the leaders, and the description of shields and other artefacts.

Definition is helped by specifying what 'mythology' may have represented for the Greek and the Roman writers. Mythological epic tends to restrict itself to a limited number of story groups (Willcock 1970: xiv–xvii adds local legends). There were four main cycles: the Trojan cycle (dealing with the war at Troy and its aftermath), the Theban cycle (events associated especially with Cadmus, the city's founder, and later with Oedipus and his sons), the stories of the Argonauts (the quest for the fleece and Jason's subsequent life), and the tales of Heracles (his labours against a number of monsters and the effects these had on his private life). The characters belonging to each of these cycles were kept more or less separate, at least in the earlier phases of epic. As the genre developed more interchange seems to have taken place. Most of the epics discussed in this book are based upon one or another of these cycles.

Miniature epic

When one compares Homer, for example, to the epics of other preliterate cultures, it is the sheer length of the *Iliad* or the *Odyssey* which stands out. Heroic epic in other cultures is frequently brief: *Beowulf*, the Old English poem, is a bare 3,000 lines. The Sumerian *Epic of Gilgamesh* is of comparable length. Many writers chose to compose epic on the small scale. The pseudo-Hesiodic *Shield of Heracles* is a mere 480 lines. There are many examples from late antiquity (discussed in Chapter 11). In the third century before Christ there developed a new style of epic poem one of whose hallmarks was brevity. The representative poem of this subgenre, Callimachus' *Hecale* (translation: Trypanis *et al.* 1975), seems to have been between 500 and 2,000 lines long. This style of epic has sometimes been termed the 'epyllion' ('little epic') or 'miniature epic' (further see Chapter 6). Length was not the sole distinguishing characteristic of the 'epyllion'. There are other important characteristics. There must be a digression (Crump 1931: 23) within the small-scale epic. And love normally has a privileged place.

3

History and the 'chronicle' epic

Epic poetry was also written about real history (for a discussion, see Ziegler 1934). There seem to have been two types of historical epic, a 'chronicle' epic (often termed 'annalistic' – this subgenre purports to offer a year-by-year narrative) and a simpler form perhaps best termed the 'commentary' epic. The chronicle epic had a long life. It is characterized by a large time frame (events usually take place over several generations) and by a concentration on the fortunes of a single city or region rather than on an individual hero. Such epics also describe 'heroes' (they are usually generals) and battles, but these heroes and battles have a reasonable claim to historical veracity. The *Annales* of the Calabrian poet, Quintus Ennius (239–169 BC), must have been as representative as any other (discussed in Chapter 5). Ennius' poem focuses on the second Punic war (218–201 BC), but manages at the same time to present highlights of the events between 1184/3 and 171 BC (Aeneas to the Istrian War). Not many such epics survived antiquity.

Mythological and chronicle epic have many shared characteristics. Both contain narratives concerning heroic actions and heroes (mythical heroes in one, real-life heroes in the other), and the relation between these heroes and the gods. Chronicle epics, like the mythological variety, are usually long, of elevated style, and have as their metre the hexameter; they may also contain such common epic features as similes, battles, set speeches, invocations of the Muses, councils of the gods and of the leaders, and catalogues.

History and the 'commentary' epic

Horace, at *Satires* 2.5.41, parodies an epic written by his contemporary, Furius Bibaculus. Bibaculus composed a poem about Caesar's campaigns in Gaul (58–50 BC). Such epic, limited to a short time-span, is not a chronicle (or an annalistic) epic, although, like its chronicle cousin, it concentrates on wars and generals. Lucan's poem *The Civil War* is an instance of this sort of epic. The time frame in Lucan is limited – ten books embrace only a two-year period (see Chapter 9). This is also the case with the historical epics of Corippus (*c.* AD 550) and Claudian (*c.* AD 400) (see Chapter 11). The commentary epic, while displaying most of the traits of mythological epic, seems to have been more partisan in its sympathies. Corippus' enthusiasm for Johannes, Claudian's for Stilicho, are balanced by Lucan's hatred for Caesar.

Didactic epic

Large-scale mythological epic, annalistic epic, and historical epic share marked similarities. These three subgenres might fairly be termed 'heroic' epic. There are, however, many examples of non-heroic epic: the ironic epyllion is an obvious example. But there is also the didactic or 'teaching' epic (surveyed by Cox 1969 and Pöhlmann 1973). It exists in bewildering array. There was scientific epic (so Lucretius, *c.* 94–55 BC, or Manilius, *c.* AD 14), the philosophical epic (so Empedocles *c.* 493–433 BC or Hesiod), the technical epic based on a variety of agricultural themes (such as Hesiod's *Works and Days*, Virgil's *Georgics*, or even Oppian's *Halieutica*, a second/third-century AD poem on fishing). Much religious writing ought be considered as part of the epic genre: Hesiod's *Theogony* is one example, the *Orphic Argonautica* (written during the second or third century of our era) is another. Thalmann (1984), by stressing the generic affinities between the various types of hexameter poetry written during the archaic Greek period (the eighth to the sixth centuries BC), indicates that it is misleading to distinguish too firmly between the didactic poetry of Hesiod and, for example, the heroic epic of Homer.

Comic epic

Aristotle (*Poetics*, chapter 4) thought that Homer could compose comic poetry:

> Just as Homer excelled in the serious style . . . so also did he first demonstrate the character of comedy, dramatizing not invective, but the ridiculous. For the *Margites* has the same relationship to comedies as the *Iliad* and *Odyssey* to tragedies.

The *Margites* was a tale of an individual, Margites, who was so out of kilter with real life that not only was he unsure of his parentage, but he also had no idea of what to do with his bride on the marriage night (Langerbeck 1958). Although Aristotle does not state that the *Margites* was an epic (its metre was a mixture of hexameter and iambs), it is difficult to imagine that he could have described a creation of Homer's in any other way (compare Newman 1986: 415). There were other comic or parodic poems associated with the name of Homer (comic passages of course occur within the *Iliad* and the *Odyssey*). There are the *The Battle of the Mice and the Frogs*, the *Cercopes*, and the *Epicichlides*. Callimachus, the leading poetic figure of the third century BC, seems to have been attracted to the comic aspect of Homeric epic (Newman 1986: 374). He is on record as having admired the *Margites*. The comic strain associated with Homer's name may have provided the inspiration for the ironic, often parodic, and often comic posture in his *Hymns*. Not enough survives of Callimachus' epyllion, the *Hecale*, to allow us to read it with any confidence. Yet its irony is clear. Ovid also, in his Callimachean epic, the *Metamorphoses*, is deliberately comic. And Statius, perhaps aping Ovid (Fantham 1979), produced a wry epic in his *Achilleid*. Comic epic has a long history (in general, see Schmidt 1953).

WHERE DID EPIC COME FROM?

Speculation concerning the origins of the Homeric epic (thus the body of classical epic) is not strictly necessary for a book which concentrates on reading epic. The topic is, however, of considerable interest. It can cast light on the thematic and descriptive strata onto which Homer and his successors built their epics.

The Greek oral epic may go back to Mycenaean times (which Greek civilization flourished in the Aegean during the period *c.* 1600–1100 BC). West (1988) maintains, although not all scholars would agree with him, that it may be traced perhaps into the fifteenth century BC. And even before that there is an ancient tradition of praise poetry – perhaps epic – rooted in an original Indo-European genre of praise poetry. This Indo-European influence was derived primarily from the arrival in Greece of the first Greek speakers, perhaps *c.* 2000 BC.

Evidence of the 'pre-Greek' origins of epic may be suggested by some Homeric motifs appearing in other Indo-European epic poetry. One especially important Homeric motif, which seems to belong to the Indo-European tradition, is that of *kleos aphthiton*, 'everlasting glory' – the fame beyond even death that accrues to a hero because of his heroic feats (West 1988: 152–6, but denied by Chadwick 1990). But such 'pre-Greek' Indo-European motifs may coexist with traces of early Mycenaean culture. One piece of archaeological evidence is Ajax' remarkable tower shield. This type of shield seems to have been obsolete as early as the fourteenth century BC (Page 1959: 232–5). Its fossilization in Homer may suggest an epic tradition dating back at least to the fourteenth century. But beyond these simple points little more can be deduced.

What happens next? The late Mycenaean world also provides influences on Homeric epic. Most obviously there is the destruction of Troy itself – an event which may have taken place *c.* 1200 BC. There may also be indications of other defunct epic cycles from the same period, most notably the Argonautic cycle. West (1988) takes the reconstruction one controversial step forward. He argues of the *Iliad* that, because of its preponderance of key Thessalian characters (Thessaly is that region of modern Greece approximately opposite Albania), it must originally have been a Thessalian (sometimes termed Aeolian) creation (West 1988: 162). That the Homeric epic ever underwent such an 'Aeolic phase', however, is vigorously disputed (Horrocks 1987).

Our Homer uses the Ionic dialect, a version of the Greek language which is associated especially with the littoral of Asia Minor. That is the sticking point. How did a mainland poetry cycle travel across the Aegean? Many believe that these Mycenaean stories were transported to Ionia directly from southern Greece (and in Ionia were confronted with a variety of Near Eastern influences). West (1988) will have none of this. He believes that our Ionian version was built upon this Thessalian poem which had been transported from the mainland through the Aeolian islands. The Ionian dialect of the Homeric epics is more to be associated with the western side of the Aegean, in particular with the island Euboea (whence the Achaean fleet set out for Troy). This may have been, in the Greek Dark Ages, the channel for the original Thessalian epic. It may be that in this period, rather than in the Mycenaean, the influence of Near Eastern poetry made itself felt on the Greek epic tradition.

Whatever the origins, there is a swelling tide of opinion which associates the world of these oral poems – even their anthropology – neither with a 'pre-Greek' Indo-European culture nor with a Mycenaean palace culture, but with the more bleak period known as the Greek Dark Ages. Despite the reservations of scholars such as Kirk (1965: 82ff.) it may have been during this period that the poems gained their peculiar sociological ethos. A brief discussion of the Dark Age world may be found in the next chapter.

A FEW EPIC THEMES

Origins may be in doubt. But it is hardly controversial to state that heroism and the hero are at the very heart of mythological and historical epic. Praise of the glory of heroes (*klea andrōn*) is perhaps the basis of the concept of heroism. In Homer we could cite such passages as *Iliad* 9.189 and 524, or *Odyssey* 8.73 (compare Virgil's phrase, *Aeneid* 1.1, *arma virum* which could be mistranslated as 'the warlike deeds of men'). But there is also late evidence. Corippus' historical epic on the exploits of the Byzantine general John Troglitha is a fine example of the eulogy of a hero. So too is Virgil's *Aeneid*: behind Aeneas there lurks the presence of Augustus. Eulogy of the hero, in an instance such as the *Aeneid*, may also imply a eulogy of the civilization. Many epics take a firm stand on the worth of the civilizing process.

Heroes had parents. Their relationship with their fathers (the epic is a patriarchal world) is continuously stressed (I suppose that the *kleos aphthiton* of the hero will also accrue to his father). For example, Achilles regularly alludes to his father Peleus. In the climactic scene in book 24 with old Priam, Achilles meets a surrogate father. In Catullus' miniature epic (poem 64) one sign of the degeneration of the era is that fathers murder sons. In the *Aeneid* Aeneas literally carries his father, Anchises, from their burning city. The death of another man's son, Pallas, provides the impulse for the troubling final scene of the poem.

Religion matters in epic poetry. Achilles has no shame before his gods: contemplate his actions in the River Scamander (it is as if the gods were like fathers). The *Odyssey* begins with Zeus outlining a metaphorical moral code for young Telemachus. The events of the *Aeneid* represent the working out of the worldplan of Jupiter. Perhaps it is the theme of hybris (presuming for oneself the prerogatives of the gods) which acts as the most frequent register for the attitude of the divine. As I will attempt to demonstrate in the next section, the hero is disposed to over-confidence. Frequently he transgresses by presuming himself almost a god.

Nostalgia and glorification of bygone eras (they must be at least quasi-historical) are in the very marrow of the strategy of epic. Nostalgia accounts, in many ways, for the appeal of the poems (the world of Odysseus or of Jason or of Aeneas seems somehow more important and more desirable than ours; issues – and the *klea andrōn* – in that heroic age were more clear-cut). The implied audience of epic, at least in the poems to be discussed here, lives much later than the events narrated in the poems. Some poets (Virgil or Valerius Flaccus) make considerable play with the theme of 'then and now'. For these poets the present is seen as a sort of a continuation or even fulfilment of the past. Glorification of the past, however, need not be uncritical. A poem such as the *Aeneid* subverts the very world it extols. This is, in a different way, true for the *Iliad*. The implicit critique of the warrior code entails a critique of nostalgic glorification of a bygone era.

WHAT WAS AN EPIC HERO?

Most of the epics which we will look at turn on the theme of heroism. They all have an implicit notion of heroes and heroism. Why did an epic hero fight? Homer provides us with one answer when Sarpedon meets Glaucus at *Iliad* 12.310–28. Sarpedon explains his motives for fighting as, first, a desire to validate the esteem in which he and Glaucus are held by their Lycian people (12.310–21) and, second, a craving to gain for himself some form of glory which will outlive him (12.322–8). That such an attitude did not always prevail amongst his Iliadic companions is apparent. Anger, a desire for vengeance, a vaulting ambition for gain drive heroes such as Agamemnon or Achilles to fight just as much as Sarpedon's motives.

The compulsion to fight has been termed the 'heroic impulse' (Quinn 1968: 1ff.). The 'heroic impulse' is an ambiguous affair. The motivations of Sarpedon are shown to be, if not productive, at least socially sanctioned. But when Achilles sets brutally to work in the River Scamander (*Iliad* 21) something has gone terribly wrong. Sarpedon and Achilles stand at two ends of a spectrum. The one character appears, within his violent world, as a possessor of a sense of shame (*aidōs*) and wisdom, the other as an overreaching, destructive scourge. The varieties and the ambiguities of the 'heroic impulse' are central for our estimation of epic heroes and epics themselves (compare Feeney 1986a).

If all heroes were like Sarpedon the epic world would have been a far more civilized place. They were not. Perhaps it is just as well, for it is their heroic barbarities which often compel the narrative interest. The misuse of the heroic impulse is a persistent, even a generic theme of epic. It is possible, however, to be a little more precise about the ways in which epic writers seem to have portrayed the ambiguities and misuse of the heroic impulse.

An epic hero is normally of superior social station, often a king or leader in his own right. He is usually tall, handsome, and muscular. He must be preeminent, or nearly so, in athletic and fighting skills. This latter ability implies not just physical skill, but also the courage to utilize it. The epic hero is sometimes outstanding in intelligence. Yet there seems to be more to the heroic character than is conveyed by such simple prescriptions. To display his heroic abilities the epic hero needs some form of a crisis or war or quest. The nature of this crisis and the hero's response are at the heart of the matter.

The hero's response to crisis may best be illustrated within the Sumerian/Akkadian poem, *The Epic of Gilgamesh* (dating, in its earliest version, from the beginning of the second millennium BC). The poem begins with its hero, Gilgamesh, alienated from his city because of his arrogance. Here we have a hero who, to put it bluntly, has too little work of a heroic nature to do. He passes time ravishing the daughters and wives of his subject city, Uruk. Enkidu, a feral creature, saves him. The two set off in pursuit of warrior's glory, a glory which will outlive their lives (*kleos aphthiton*). The heroic impulse drives Gilgamesh to fight the monster of the cedar forest, to kill a heaven-sent boar, and to log the cedar forest. But his selfish pursuit of glory alienates the gods. They cause the death of Gilgamesh's most loved friend, Enkidu. After a long period of grieving and fruitless wandering in the pursuit of literal immortality (even to the land of the dead itself) Gilgamesh gains some sort of a comprehension of his own nature and of his own mortality. He returns to Uruk and becomes, in some versions at any rate, a reformed ruler.

One very simple reading of *Gilgamesh* goes like this. At first the hero is at odds with his community. Personal tragedy, brought on by a lack of respect for the gods and his companions, and subsequently accompanied by long wandering, allows him to gain a deeper understanding of his own nature. Having become the possessor of such qualities as loyalty, patience, endurance, empathy, and a proper sense of shame before his community and his gods, the hero returns to his people where he occupies his rightful place. The process depicted in the Gilgamesh story can be read as one of personal 'moral' growth.

Gilgamesh allows us to make more precise the tentative definition of an epic hero and through this an understanding of the inherent ambiguity of the heroic impulse. An epic hero will indeed be of superior social station and physique, he will be preeminent in fighting, courage, and, maybe, even in intelligence. But, perhaps as a result of a quest, this hero will undergo some form of moral maturation. After being initially at odds with his human and divine community (misusing the heroic impulse) he will develop a deeper understanding of his duties towards both groups.

What an epic does with the heroic impulse is what makes it interesting. Most epics treat the theme critically. There is a pattern by which the theme is outlined. I believe that it is part of the epic 'genre'. The pattern, as I have argued, may be detected in *The Epic of Gilgamesh*. I will argue, in later chapters, that the pattern may be detected in other epics (compare Toohey 1990b). It is of especial importance in Homer's *Iliad* and in Virgil's *Aeneid*.

THE STYLE OF ORAL EPIC: MILMAN PARRY

Two broad categories of ancient epic are the 'oral' or 'primary' epic, and that composed with a pen, termed 'secondary' or 'literary' or 'written' epic. In the next few pages I would like to look at some of the more prominent aspects of the style of the oral and the written epic. This will mean, at first, concentrating on Homer's oral epics. There are two reasons for this. First, the constraints placed upon a poet by oral composition are, to our 'literate' way of thinking, unusual. They need considerable clarification. Second, epic after Homer is in constant dialogue – technically and thematically – with the *Iliad* and the *Odyssey*.

Words, phrases, whole lines and even whole passages are frequently repeated in the *Odyssey* and the *Iliad*. Why Homer should have composed in this way was explained in the 1920s and 1930s by the young American scholar Milman Parry (1902–35). Research on the text of Homer and field studies of the oral poetry of Yugoslavia convinced Parry of the traditional oral and formulaic style of the Homeric epics. In his work on Homer Parry had noticed that certain words, phrases, and lines recur. The simplest instance is the repetition of a whole line. For example, this line (*Iliad* 1.130) appears again at *Iliad* 1.285 and elsewhere: 'in answer to him spoke lord Agamemnon'. In fact 'one in eight of all the verses in the *Iliad* recur at least once elsewhere in the poem' (Silk 1987: 17). Parry paid close attention to the repetition of noun and adjective combinations. These he termed 'formulas'. Typical examples are 'Achilles of the swift feet', 'godlike Achilles', 'the goddess, grey-eyed Athena', 'powerful Agamemnon', 'long-suffering, great Odysseus', 'circumspect Penelope'. Parry came to see such formulas as the building blocks of an improvisatory medium.

How do these building blocks operate? The metre of epic is the dactyllic hexameter. It is constituted of a combination of between twelve and seventeen long or short syllables. Here is the approximate pattern:

$$-\,^{\wedge\wedge}\,-\,^{\wedge\wedge}\,-\,^{\wedge\wedge}\,-\,^{\wedge\wedge}\,-\,^{\wedge\wedge}\,--$$

A long syllable is represented thus: $-$; a short syllable is represented thus: $^{\wedge}$. For each combination of two short syllables a single long syllable may be substituted. Each hexameter line, furthermore, is made up of metrical subgroups entitled 'cola' (singular 'colon'). Their nature may also be defined semantically. Parry discovered that some of these metrical cola were filled by 'formulas'. A formula, therefore, can be defined as a group of words used to express an idea in an unvarying metrical position wherever that idea occurs. Here is a typical formula: 'the goddess, grey-eyed Athena'. This word-group fits at the end of a hexameter line and occupies a metrical sequence of $^{\wedge}---^{\wedge\wedge}--$. It appears in the *Iliad* nineteen times, and in the *Odyssey* thirty-one times. Schein (1984: 5), whose excellent summary I am following, observes that: 'the words "grey-eyed Athena" alone occur another nine times in the *Iliad* and nineteen times in the *Odyssey*, also at the end of the line.' The formula, therefore, is a utilitarian item. It exists not so much to provide detailed description as it does to expedite extempore composition while at the same time facilitating in the listener an ease of comprehension and a sense of regularity.

Repeated lines and repeated phrases represent two types of formulas. Parry and his followers have argued that Homeric verse as a whole is formulaic. A third type of formula is created by analogy (Silk 1987: 20; compare Parry 1971: 41ff.). A phrase such as 'great Achilles' may be added to a verb such as 'killed' or 'commanded' or 'exulted' or 'raised' (each of which verbs are in the Greek of identical metrical shape). Thus a very loose family of formulas is created. Not all scholars believe in this third type of formula. Its conception is over-generalized (see Finnegan 1977: 71): common word patterns and metrical cadences are to be expected of all types of poets, oral or literate. Reservations have also been expressed concerning the repeated lines and phrases. These appear to accumulate at the beginnings and ends of speeches and at new departures in the narrative. It is possible that Homer's verse is only part formulaic and 'embodies a perpetual oscillation between the fixed and the free' (Silk 1987: 24).

THE STYLE OF ORAL EPIC: INACCURACY AND IMPROVISATION

In the nineteenth century certain 'analyst' critics (fathered by Wolf 1985) posited multiple authorship of the *Iliad* and the *Odyssey* as an explanation for redundancy and inconsistency of detail (a modern-day analyst of considerable influence is Page 1955 and 1959). A typical instance of such a 'fault' is the clumsy repetition of the proceedings of divine assembly at the opening of *Odyssey* 1 and 5 (Kirk 1965: 169). Oral composition makes comprehensible such a redundancy. The oral poet has adapted the typical opening pattern of epic narrative (confrontation, divine assembly, voyage, etc.) to mark the beginning of Telemachus' tale, then later the beginning of Odysseus' tale. Redundancy is caused here by the persistence of this stylized opening sequence. A famous example of inconsistency is the use of the dual verbal form (indicating a pair of subjects) for the trio of envoys in *Iliad* 9. In this case Homer may have conflated two perhaps imperfectly remembered traditions, one with two ambassadors, the other with three. Redundancy and inconsistency are probably to be expected of an improvisatory, oral poet. This is especially the case when such a poet is working with large-scale narratives.

THE STYLE OF ORAL EPIC: PARATAXIS

So he spoke praying, and Phoebus Apollo heard him,	43
and he came down from the peaks of Olympus, angered at heart	44
holding his bow on his shoulders and the covered quiver.	45
And the arrows clashed on the shoulders of the angered god	46
leaping; and he came like the night	47
then sat apart from the ships and shot an arrow;	48
and terrible was the clash from the silver bow.	49
First he went after the mules and the swift hounds,	50
but then shooting a piercing arrow against them	51
he struck. And continuously burnt the crowded pyres of corpses.	52

(Homer, *Iliad* 1.43–52)

The linking of the clauses and participial phrases is done simply in this impressive passage. Eight clauses are linked by the conjunction 'and' (lines 43, 44, 46, 47, 48, 49, 52); two are linked by the temporal conjunction 'then' (48, 51); in six cases a participial phrase is used instead of a clause (43, 44, 45, 46, 47, 51). There is no attempt to build up complex sentences through subordination (hypotaxis). Homer does not write 'after he had spoken in prayer, and after Phoebus Apollo had heard him, he came down from the peaks of Olympus, and, because he leapt in his anger, the bow and the covered quiver which he carried across his shoulders clashed'. Homer's syntax is simple. It is built up by the use of conjunctions and participial phrases. This is termed 'parataxis'.

Parataxis is a key feature of Homeric style (Notopoulos 1949). It is frequently and justly invoked in discussions of epic (Thalmann 1984: 4–6): parataxis is often nominated as a characteristic of oral epic; hypotaxis is characteristic of the written epic. Parataxis is not limited to the verbal and syntactic texture. There is in Homeric oral epic a repetitious stylization of narrative, of the deployment of themes and thought, of characterization, and a stylization of the shape of the poem itself which seems to mirror the cumulative nature of paratactic syntax. Analogy or at least parallelism, to put it another way, seems a prominent feature of the Homeric epic. Simple contrast or polarity (Fränkel 1975: 525–7) is also a feature of 'paratactic' early Greek hexameter poetry.

The repetitious, stylized nature of oral narrative is especially evident in the battle scenes of the *Iliad*. For example, the *aristeia* (when one fighter dominates the battlefield), like the battle scenes, are also stylized and often fall into five sections (Schein 1984: 80). First, the hero arms himself (stress is placed upon his impressive armour); second, the hero turns the battle by killing an opponent; third, the hero causes his opponents great damage when he breaks their ranks; fourth, he is wounded, but supplication of a tutelary god allows his reentry to the battle where he slays a prominent opponent; fifth, there is an all-out battle over the corpse of the slain opponent which is only just rescued by its defenders.

Narrative repetition is not restricted to battle scenes. It may also produce what some call the 'situational parallel' (sometimes termed 'symbolic reenactment'). Such parallels often provide the thematic and conceptual basis for the poem. Perhaps the most instructive instance of the 'situational parallel' is the analogy drawn in the *Odyssey* between the house of Agamemnon and that of Odysseus (*Odyssey* 1.32–44: Olson 1990). The comparison, never made explicit, acts as a commentary on the situation in which Odysseus now finds himself (see Chapter 3). Related to the situational parallel is stylization of character. Here is a simple instance from the *Odyssey*. Eumaeus (book 14), Odysseus' loyal goatherd, reflects all of the virtues of mercy, loyalty, endurance, and gentleness which the poem seems to recommend. Eumaeus has his polar opposite displayed when he and Odysseus meet the goatherd, Melanthius (book 17). Melanthius attempts to do violence to Odysseus. Melanthius has a remarkable analogy in the next book of the *Odyssey* in the sneering, similarly named female servant, Melantho.

Does paratactic composition shape Homer's poems? The *Iliad* and the *Odyssey* both exhibit a compositional style which links or juxtaposes large narrative blocks. Thalmann (1984: 1ff.) describes a number of methods of paratactic arrangement. Here we might emphasize just two: 'ring composition' (which takes forms such as A–B–C–B–A) and 'spiral form' (which takes forms such as A–B–A–B). These devices may shape the individual passage of the poem as a whole. For example *Iliad* 24.599–620, the story of Niobe, shows ring composition (Schein 1984: 33) as follows: A (24.599–601: tomorrow you will ransom your son), B (24.601: now remember to eat), C (24.602: Niobe remembered to eat), D (24.603–12: Niobe's story), C (24.613: she remembered to eat), B (24.618–19: let us remember to eat), A (24.619–20: weep for your son tomorrow). Nagler (1974: 191ff.) claims that there can be ring composition between speeches within a book. He has argued that Achilles' speech at 24.599–620 is a mirror image of Achilles' speech at 24.518–51. These local structural devices can condition the structure of the whole poems. Whitman (1965: 249ff.) observed that the outer three books of the *Iliad* balance one another: book 1 (a quarrel) balances book 24 (a reconciliation), book 2 (an assembly of the Achaean army) balances book 23 (the assembly of the Achaeans for Patroclus' funeral), while book 3 (the 'first' duel of the war, between Paris and Menelaus) balances book 22 (the 'last' duel of the war, between Achilles and Hector). Thalmann (1984: 52) believes the *Odyssey* is shaped in a spiral (A–B–C–A–B–C): books 1–4, describing events on Ithaca and Telemachus' journey, match approximately books 13–16 (the return of Odysseus and his reunion with Telemachus); books 5–8, describing Odysseus' arrival at the Phaeacian court, match approximately books 17–20 (where Odysseus arrives back at his own court); books 9–12, describing Odysseus' wandering and his rescue to Phaeacia, match approximately books 21–4 (Odysseus' 'rescue' of his own home).

Parataxis, finally, may help explain the nature of one other

especially typical feature of Homeric epic, the simile. (Camps 1980:
55 tells us that there are about 200 examples in the *Iliad* and about
forty in the *Odyssey*.) The simile, after Homer, became almost a
compulsory element of ancient epic. But the Homeric simile is
unlike later products: it is occasionally stated that it is less complex
than that of the written epic (for example, by Pöschl 1962: 45–7).
Camps (1980: 59f.) believes that the Homeric simile adds a 'purely
decorative element' to its texture. Mueller (1986: 108–24) correctly
rejects such an extreme position.

Here is a lion simile (*Iliad* 3.23–6). It is applied to Menelaus
advancing to duel with Paris:

> like a lion takes pleasure when it comes upon a great corpse,
> when it finds a horned stag or a wild goat,
> in its hunger. The lion eats it down, even if
> swift hounds and bold young men rush at him.

The emotional force of the simile resides in its length (almost stately,
it retards and punctuates the narrative, thus allowing the listener to
savour the prospective encounter) and in its detail (Menelaus is like a
lion, Paris like a dead beast, the Trojans are 'swift, active hounds').
The simile deepens our emotional response to the text. Yet not all of
its constituents are contextually apropos: the rush of the hounds and
of the young men is out of place, for this is a sanctioned one-to-one
duel. Strict logic is sacrificed to emotional force in this simile (here
reducible to 'Menelaus is like a dangerous lion'). The peculiar force
of this Homeric simile derives from its being almost detachable from
its context. Were it removed, ethos might suffer, but logic would
remain unharmed. I doubt that we would notice its absence. The
simile, like so much in Homer, is juxtaposed with its surrounds
(rather than intertwined or subordinated). This is a peculiarly paratactic mode of expression.

THE STYLE OF WRITTEN EPIC

Wars and a hero I sing, who first from the coasts of Troy   1
came to Italy and to the Lavinian shores, exiled   2
by fate, and, much buffeted on land and on sea   3
by the gods' violence, because of cruel Juno's unforgetting
    anger,   4
greatly did he suffer in war, to found his city,   5

and to bring his gods to Latium – whence the Latin
people,   6
the Alban lords, and the walls of lofty Rome.   7

These lines are the first seven of Virgil's *Aeneid*. The deliberate and allusive texture captures many of the most prominent aspects of written epic. Let us look at the syntax first. It is loose – not quite paratactic, or quite matching the complex period of contemporary prose. Yet it does produce the timbre of hypotaxis. These seven lines comprise one sentence: 'I sing' (line 1) is the core of the main clause and to this are loosely attached adjectival clauses (1–2) and phrases (6–7), participial phrases (2, 3), and adverb phrases (4, 5, 6). The hypotactic flavour is made evident in another way. These seven lines form a 'verse paragraph': metrical pulse and syntax disallow pause within the lines; light enjambment and syntax do the same at the endings of lines 1–6. Within this paragraph Virgil deliberately paces his information (it builds up: Troy – exile – wandering – Juno's hatred – war – Latium – Rome), and frames the passage by 'Wars and a hero' and 'Rome'. Notice also that, like most Latin prose sentences, this one saves its climax until the end: Rome, the crowning point of Trojan migration, is the last word. Rome, of course, is the real focus of Virgil's poem.

Syntax (the deliberation with which it is employed) exhibits one difference between the written and the oral epic. Structure exhibits another. I have tried to show this in the *Aeneid* passage. The syntax is visibly structured: there is a two-line statement which spills over into the third ('Wars . . . by fate'), then, in approximately three lines ('and, much buffeted . . . Latium'), a narrative encapsulating the contents of the epic as a whole, and finally there is a conclusion ('whence . . . Rome') in a line and a half. Such a preference for deliberate balance is evident in the structure of the poem as a whole. The epic is divided into two matching halves, books 1–6 (broadly modelled on the *Odyssey*), books 7–12 (modelled on the *Iliad*). Coexisting with this dynamic pattern is a static one (the terms are those of Kenney 1977: 18ff.) which pairs books 1 and 7, books 2 and 8, books 3 and 9, books 4 and 10, books 5 and 11, 6 and 12 (see also Duckworth 1962).

Such deliberation is not restricted to the verbal texture and to the structure of passages such as *Aeneid* 1.1–7. Allusion (sometimes termed 'intertextuality') permeates written epic (Conte 1986 is good on this). Homer is the most common point of reference. The very length of this exordium implies a link with Homer – the introduction to the *Iliad* is also seven lines. The first words of the passage point to the *Iliad* ('arms') and to the *Odyssey* ('hero'). Homer is again picked up in lines 3 and 4: in 3 the description of the much buffeted hero could as well be of Odysseus and his wanderings; in 4 the reference to Juno's anger seems to reflect that of Poseidon in the *Odyssey*. Allusion, however, implies contrast, for this is a Roman poem. Roman elements are stressed in line 2 ('Italy' and the 'Lavinian shores'). These are especially prominent in lines 5–7. Here we might have expected a parallel to be drawn with the *Iliad* (balancing that to the *Odyssey* of lines 3–4). Instead there is a statement of the exiled hero's Roman mission: to found a city and to bring his gods to Latium.

That is perhaps enough of *Aeneid* 1.1–7. My point is a simple one: to demonstrate the deliberation and allusion evident in the written epic. Were there space we could look in more detail at how such deliberation ('hypotaxis') permeates the texture of ancient written epic in general (Bowra 1972 is useful). We could look at how words matter more and how their patterns within a line become important and how words interact with themes (imagistic tags often help us interpret the actions and reactions of the main characters). We could look at how language becomes more learned and allusive (Virgil echoes not just Homer, but Ennius, Lucretius, and Catullus) and how the poet also becomes more ostensibly learned (in *Aeneid* 6, Aeneas' descent into the underworld becomes almost a literary *tour de force*). We could look at how deliberation is evident in the treatment and selection of characters and situations. Homer's characters and situations are deployed in analogous or antithetical combinations. A 'reading' of the poem may emerge from these combinations. Simple juxtaposition (polar or antithetical) is far less common in written epic.

WHY READ EPIC?

The question, like its answer, is too generalized. Yet it is possible to reach some tentative conclusions. Epic has been, has become, important for historical reasons – for what it has contributed to the Western tradition. Almost until the invention of printing epic acted as the major non-dramatic mode of presentation of the serious side of life. This seriousness, in the best of epics, has been felt to catch something of what is essentially Greek or essentially Roman. These epics helped shape Greece and Rome (the Greeks thought that they learned from Homer) and they helped shape the European mind. Reading epic, therefore, allows one entry into the 'mind' of great ages.

But the best of epic would work if one had never heard of Europe. Much of the attraction of the genre resides in the fact that it evokes a self-contained and appealing 'world'. The 'world' of epic will often represent a past time that is in some way more desirable than the present (heroes were braver and more numerous; the events in which these heroes participated were in some way a 'beginning' or an 'end' of things; issues then were more clear-cut). The past is therefore glorified (or in Lucan's case vilified). The mythological story often seems to tell of how it was in better times.

Such a contrast between 'then and now' is a sleight of hand and requires the collusion of the listener. There is, therefore, a high degree of aesthetic play involved in a successful epic. The most obvious manner by which this aesthetic play is achieved is through descriptive and situational variety. More precisely one could say that an epic poem, if it is to be a real success, must contain a fair level of generic variety and even generic play.

Mythological epic must also have its human side. It must catch a variety of human voices and human circumstances. If the epic world is admirable because it is larger than life, it must nonetheless present characters with whom, as Aristotle would have said, we form identification. This is most frequently obtained by the use of a flawed, erring hero – in the broadest sense, by a focus on tested heroes (it seems that testing and regeneration rather than 'characterization' are what matters in ancient epic). The poem also needs to present a distinctive attitude, voice, or perhaps a world view. Virgil's 'private' voice (Williams 1990) is an outstanding example. This plangent, melancholy, yet humane voice is one of his most attractive features for many modern readers. Most modern critics also insist that a poem should present us with a coherent, convincing, and humane set of ideas or ideals. That may be. It cannot, however, be sufficiently stressed that ideas and ideals are not what makes a literary work a success. Epic, like all great literature, is rooted in aesthetic play.

2

HOMER, *ILIAD*

THE WORLD OF THE *ILIAD* AND THE *ODYSSEY*

What sort of a world produced the *Iliad* and the *Odyssey*? The poems were probably composed between 750 and 700 BC, with the *Iliad* preceding the *Odyssey* by a generation (Kirk 1965: 197). If the compositional date of the poems was in the mid 700s, the events they describe took place during the Mycenaean period (1600–1100 BC). Mycenaean civilization, located in the Greek Peloponnese, gives the appearance of being an advanced culture: palace-based, possessing its own bureaucracy, it had even developed a syllabic form of writing known as Linear B (Kirk 1965: 45ff.). Commerce may provide the link between Mycenaean civilization and Troy. The Mycenaeans were active maritime traders. One of their trading regions was the littoral coast of Turkey. Archaeological research suggests that it was here in north-western Asia Minor, not far from the Aegean and the Hellespont, that Troy was situated. The ruins of an ancient stronghold, these days called Hissarlik, may represent the site of what was once Troy. In the remains preserved there, at what archaeologists term Troy VIIa, there are the traces of a city which suffered a violent sack (Kirk 1965: 39–44), perhaps in the 1100s. That is the period during which Mycenaean civilization disappeared. Perhaps the events are linked. The reasons for this eclipse are unclear. The epic sack of Troy may preserve traces of the cataclysm.

Armoury, battle tactics, names, burial habits – many of the details of the Homeric poems preserve traces of the Mycenaean era. Yet, detail also mirrors the bleak period (*c.* 1100–800 BC), known as the Dark Ages, which followed the Mycenaean civilization. Many historians believe that the *Iliad* and the *Odyssey* show more of the Dark Ages than of Mycenae (Thomas 1970). Historians point to two

20

aspects: first, the society is essentially aristocratic and, at that, based on the rural estate; second, many of the customs described in the poems persist into the classical period of Greek history. Two strands particularly, Mycenaean and late Dark Age, are jumbled together. Such a farrago is to be expected of oral poetry.

Oswyn Murray (1980: 38–68) provides a useful reconstruction of the late Dark Ages. This rural, estate society is dominated by a group of hereditary nobles (in Homer the *basilées*) who seem to hold an 'ill-defined and perhaps uneasy' position within their community. It is their wealth and their martial style of life which sets them apart from the rest of the community – landed peasants (the *dēmos*), hired labourers (*thétes*), artisans (*demiourgoi*), and slaves. The *basileus* commands a family (*genos*) and a household (*oikos*). The *genos* is not especially extended (and ought not be confused with the clan) and constitutes father, wife, adult sons and their wives, and any immediate kin. Distant relatives are moderately unimportant. Property in this patriarchal society passes from father to son.

The *basileus*, helped by hired labourers and slaves, ran the estate economy of the *oikos*. The slaves were likely to have been female and often obtained by piracy, kidnapping, or trade. Few slaves were male. (In raids the subject male population normally perished.) The wife of the *basileus* probably had charge over household duties pertaining to the female slaves. Chief crops of the estate were barley, wheat, flax. The estate would also have had its own vegetable garden and orchards of pear, pomegranate, apple, fig, and olive trees. The diet of the *oikos* was meat rather than cereal based.

Prestige defined the position of the *basileus* within the wider community. Homer shows us that. A legislative meeting of the community (termed an *agora* – there is a wartime version of one in *Iliad* 2) was dominated by the kings whose prime functions in life seem to have been warfare and debating. Public opinion mattered, but as the reception of Thersites in *Iliad* 2 demonstrates, it could easily be overridden. The *basileus* was also responsible for arbitrating community disputes. Penalties, as *Iliad* 1 shows, were fiscal and one method of arbitration was for the contestants to swear oaths.

The *basileus* establishes his prestige and social standing (*timē*) by attracting followers (*hetairoi*). *Timē* increases the capacity of the *basileus* to attract still more followers. Homeric society was highly competitive. The loyalty of adherents was encouraged by the provision of feasts and gifts. These are 'financed' by raiding expeditions on land but especially on sea (Achilles refers to such raids). Society

21

was cemented by a complex system of mutual obligations (Finley 1962: 110ff.). Nobles established ties and obligations through guest-friendship (*xenia*). This involved the provision of accommodation and of gifts to visiting strangers and friends. Thus were produced bonds and obligations which in times of need could be called upon. A breaching of the bond of guest-friendship at the court of Menelaus started the Trojan war.

THE HEROIC CODE

The heroic code of the *Iliad* or the *Odyssey* derives from the martial, competitive world of the *basilées*. The maintenance of *timē* is central. The code is based upon face saving (this was a 'shame society' according to Dodds 1968: 28ff.). *Timē* rests upon martial excellence (*aretē*). *Timē* and *aretē* appear to have a concrete manifestation in the accumulation of booty. Booty enables the maintenance of followers through guest-friendship. Achilles' wrath in *Iliad* 1 shows that if booty is withheld or taken back, then *timē* and *aretē* have been impugned. In the *Iliad* this heroic ideology is taken one step further. The aristocratic notion of prestige (*timē*) extends beyond the grave. The art of the poet (Homer) provides glorious death with a kind of immortality. Silk (1987: 70) paraphrases: 'certain acts, especially those that risk or incur death, can achieve the glory that outlives finite life, so long as they are perpetuated in art.' The immortal fame and prestige that accrue to a person of preeminent *timē* and *aretē* is designated by the Greek word *kleos* ('glory' – sometimes *kudos*). Inherent in this code, however, was a too-ready acceptance of blood-shed and carnage: without violent death there can be no *kleos*. Much of the force of the *Iliad* derives from its playing off of the desire for *kleos* against the human cost thereby incurred. The tension is caught vividly in the final two lines of *Iliad* 20: 'The son of Peleus strove to gain glory (*kudos*), and he defiled his invincible hands with bloody gore.'

THE GODS

Homer's gods did matter. But their depiction is influenced markedly by two factors. First, because these poems are oral they preserve a variety of anachronistic features. Mycenaean elements, for example, are jumbled with Dark Age elements. Second, because the epics are poetic creations, the vision of the gods is constrained by a poetic vision. The concept of the gods must fit a thematic, intellectual, and dramatic design (Edwards 1987: 131).

The gods can resemble the Dark Age *basilēes*. The divine world was dominated by a group of hereditary nobles (Zeus and his family) who lord it over many lesser gods (river gods, for example, like the Scamander). If Zeus and his *genos* are the *basilēes*, then humans are at the bottom of the social scale – the hired labour and the slaves. Over the divine *genos* ruled a patriarch, Zeus. His wife, Hera, had considerable power and prestige. Zeus' position seems based in part upon innate power and in part upon the resultant prestige (*timē*). Like a mortal *basileus* Zeus exercised his prestige in the settlement of disputes amongst fellow gods and mortals. *Timē*, which mortals pay the gods through sacrifice, indicated the standing of the divine *basileus*. Yet Zeus and all of the Homeric gods are subject to the demands of Fate (*moira*). Fate was little more than a retrospective perception of history.

Aristocratic warrior-gods in these poems seem to displace chthonic (fertility) elements. Lack of fertility or agricultural divinities seems to preclude any clear conception of the soul or of a significant afterlife other than that provided by *kleos*. Furthermore, these aristocratic warrior gods are essentially amoral. They administer justice in much the same way as does an Agamemnon. Their capacity to administer justice is not determined, that is, by their own personal morality. But it is natural to expect some moral probity from superiors. This seems as true for Agamemnon as for Zeus. Though sexually immoral, he increasingly comes to embody a notion of justice and fair play. Important to the *Iliad* and the *Odyssey* is the notion that human affairs ought be brought into line with the will of Zeus (Lloyd-Jones 1971: 1ff.).

ILIAD 1–4: REENACTING THE CAUSES OF THE WAR

It is the tenth year of the war; the Greek army is established on the shore near Troy. The god Apollo has sent a plague on the Greek army because Agamemnon offended Apollo's priest Chryses by refusing to let him ransom his daughter Chryseis, Agamemnon's slave. At an assembly Agamemnon agrees to give the girl back. But, provoked by Achilles, he demands as a compensation Briseis, Achilles' concubine. Angered and believing he has been dishonoured, Achilles and his companion Patroclus (and their troops) withdraw from the conflict. Achilles appeals to his mother, the goddess Thetis, for assistance. He asks her to request Zeus to avenge him by supporting the Trojans (1.407–12). These events (1.1–430) set the *Iliad* in motion.

The clash between Achilles and Agamemnon is at the heart of things. It is more the result of the heroic code than it is of character or temperament. Agamemnon's prestige (*timē*) rests on his ill-defined position as chief of the expedition. The *timē* of the leader must be preeminent. Yet in this case it is not founded on a comparable martial ability (*aretē*). In this sphere Achilles is preeminent – as he angrily asserts. There is a clash between rival claims of *timē* and *aretē*. It is further aggravated by Agamemnon's claiming Briseis. Achilles, perceiving his *aretē* impugned, has two choices: he can fight (which psychological dilemma is dramatized by the appearance to Achilles of Athena), or withdraw from the army (1.169, 1.298; Whitman 1965: 181ff.).

Yet temperament is important. Both Achilles and Agamemnon are tested and found wanting. Achilles, tall, handsome, excelling at war, has no sense of obligation to his community (*aidōs*; on this concept, see Redfield 1975: 115). This is something he must learn. This is apparent in his prayer to Thetis for the destruction of the Achaeans – 1.407–12 and 1.505–10 (compare 18.73–84). In the clash with Agamemnon Achilles' sense of shame (*aidōs*) before his community and his gods is tested. He fails. Martial prowess is not balanced by such moral virtues as endurance, self-control, patience, empathy, gentleness, loyalty, friendship, and honour. Agamemnon, on the other hand, fails to respect the needs of his companions. By demanding Briseis (and by dishonouring Chryses), he marks himself as brutal, authoritarian, quarrelsome, self-centred, and proud. Preeminent neither as a fighter nor as a counsellor, his power is based on ill-defined hereditary privilege.

Olympus is where the third section of *Iliad* 1 (1.493–611) takes place. Thetis recounts to Zeus Achilles' prayer (1.505–10). Zeus, her father, accedes to her wishes and sets in motion the events which will lead to Patroclus' death (his plan is clearly expressed at 15.63–77). The charming world of the gods provides an ironic reflection of the human world. Confrontation between Hera and Zeus resembles the quarrel between Agamemnon and Achilles; the peace-making overtures of Hephaestus may be compared to those of Nestor (the one ignored, the other heeded); the beguiling calm of the last description of events in Olympus – 1.595–611 – has its parallel in the Achaean feasts of 1.467–74. Part of the poignancy of the *Iliad* results from the implicit comparison between the calm, the carelessness, the triviality of life on Olympus and the disorder and rancour of the human world.

Two aspects of book 1, in the larger context of the poem, deserve mention. First, book 1, like each of the first four books of the *Iliad*, recapitulates the origins of the war. In this book there is a (symbolic) reenactment of the initial conflict over a woman. Here it is not Helen, but Briseis, Achilles' concubine. The combatants are not Menelaus and Paris, but Achilles and Agamemnon. Homer is, therefore, setting the larger scene against which Achilles' wrath is depicted. The second aspect concerns structure. It has often been said that book 1 balances book 24 (providing a frame for the poem as a whole): the ransom of Chryseis and the ensuing argument over her fate matches the ransom of Hector and the 'argument' between Achilles and Priam (Whitman 1965: 260). The technique is typically oral.

Agamemnon's dream; the catalogue of ships

Agamemnon is sent a deceptive dream – part of Zeus' plan to get the Achaeans to fight? – indicating that he will at last take Troy (2.1–34). He calls an assembly to test his army (it seems) by proposing return to Greece (2.35–454). That the proposal so easily misfires tells much of Agamemnon as a leader. He is intemperate, not clever, and he is an inept manager of men (Odysseus tells us what he ought to be like at 2.200–6). When Agamemnon's assembly misfires and the troops rush eagerly to get ready to go home, Hera sends Athena to urge Odysseus to stop them. He does this efficiently, but at the resulting assembly Agamemnon is reviled by the *déclassé* Thersites (2.212–42). The means and the ease by which Odysseus restores order illustrate the firm class divisions within this hierarchical society. Notwithstanding the army's acquiescence in Odysseus' action, Thersites does seem to mouth the common view. But his speech may echo that of Achilles to Agamemnon at 1.149–71. There Achilles, rejecting the power of Agamemnon, steps beyond the proper limits of society.

The remainder of the book provides catalogues of the Greek (2.494–759) and Trojan forces (2.816–77). Willcock's sums (1976: 22–4) show how the detail wearies: from Greece we hear of 29 contingents, 44 leaders (of whom nine are not mentioned again and eight only once – five when they are killed), 175 towns or localities, 1,186 ships, and upwards of 100,000 troops. The regions covered in the first catalogue are Greece north of the Isthmus (2.494–558), the Peloponnese (2.559–624), the western islands and western Greece (2.625–44), the south-eastern islands (2.645–80), and northern Greece (2.681–759). The catalogue represents a circumnavigation (a *periplus*) which begins and ends with Boeotia. Why Boeotia? Some have speculated that Homer was Boeotian. The simplest explanation is that it was from Aulis in Boeotia that the original expedition set out. The genuineness of the catalogue has often been doubted, but its overall historicity is probably to be accepted (Hope Simpson and Lazenby 1970). As to the function of all this tedious detail, again it seems to be reenactment. Just as in book 1 we have Helen and Paris reflected in the conflict over Briseis, here we have reflected the beginning of the expedition. The catalogue also links with book 23: here we have the 'first' great gathering of the Greeks, there, at Patroclus' funeral, the last. Furthermore the catalogue serves as a sort of a playbill in which are mentioned the major Greek fighters. It is also universalizing. By mentioning most of the major regions of Greece the conflict assumes global or universal status for the Greeks.

The *teichoscopia*; Paris and Menelaus' duel, and Pandarus' arrow

The two armies advance onto the plain outside Troy, and, after a humiliating encounter with Menelaus (3.21–37) and a scolding from Hector, Paris offers to fight a duel with Menelaus for Helen (3.58–120). Helen, in the meantime called to the walls of Troy by a disguised Iris (3.120–60), points out the Achaean leaders to Priam. This famous *teichoscopia* ('viewing from the wall') surveys Agamemnon (3.161–90), Odysseus (3.191–224), then Ajax and Idomeneus (3.225–33) (Helen's absent brothers Castor and Polydeuces are mentioned at 3.236–44). The clue to what is taking place is provided by Antenor's recounting of an embassy by Odysseus and Menelaus to Troy concerning Helen before the war (3.203–24): there is a reenactment of events leading up to the war. In this *teichoscopia* there is recreated (in this tenth year of the war) the first marshalling of troops on the Trojan plain.

After long preparations and oath taking (3.245–339) the duel between Paris and Menelaus is set to begin. With the duel between

Paris and Menelaus we seem to be recreating symbolically what took place years before in Sparta when Paris came as Menelaus' guest (Edwards 1987: 189). (The duel between Paris and Menelaus, which 'inaugurates' the conflict, also looks to the duel in book 22 between Achilles and Hector which 'finishes' the conflict.) Naturally the effete Paris cannot contain Menelaus; he is saved from defeat by the goddess of love, Aphrodite, who takes him back into the city to Helen (3.340–82). Paris' being saved is another example of the heartless caprice of the gods (note that it is not Zeus who does the saving), a caprice that emphasizes the frailty of human life: this is part of the force of the final description of the two armies angrily looking for Paris (3.449–54). But there is also a logic in having the effete lecher (see 3.421ff.) saved, especially by the goddess of love, and the honest husband Menelaus frustrated. Aphrodite literally forces (3.383–20) an unwilling Helen back into Paris' arms. Does this scene reenact the original seduction of Helen (Edwards 1987: 196)?

The gods begin book 4: their ease, the ruthless triviality of their concerns – they are bargaining over the fate of cities – as they watch the Trojan plain from Olympus (4.1–67) emphasize again the helplessness, vulnerability, and insignificance of humans and their concerns. Hera's hostility to Troy – roused by Zeus – causes the truce to be broken. She sends Athena to persuade Pandarus, a Lycian ally of Troy, to shoot at Menelaus (4.68–103). Pandarus (a bowman like the unheroic Paris) precipitates the conflict. His action (4.104–47) echoes the outbreak of hostilities nine years previously. It completes the chain of reenactments begun with dispute between Achilles and Agamemnon, the catalogue of ships, and the *teichoscopia*.

Agamemnon's reactions are important. After damning the actions of the Trojans (4.148–82) and calling for the doctor Machaon (4.183–219), he ranges amongst his troops urging them to battle. He encounters Idomeneus (4.250–71), the two Ajaxes (4.272–91), Nestor (4.292–325), Menestheus and Odysseus (4.326–63), and finally Diomedes (4.364–421). Again, there is reenactment. Here there is a third catalogue, capping that of the ships and the *teichoscopia*. Here we witness, as it were, the marshalling of the troops for their first conflicts. The Danaans and the Trojans finally go to war in 4.421–544. The battle is indecisive. This is most graphically illustrated by the conflict at 4.517–44 where Diores and Peirus, victor and vanquished, lie dead. The battle, but for Achilles' prayer at 1.407–12, seems equipoised.

ILIAD 5–7: DIOMEDES' ARISTEIA; HECTOR, ANDROMACHE, AND AJAX

The fighting in *Iliad* 5–6 belongs to Diomedes. Diomedes functions as a foil for Achilles (Mueller 1986: 157). He embodies the temperance and good sense which may be described by the Greek word *sophrosynē*. He epitomizes the virtues of endurance, self-control, loyalty, honour, respect for the gods and his community (*aidōs*) which Achilles learns too late in book 24. Book 5 enacts the most dramatic portions of Diomedes' remarkable *aristeia*. Motivated by the unfounded accusations of Agamemnon at 4.370–400 the hero battles in the company of Athena. He is wounded and revived (by Athena at 5.121–32) and urged not to fight gods unless he sees Aphrodite (5.130–2). At 5.330–51 Diomedes attacks and wounds the goddess Aphrodite. The battle has been described as comic (Owen 1966: 50ff.). Rather, here a hero runs amok and, by challenging a god, overreaches mortal limits. Diomedes' attack on Aphrodite is noteworthy in another way. It was the judgement of Paris in awarding the beauty prize to Aphrodite which caused the war. In that sense Diomedes is confronting the very origin of the conflict. But, unlike Thersites, Diomedes does know his limit. He heeds Apollo's advice not to challenge him at 5.440–2. Diomedes makes one further attack on a god when, at the behest of Athena, he worsts Ares (5.825–63).

Diomedes' encounter with Glaucus and Hector's return to Troy dominate *Iliad* 6. Diomedes and Glaucus meet expecting to duel (6.119–236). But Diomedes, impressed with his adversary's deportment, asks his lineage. He discovers that they are linked by the bond of guest-friendship (*xenia*). They forbear fighting and exchange gifts (6.226–36). The honour and humanity of the social order, and of Diomedes in particular, are prominent – despite the fact that Diomedes gulls his guest-friend. Glaucus' speech of 6.145–211 is frequently singled out, especially his famous 'generations of leaves' simile at 6.146–9. The bleak but strangely consoling pessimism of these lines is typical of the pathetic timbre of the *Iliad* as a whole.

Hector returns soon after to Troy. He meets his mother Hecabe (6.251–85), Helen (6.312–68), and finally his wife Andromache (6.390–502). We know that Hector's life with Andromache will not last much longer. (At 6.494–502 Andromache and her attendants mourn Hector as a dead man.) Hector in his famous lines of 6.447–8 seems to recognize this, but still prays for good fortune for Astyanax (6.476–81). It is in this context of dramatic foreshadowing that the previous meeting with Hecabe should be understood. Her pleas look to his eventual death in book 22. This in turn reflects on Astyanax. Like his father, Astyanax will perish. Like his father, he will leave a grieving mother in the ruins of Troy. Such foreshadowing affects our reading of the encounter between Helen and Paris. Helen, the source of all this evil, the family destroyer, the city destroyer, could not be further from Andromache. The same is true of Paris.

The action of *Iliad* 7 is slight. At the instigation of Athena the armies determine to arrange a single combat. Hector makes the challenge. Ajax is chosen as his opponent, but the duel is indecisive. (They fight to a stand-off; then, in a scene very like that between Diomedes and Glaucus, they acknowledge one another's abilities and exchange gifts. Once again a model of heroic behaviour is emphasized – not one to be respected by Achilles.) Night begins to fall (the end of the long day which began in book 2) and a truce for the burial of the dead is arranged. On Nestor's advice, the Achaeans fortify their camp. The Trojans, as part of the same truce, attempt to strike a bargain over Helen and her possessions: Paris would keep Helen but return the possessions if the Achaeans called off their armies. Agamemnon, following Diomedes, firmly rejects the bargain (7.406–11). Such bargaining clearly establishes the Trojan guilt (Owen 1966: 77), but this is a guilt in which paradoxically Hector does not share.

ILIAD 8–9: GREEK SETBACKS AND THE APPEAL TO ACHILLES

In *Iliad* 8 the will (*boulē*) of Zeus finally becomes active (and Thetis' request is answered; see 15.63–77 for a clear enunciation of his will). The Trojans begin to gain the upper hand and, driving the Achaeans back inside their fortifications, even manage to camp overnight on the plain. Zeus' will is made even more apparent by the manner in which he controls recalcitrant Hera and Athena (8.397–437). This is further underlined by the prediction (8.473–7) concerning the defeat of the Achaeans and the return of Achilles.

Why has the will of Zeus taken so long to come into effect? The simplest answer is that we need to be convinced that the Trojans are worthy opponents for the Achaeans. But a glance back at the contents of books 2–7 will demonstrate that Homer had other duties to fulfil before he could resume the story of the wrath of Achilles. He needed first to set the scene against which the wrath can be carried out. This is done in part through symbolic reenactment and in part through the provision of suitable foils for Achilles. Thus the significance of the quarrel over a woman in book 1, the catalogue of ships in 2, the *teichoscopia* in 3, the folly of Pandarus in 4, the foil of Diomedes' *aristeia* in 5–6, and, in 6, the moving scene between Hector and Andromache.

In *Iliad* 9 we are ready again for Achilles. The book begins with Agamemnon's concern at the Trojan advance. He calls an assembly and once again (compare book 2) suggests return home (9.9–29). Nestor urges conciliation with Achilles (9.89–113) and Agamemnon agrees (9.114–61). He offers compensation (the return of Briseis, one of Agamemnon's daughters in marriage, generous gifts) but no apology (9.157–61). Odysseus, Phoenix (Achilles' tutor as a child), and Ajax are sent as ambassadors. Their pleas to Achilles – and Achilles rejects them all – range from the official (Odysseus, 9.225–306) to the parental (Phoenix, 9.434–605) to the comradely (Ajax at 9.624–42). Achilles' resistance gradually softens (something not picked up by Odysseus in his recounting of the embassy at 9.676ff.) He reacts passionately to Odysseus' speech (9.308–429) and seems to reject the heroic code upon which the dilemma of the *Iliad* is built (especially 9.401–9). This point is especially important. At 9.410ff. Achilles speaks of the two futures which Thetis predicted for him: there was Troy, glory (*kleos*), and an early death; or he could stay at home and live to a ripe but hardly glorious old age. That Achilles is at Troy indicates that he had chosen the former. That he now absents himself from the war indicates that, in the face of Agamemnon's violation of the heroic code, he has come to question the latter. This is also made clear in his response to Ajax (9.644–55) where he indicates that, although he will not leave Troy, he will resist Hector's advances should they reach his ship. (When, in book 18, Achilles determines to reenter the conflict, he is driven by a new priority: this time it is a desire for vengeance.)

ILIAD 10: DOLON

It begins with Agamemnon awake at night, still worrying over the reverses suffered by his forces – the overconfident Trojans are now sufficiently bold to bivouac outside the walls of their city, Ilium (10.1–24). After conferring with Menelaus (10.25–71), Agamemnon consults Nestor. The pair determine to hold a council (10.72–130) and to call for volunteers (10.202–17) to scout out the situation of the

Trojan forces. Diomedes volunteers, choosing Odysseus as companion (10.218–53). There follows a council amongst the Trojans: wanting to reconnoitre the disposition of the Greek forces they send out the unlikeable Dolon (10.316–17 and 319–27) as their spy (10.299–331). The doublets meet: Odysseus and Diomedes capture Dolon and extract information concerning the Thracian camp. Then Diomedes kills him (10.446–57). Odysseus and Diomedes attack the camp of the sleeping Thracians. Diomedes murders the sleeping king, Rhesus, along with a dozen of his companions, while Odysseus steals Rhesus' remarkable horses (10.469–525). *Iliad* 10 is a powerful book. The manner by which our sympaties for Dolon are persistently suppressed almost until his death but then kindled as he is brutally slain by Diomedes, the oblique narration of Rhesus' death, the characterization of Agamemnon and Menelaus, of Odysseus and Diomedes, of Dolon, are detailed.

Aristarchus, the Hellenistic Homeric scholar, believed that Homer did not compose *Iliad* 10. The majority of modern scholars follow Aristarchus. Their reasons are straightforward: the events of this book are not 'organically' related to those which surround it; there are also said to be late linguistic forms in its language; the remarkable Thracian horses taken away by Odysseus are never mentioned again. Notwithstanding these objections, the function of the Doloneia is plain: the brutality of the slaughter of Dolon and of the Thracians by Diomedes acts as a means of easing the poem from the gloom of books 8–9 to the violence of the books to follow. Conflict up to now has been largely honourable (recall Diomedes and Glaucus). In the books to follow it becomes brutal and climaxes in the violent rage of Achilles. The book also acts as a chilling depiction of a heroic code that rates an individual's worth in material booty (10.211–17, and 10.305ff.) – where *timē* is reflected not by a man's compassion, empathy, and mercy, but by his capacity to kill.

ILIAD 11–15: ACHILLES' PRAYER CAUSES THE GREEKS TO FACE DEFEAT

Next morning the fighting resumes (the day lasts until 18.238). Hinted at in book 8, but anticipated since book 1, the climax of Achilles' baleful prayer is finally beginning to be realized. (Zeus' 'tomorrow' of 8.470 is 11.1–18.238.) After the intervention of Zeus (11.181–209) there ensues a sharp reversal in the fortunes of the Achaeans: in quick succession the heroes are wounded and retreat:

Agamemnon (11.218–83), Diomedes (11.368–400), Odysseus (11.401–71) and Machaon (11.504–20). Even the redoubtable Ajax is halted by the ferocity of the Trojan onslaught (11.544–95). The fighting is particularly brutal, Agamemnon's *aristeia* (11.84–283) especially so, looking to that of Patroclus in book 16 and that of Achilles in books 19–22. This is not how Diomedes fought in books 5–6.

Agamemnon is unpalatable. Achilles is now (compare 11.104–6) no better. Watching the Greek retreat from his camp, Achilles gloats, then sends Patroclus to Nestor's tent to inquire whether Machaon was one of the casualties (11.596–617). Achilles' prayer to Thetis is beginning to receive its answer. When Patroclus reaches Nestor's tent an appeal is made for him to rejoin the battle (11.618–803) and to wear Achilles' armour. This, Nestor believes, will frighten the Trojans (11.796–803). Zeus' predictions of 8.470–7 are moving a step closer to completion. Patroclus' willingness to enter the conflict marks a turning point in the epic.

The Trojans attack the Achaean camp before Patroclus can return. The attack is made against the advice of the seer Polydamas. He interprets an eagle dropping a huge snake within the Trojan army as a sign that they should not attempt to breach the Achaean camp (12.211–29). Hector scornfully rejects Polydamas' interpretation, accusing him of cowardice (12.231–50). In rejecting the seer's advice is Hector rejecting the advice, even the will, of the gods (see especially 12.234–5; compare Mueller 1986: 43)? Or is he merely furthering the will of Zeus and, therefore, to be viewed in an unjudgemental manner? Hector does further Zeus' will. Yet his determination to attack the Achaean camp – not the Achaeans themselves – seems mistaken. His desire for glory (*kleos*) is excessive and ill-considered. Thus when he smashes open a gate in the Achaean wall (12.459), he is, as we would say, an almost demonic figure.

Sarpedon, acting as a foil, helps us place Hector's rash plan in perspective. This is clear in his famous speech to Glaucus at 12.310–28. The speech is more than a mere *locus classicus* for the enunciation of the 'heroic code' and warrior notions of *noblesse oblige* (Achilles' rejected this code at 9.318–22 and 401–20). It embodies aspects of the notion of *sophrosynē* which we associate with Diomedes. Sarpedon explains his motives for fighting: not anger or a desire for vengeance (like Agamemnon, or Achilles), but first a desire to validate the esteem in which he and Glaucus are held by their Lycian people (12.310–21), and second a craving to gain for himself some form of glory which will survive his own life (12.322–8). These are not the desires of Hector.

The death of Patroclus is now unavoidable. Books 13 and 14 merely delay the inevitable. In book 13 the two armies fight on the beach, as the Trojans strive to reach the Achaean ships. In Zeus' absence, Poseidon encourages Achaean resistance. Individual combat after individual combat takes place (in an almost leisurely, but often tedious manner), but increasingly to the disadvantage of the Trojans. The necessity for Patroclus' entry becomes less acute, if no less inevitable: near the end of the book we find Hector's advance checked by Ajax. The will of Zeus (clearly enunciated at 15.63–77) has been frustrated, but only temporarily, for it is too soon for the Achaeans to take the upper hand. Achilles' prayer must be answered, then, according to the prediction, Patroclus will die. Only then will Achilles put aside the quarrel with Agamemnon.

Not what will happen but the manner in which it will unfold provides the narrative drive for book 14. The Trojans have not quite gained the upper hand. Nestor meets with Agamemnon, Diomedes, and Odysseus. They debate (14.1–152). Agamemnon is all for quitting (14.74–81: for the third time; is he weak or testing his companions?) but is angrily rebuffed by Odysseus (14.82–102). Diomedes wants to keep on fighting (14.110–32). He remains a paragon – unlike his chief or his chief's opponent, Achilles (who receives from the disguised Poseidon an accurate description at 14.139–41).

There is a momentary reprieve for the Achaeans. This is provided by Hera's collusion with Poseidon. To keep his eyes off the battlefield and away from Poseidon's meddling she seduces Zeus in a long, comical scene (14.153–351). The humour palliates the grim battlefield descriptions. Pathos, however, is close to the surface. It is impossible not to allow the levity of such scenes to colour a reading of the violence and conflict of sections such as 14.440–522. This becomes particularly apparent in ironic parallels such as that of Hera readying herself for Zeus (14.166–86). It is sometimes pointed out that her preparations match those of a warrior for war (compare 3.330–8).

The climax of this book comes while Zeus sleeps. Poseidon first encourages the Greeks to rally (14.352–401). Then Ajax at 14.402–32 knocks Hector senseless with a large rock. For a time the battle seems evenly pitched, but, with their Trojan bulwark gone, the tide begins to change (14.440–507). The final scene of the book has the Trojans in complete rout (14.508–22).

The Trojans gain the upper hand in *Iliad* 15. The book begins by showing the after-effects of Zeus' deception: the Greek advance must be turned (15.281–366) and the Trojan rout neutralized (15.1–11). Zeus' intervention is followed by short scenes with Nestor and Patroclus (15.367–405), and by the eruption of battle at the Greek ships (15.406–591). The ending of the book presents a scene that could not be worse: Hector manages to reach the Greek ships (15.592–746).

In *Iliad* 15 the theme of hybris (or is it treachery?) is important. The narrative begins with Poseidon flouting the will of Zeus (15.8). The theme is repeated by Zeus' reference to the persecution by Hera of Heracles (15.14–33), and by the description of the near revolt of Ares at 15.101–41. Ares' revolt introduces another important theme, that of fathers and sons – so Zeus and Heracles (15.14–33), and Ares at 15.110–41. Ares wanted to join the conflict because of the death of his son, Ascalaphus (13.517–20). His grief will have parallels in Zeus' for his son, Sarpedon, Priam's for Hector, or Achilles' for Patroclus. Ares' reaction to the death of Ascalaphus (13.517–20 and 15.110–12) is important in another way. This death is the first in the chain of killings which climaxes in the death of Hector: Sarpedon dies in book 16, then Patroclus also in 16, then Hector in 22, and, finally, there is the prefigured death of Achilles himself. Hector's death especially is foreshadowed. When at 15.704 he finally lays hold of an Achaean ship (that of Protesilaus, the first Achaean man ashore at Troy and the first to be killed) the full force of Zeus' predictions becomes apparent. Hector is now a doomed man – a tragic figure. His action has cleared the way for Patroclus' reentry into the war which in turn will draw Achilles back to kill him. This makes his impassioned actions all the more significant. Hector may have fulfilled the will of Zeus, and he may even have had little choice in the end of his action. But the means by which he pursues Zeus' end seem excessive. Hector (like Achilles) has gone too far. The moderation he showed at the end of book 8 has been replaced by violence and over-confidence (15.604–6; compare Rutherford 1982; Mueller 1986: 43). Does this echo the notion of hybris?

ILIAD 16–17: THE DEATH OF PATROCLUS

Iliad 16 divides into six sections (Willcock 1976: 176). In the first (16.1–100) Patroclus returns to Achilles, who allows him to borrow his armour and lead out the Myrmidons. Achilles also warns Patroclus against pursuing the Trojans too far. In the second section of the book, 16.101–23, Achilles' prayer has finally been answered: Hector drives back Ajax and the first ship is set on fire. In the third and fourth sections are narrated the results of Patroclus' intervention: in the third he leads the Myrmidons into battle and, eventually, causes the Trojan repulse (16.124–283); in the fourth is his *aristeia* (16.284–418). For the first and last time Patroclus is depicted, not just as an appendage of Achilles (compare his role in books 9 and 11), but as a fighter of considerable power and brutality (16.364–418). In the fifth section Sarpedon provides a tragic alternative to Patroclus' violence. This climaxes in his death and in the fight over his corpse (16.419–683). Sarpedon, a doublet for Hector (suggested by 5.480 and 5.688), is a paragon. He acts not from anger or a longing for vengeance, but from a desire to validate the esteem in which he is held by his Lycian people (12.310–21), and from a craving to gain for himself some form of glory (12.322–8). Sarpedon reflects many of the virtues which this epic poem recommends. His death is a potent commentary on their chances of survival.

The death of Patroclus occupies the final section (16.684–867). Ignoring Achilles' warning, Patroclus drives the Trojans back to their city wall, and is confronted by Apollo, who stuns and disarms him. The Trojan Euphorbus wounds him and Hector moves in for the kill. Patroclus' death reenacts that of Sarpedon (Thalmann 1984: 46). It also looks forward to the narrative of book 22 in which Achilles kills Hector (Rutherford 1985: 134f.). Hector's part in Patroclus' death is nugatory. Apollo initiated the kill, Euphorbus capitalized, and Hector attacked third – as the dying Patroclus points out (16.844–54). Hector's vaunting (16.830–42) therefore rings more than hollow. It reflects the same misjudgement that led him to attack the Achaean ships in book 15.

The indistinguishable combats of *Iliad* 17 (Fenik 1968: 159–60), like those in books 13 and 14, become wearisome. But 17 does introduce the crucial theme of the proper disposal of the corpse, a theme which will climax in the return of Hector's body to Priam in book 24. This theme – evident in the battle for the corpse of Patroclus – animates most of the book. After preliminary skirmishing over the body and after preparations for battle have been made (17.84–261), the drawn-out fight for Patroclus begins (especially 17.262–425). But, with Zeus openly favouring the Trojans, the Achaeans perform so badly (17.543–699) that they are forced to send Antilochus to Achilles, to break the news of Patroclus' death. (In the meantime the Achaeans barely manage to rescue Patroclus' corpse and to withdraw, 17.700–61.) Thus book 17 also signals a new phase in the development of the epic: once Achilles has learnt of the death of his friend, the 'dénouement' of his wrath becomes inevitable.

Willcock (1976: 193) believes that two elements of this book may look to the lost epic, the *Aethiopis* (see my Chapter 3). The fight for the corpse of Patroclus may foreshadow the fighting over the corpse of Achilles in the *Aethiopis* (compare *Odyssey* 5.309–10, 24.39–41 and *Iliad* 22.359–60). The depiction of Ajax carrying away Patroclus' body may mirror that of Ajax carrying away the body of Achilles in the *Aethiopis*. Such foreshadowing may add Achilles' death to the chain begun with Ascalaphus, and may reemphasize that Achilles' choice to fight, as Thetis foretells at 18.95–6, means a shortened life.

The foreshadowing of the *Aethiopis* tells something of Homer's attitudes. It would be easy to conclude from reading *Iliad* 17 that Homer's is a very bleak and pessimistic vision (so the death of Patroclus, the foreshadowed deaths of Hector and Achilles, scenes such as 17.426–40 – Achilles' immortal horses weep for dead Patroclus – or Zeus' doleful generalization on the lot of humans at 17.446–7). The vision of the poem is tragic, yet it is also profoundly moralistic: know your limits in the human sphere and, especially, in those situations relating to the divine. Overstepping the mark leads at the simplest to the punishment suffered by Thersites (2.265–9) or by Hera at 15.18–21. But on a more profound level it is intertwined into the deaths of Patroclus, Hector, and Achilles. Hector's conduct in this book is illustrative. Menelaus, after he has killed Euphorbus, attempts to protect the body of Patroclus. But he is alone. The Trojans drive him back. Hector then strips Patroclus' corpse of its armour and makes to mutilate it (17.125–7). Ajax intervenes. Hector soon after leaves the battle and changes into Patroclus' armour (17.192). Zeus makes the moral (17.201–8): Hector ought not to have stripped the corpse, nor, it seems, ought he, the son of mortals, to have put on the armour of the son of an immortal (Patroclus was wearing the armour of Achilles). Hector, like Patroclus, like Achilles, has overstepped the mortal mark.

ILIAD 18–22: ACHILLES TURNS THE TIDE AND KILLS HECTOR

Achilles finally learns of the death of Patroclus and learns too of the battle for possession of his corpse. The full consequences of Achilles' prayer to Thetis of 1.407–12 have been brought to fruition.

Achilles determines on revenge against Hector. His mother, Thetis, promises that Hephaestus will make him new armour. There follows one of the most transcendent moments in ancient literature. Lightly armed, Achilles stands in the ditch separating the two armies – the venue for so much Achaean bloodshed – and, with his head miraculously wreathed in fire, roars (18.203–38). The extravagance of the sound terrifies the Trojans and forces a halt to the combat. The Trojans retreat. Achilles regains the corpse of his friend, and night falls (18.239–42) on the long day begun at 11.1. It is important to be clear why Achilles has reentered the conflict. Formerly he was motivated by a desire for *kleos*. (Of the choices referred to at 9.410ff. he formerly opted for Troy and a short life: this offered *kleos*.) To be sure, Achilles' reentry spells his supremacy over his rival, Hector, and the destruction of Troy, and it does guarantee him *kleos aphthiton*. But these things are no longer at issue. Achilles now is dead to his former desires: his willingness for combat is now controlled by a desire for vengeance.

The three most important sections to follow are Hector's reaction to the reappearance of Achilles (18.285–314), the mourning for Patroclus and Achilles' vengeful promise to the dead Patroclus (18.314–67), and the making and description of the shield (18.368–613). In the first Hector confronts his opposite, the pacific seer Polydamas (18.249–83), who suggests they should regroup inside the city walls. The prudent suggestion is bitterly rejected (18.284–309). The Trojan leader succumbs to an arrogant impulse towards an ill-considered heroism (Rutherford 1985: 135). Homer, at 18.310–13, states as much. Hector's folly will be the ultimate cause of his death and with it the destruction of Troy. Achilles is no more to be admired. The violence presaged in his promises of human sacrifice for Patroclus surpass any standard of acceptable behaviour (18.333–7). There is, in Achilles' behaviour, a recapitulation of that same excess which led to Patroclus' death.

The depictions (ecphraseis) on the shield of Achilles relate to the immoderate behaviours of Hector and Achilles: they dramatize the results of the actions of natures and attitudes which live or do not live within their allotted stations. Broadly speaking the shield depicts two situations: that of a city and region at peace (18.490–508 and 541–606), and that of a city besieged and at war (18.509–40). The relevance of the latter for Troy hardly needs stressing. As for the former, critics have rightly pointed out that this is the world as it ought to be, the doomed world of Hector, Andromache, and Astyanax in book 6 (Taplin 1980).

Iliad 19 acts as an intermediary between the announcement of Patroclus' death and Achilles' reentry into the conflict. At Thetis' instigation (19.29–36), Achilles finally has a public and formal reconciliation with Agamemnon (19.40–275). He accepts the gifts promised in book 9 and the return of Briseis. This does not, however, indicate Achilles' acceptance of the heroic ethic rejected so forcibly in his response to Odysseus in book 9.

Before Achilles puts on the new armour at 19.349–91 (a process which closely recalls the arming of Patroclus in book 16, and hints, like much of book 17, at the eventual death of Achilles), and before Xanthus, his immortal horse, foretells his death (19.392–424), Agamemnon makes his remarkable apology (19.78–144; Dodds 1968: 2–8). Achilles' subsequent reconciliation with Agamemnon is motivated by no sense of empathy with his community. It does not reflect a perception of the danger of extremes and of the rhythm of human life (compare *Iliad* 24.518–51, *Odyssey* 18.130–142). Achilles has learnt no sense of shame or responsibility before man and god. His reconciliation is motivated by a desire for vengeance.

Reconciliation means that Zeus no longer needs to follow his promise of book 1 (Edwards 1987: 288). *Iliad* 20 begins with Zeus in council giving the gods permission to take part in the fighting. As the gods descend to earth, Achilles begins a murderous assault on the Trojans. The book's most significant encounter occurs within this assault. It is between Achilles and Hector's foil, Aeneas (20.75–352). The combat does not go well for Aeneas (something he understood would happen: 20.86–102). Aeneas' protector Poseidon is forced to waft him to safety (20.318–52). This encounter reenacts that encounter between Diomedes and Aeneas in book 5 (Owen 1966: 203): that fight took place on the first day of battle, this on the last; in that battle Aeneas was spirited away by Apollo, in this one he is by Poseidon. Does this signal that the poem is moving towards its climax?

Hector encounters Achilles towards the end of the book (20.419–54). (Owen 1966: 204 compares it to the encounter between Diomedes and Glaucus in book 6.) It is too early for this climactic conflict to reach a conclusion. The duel is forestalled by Apollo. More needs to be made clear concerning the reversed fortunes of the Trojans, more needs to be shown of the horrific power of Achilles' assault on the Trojans, and more needs to be made clear of Achilles' new attitude to the war (evident in the killing of Tros, 20.463–72, and particularly in the encounter with Lycaon in the next book). Before the conflict between Hector and Achilles takes place Achilles' alienation must be shown to be complete. With the disappearance of Hector, Achilles resumes his rampage. The descriptions here (20.455–503 and in the sections preceding the encounter with Hector at 20.381–418), even by the standards of the *Iliad*, are particularly horrifying (Segal 1971).

This is nowhere more apparent than in the extraordinary conflict between the River Scamander and Achilles (21.136–382). Achilles had clogged the river with Trojan dead: corpses are left, mutilated, to be eaten by river eels and fish; twelve young Trojan warriors are bound and led away for later immolation to Patroclus (21.22–33); the death of the pathetic Lycaon (21.34–135) is described at remarkable length. The river, in revulsion, rises against Achilles.

Lycaon's killing should be singled out: previously a captive of Achilles, he had been ransomed back to his parents. Return to Troy brought him again into the hands of Achilles. But now the Achaean is a changed man (21.100–5) and mercilessly kills the hapless Trojan. The listener is revolted (note especially the violent sentiments of 21.122–35; these look to 22.347). Mercy has been replaced by a frantic desire for vengeance. Ironically Achilles sees his own death presaged in that of Lycaon (21.106–13).

After the gallows humour of the petty squabbles between the gods (21.383–520) the book concludes with the conflict between Agenor and Achilles (21.544–611). The key section is Agenor's speech at 21.553–70. Agenor nervously weighs the odds and, if anything, seems to prefer flight. Apollo's inspiration, however, strengthens his resolve and he determines to stand firm and to allow his fellow Trojans to escape inside the city walls (which, thanks to Apollo's impersonation, happens). By any account, it was a selfless action and a type of heroism of which Homer appears to approve. It is a selfless heroism which contrasts sharply with that of Hector or Achilles. Agenor deserves his miraculous rescue.

The narrative climax of Achilles' *mēnis* ('wrath') comes in *Iliad* 22: this is where he kills Hector. The events of the book are poignantly simple: Achilles hurries back and finds Hector alone outside the wall, prepared to meet him. As Achilles comes near, Hector takes flight and, with Apollo's help, stays out of reach. Then Apollo leaves him and Athena induces him to stand and fight. In single combat Achilles kills Hector and fastens the body to his chariot. Dragging it behind him, he drives to the Achaean camp, while Hector's family watch in distress from Troy. The structure of book 22, as Willcock notes (1976: 240), is carefully elaborated. Three speeches at the beginning (by Priam, Hecabe, and Hector, 22.25–130) balance three at the end (by Priam, Hecabe, and Andromache, 22.405–515). In the centre is the chase (22.131–246) and the battle (22.247–404).

Much of this book is narrated from Hector's point of view. The effect is to produce a more vivid and sympathetic portrait of the combat. It also mirrors the distance, even revulsion, now felt for Achilles. But by concentrating on Hector Homer is able to highlight the fact that his death represents or prefigures the destruction of Troy itself. This is nowhere more apparent than in Andromache's prediction of the fate to come for the fatherless Astyanax (22.477–514). Troy's fate, in a sense, is his fate.

The circumstances of Hector's death require consideration. Hector, up until the last moment, appears to be about to die a most unheroic death. This is to be expected: he withdrew from Agamemnon and from Ajax in book 11. He killed Patroclus by stealth. Comparison with Agenor's stand against Achilles at the close of the last book does Hector no honour. Only at the end is he ennobled. Unlike Lycaon he does not plead for his life. But Hector's motives to the end are at fault. At 22.337–60 he tries to save face rather than his people. Contrast Agenor. Were Hector more concerned for his community, he would have responded to the justifiable requests of his father, Priam (22.38–76). Priam's advice may seem unheroic. Yet he is correct to state that in Hector lies the city's salvation (22.56–8).

Hector's death recapitulates that of Patroclus – which looked back in turn to Sarpedon and Ascalaphus. What is the message? Achilles must learn the lesson that Ares needed to learn at the death of his son (15.138). Repetition points to a vicious circle which must be broken. How this may happen has been demonstrated on the divine level by Zeus' acceptance of Sarpedon's death. On the human level this lesson will be repeated in book 24.

ILIAD 23–4: PATROCLUS' FUNERAL AND THE RECONCILIATION OF ACHILLES

Book 23 depicts the funeral games held by Achilles for Patroclus. (Funeral games are a traditional part of the epic genre – compare Virgil, *Aeneid* 5, Statius, *Thebaid* 6, Silius Italicus, *Punica* 16.) Some argue that they prefigure the funeral games celebrated for Achilles' own death and thus allude to the *Aethiopis*. Events unfold as follows: during the night Patroclus' ghost appears to Achilles requesting immediate burial (23.54–107). The funeral rites are held the next day (23.108–257), presided over by Achilles. They are followed (the second two-thirds of the book, 23.257–897) by a series of athletic contests: chariot racing (23.261–650), boxing (23.651–99), wrestling (23.700–39), foot racing (23.740–97), sword fighting (23.798–825), the shot (23.826–49), archery (23.850–83), and javelin throwing (23.884–97).

Why is book 23 here? It acts as an envoi to the *Iliad*. It provides a farewell to the major heroes such as Agamemnon, Menelaus, Diomedes, Odysseus, Nestor, Ajax, Idomeneus, and Meriones. The final 'parade' of these Greek heroes matches the initial parade of the Greek (and Trojan) forces in book 2. Book 23 also provides tonal respite between the intense books 22 and 24. A further point: funeral games were a traditional, civilized way of marking the passing of a great individual. Behind the process of this book is the defiled body of Hector. Achilles' espousal of civilization is limited – even in the context of this brutal world. It is limited in the same way as his vision has been from the outset of the poem. If Hector, at various points in the poem, seems to embody civilization, then the defiled presence of his body acts as a tragic parody of the civilized notions of the funeral games.

A bald outline to the final book of the poem does little justice to its complexity: Hector's body, twelve days after death, remains unburied and defiled. Apollo, however, has protected it from permanent damage. Zeus, through Iris, charges Priam to bring Achilles a ransom for his son's body. Achilles, similarly charged, agrees to accept it. With Hermes' guidance Priam visits the Achaean camp and meets with Achilles. Before daybreak the old king returns to Troy with Hector's body. Back in the city the women, led by Andromache, lament over the body. The poem concludes with Hector's funeral.

The core of the book is the interview of Priam with Achilles

(24.468–676). Priam begins his address with an appeal to Achilles' father: 'Remember your father, god-like Achilles, a man who is of my age, on the woeful door-sill of old age' (24.486–7). The force of the appeal (which continues for some lines in this vein) is to create in Achilles an identification of Priam with Peleus. By the end of this speech Achilles weeps for his own father. In a subtle shift Achilles begins to assume the role not just of Priam's host but of his son, Hector (thus the force of 24.531–51 where Achilles makes a clear, though implicit, parallel between the fates of Peleus and Priam). What has happened in this exchange may best be described as emotional transference. By identifying Priam with his father, Peleus, Achilles identifies with, even 'becomes', Hector. Thus the desire for vengeance which has led to so much violence is turned in on itself. In slaying Hector Achilles has slain himself (there are frequent reminders of Achilles' impending death: 18.95–100, 22.356–60, 24.85–6, 24.130–1). In this way he recognizes he is a part of 'the community of human suffering'. In this way he learns the sense of pity for one's comrades which such fellowship engenders.

Achilles' subsequent advice to Priam is startling. It represents a *volte-face*: 'Endure, do not mourn endlessly in your heart, for you will gain nothing in your grief for your son, nor will you bring him to life. Sooner will you suffer another sorrow' (24.549–51). The forbearance urged upon Priam is exactly that of which Achilles was incapable after the death of Patroclus. (Again compare the ideal of Zeus' reaction to the death of Sarpedon.) To be capable of giving this advice Achilles must have begun to perceive the meaning of *aidōs*. This is further borne out in Achilles' next remarkable speech (24.599–620). Here he adduces the parallel of Niobe who vaunted her own maternal fertility over that of Leto, the mother of the gods Artemis and Apollo. Niobe had her twelve children killed by Apollo. But in spite of her grief, after nine days and after the burial of the children by the gods, she ate. So too, urges Achilles, should Priam. But food did not assuage Niobe's grief. Sorrow turned her to stone 'in the lonely mountains, in Sipylos'. To whom does this parallel best apply? Certainly to Priam on the first reading. But knowing what we know now, it seems to apply with more certainty to Achilles. The initial act of hybris, Niobe's vaunt, parallels Achilles' prayer to Thetis. The slaughter of her children represents, for Achilles, the death of Patroclus – both sets of deaths may be taken as a type of divine or even cosmic punishment. The petrifying grief of Niobe represents that to which Achilles has also been subject. But it is a grief which he, unlike Niobe, seems now capable of growing beyond.

Much of the lesson learned by Achilles is summed up in a complaint made by Apollo at 24.44–9:

> Achilles has lost his pity, and there is in him
> no shame (*aidōs*), which greatly harms men and also profits
>   them.
> For a man may have lost someone even dearer,
> a brother from the same womb, or even a son,
> and yet, after weeping and grieving, he lets go.
> For the Fates made for humans a heart of endurance.

Achilles, by the end of book 24, has learnt what Apollo says he lacks. Perceiving that he is not alone in his loss and by perceiving through Priam the strength of endurance, he becomes reconciled within his community and within his place in the divine scheme. He gains a sense of *aidōs*. Achilles, though too late, has learnt the sympathy, humility, pity, and a perception of the community of human suffering. The ending of the epic is not happy. Troy will soon fall and Achilles' own death has been foreshadowed. But if the ending moves and uplifts, it is because of the force of the tardy, but real perceptions learnt by Achilles.

3

HOMER, *ODYSSEY*

FROM THE *ILIAD* TO THE *ODYSSEY*

What happened after the *Iliad* finished? The events were recounted in a series of oral epics (termed the Epic Cycle and dated to the eighth, seventh, and sixth centuries). They survive only in an outline provided by the ninth century Byzantine grammarian, Photius (Davies 1989 provides a discussion of the Cycle). In fact the Cycle seems to have told also what happened before the *Iliad*. There was one poem, called the *Cypria*, which narrated why the gods caused the Trojan war. Much of the remainder of the cycle recounts events following the burial of Hector. We have already mentioned the *Aethiopis*: it told how the bare-breasted Amazon women came to help the Trojans and of Achilles' death. Next is the *Little Iliad* (outlining events from the death of Achilles to the fall of Troy) and the *Sack of Troy* (covering much of the same ground: the building of the wooden horse, the sack of Troy, and the departure of the Greek forces). How heroes such as Odysseus, Menelaus, and Ajax returned home after the war is told in the *Nostoi (Returns)*. The *Odyssey* comes in here. It retells the 'return' of Odysseus.

The *Odyssey* alludes to and may have been influenced by much of the cyclic material (Griffin 1977). Simple examples are Demodocus' songs in *Odyssey* 8: the first and last of his three songs point to the *Aethiopis*, the *Little Iliad*, and *The Sack of Troy*. There are other references such as the 'returns' of heroes like Ajax and Menelaus. There are even references (in Tiresias' predictions of book 11) to what will happen after the *Odyssey*. A version of that material was put together during the mid-sixth century in the *Telegony* of Eugammon of Cyrene.

The *Odyssey* was composed perhaps a generation after the *Iliad*. It may or may not have been the work of the same poet. The *Odyssey* was not only influenced by stories from the Epic Cycle. The pressure of the older Argonautic legend is often detected. Folk tales are important. There are many parallels in 'popular' literature for the tale of the 'Returning Hero', or the Cyclops tale, or the vision of Hades in book 11 (Page 1955; Lord 1960; Carpenter 1962). There are, however, marked similarities between the *Iliad* and the *Odyssey*. I believe that the *Odyssey* recommends much the same code of behaviour as does the *Iliad*. Like the *Iliad*, it charts the development of an outstanding individual to hard-won maturity. In the *Odyssey* and the *Iliad* a remarkable man, through his own folly, participates in the destruction of many of his companions (Achilles and the Achaeans; Odysseus and his crew). In both poems the hero must learn a sense of shame and responsibility before man and god. Odysseus must learn of the folly of his provoking Poseidon; Achilles, of his indifference to his companions. Both heroes are brought low: one becomes a beggar in his own court, the other destroys the individual he loves most. Both must learn that friendship requires reciprocation and mutual respect, and that the will of Zeus is paramount. After a series of misadventures both heroes come into the uneasy possession of the virtues of endurance, self-control, gentleness, loyalty, and a restraint which may provide an alternative to the violent and greed-driven *mores* of the harsh society in which they dwelt. When Odysseus finally doffs his disguise in *Odyssey* 22 it is as a far wiser individual. Like the Achilles of *Iliad* 24 he has come to understand the danger of extremes.

But we ought to be clear on this matter. If Odysseus, like Achilles, shows the outlines of the paradigmatic epic hero, he does so in a far different context. The *Iliad*, gloomy and realistic, is a tragedy: it looks to the end of a great man. Odysseus may, on my reading, undergo moral rehabilitation, yet his downfall is never at issue. The *Odyssey* is a moralistic romance: 'its moral tells us what, in this confusing world, we want to hear, that god is on the side of virtue and justice and that wickedness will be punished' (Hainsworth 1991: 33).

ODYSSEY 1–4: TELEMACHUS' WANDERINGS

Telemachus, Penelope, and the Suitors

The opening twenty-one lines of the *Odyssey* summarize what is to follow. This 'narrative summary', however, is limited to books 5–12, the most famous portion of the epic. These lines are also of considerable thematic significance. Two statements deserve singling out. First, Odysseus' companions perish through folly or wickedness (*atasthaliē*, 1.7) (they ignored repeated warnings, 12.271–6, and slaughtered the cattle of the sun god, Helius). Second, Odysseus is being kept from his home by the wrath of Poseidon (1.19–21), angered at Odysseus' blinding of his son, Polyphemus (1.68–71). Thus is established a basic pattern of transgression and divinely sanctioned punishment. The pattern, which repeats throughout the poem, is taken up at once in the first scene, the assembly of the gods (1.26–95). They are considering Odysseus' lot. Athena asks Zeus why he has forgotten Odysseus (1.45–62). Zeus replies that Poseidon's anger still pursues the hero, but, since Poseidon is away, the hero's return can begin (1.64–79). Athena's questions come after Zeus' reference to the problems of the house of Agamemnon (1.32–47). The speech of Zeus and the example of Aegisthus embody the prologue's notion of justice (Fenik 1974: 210). Aegisthus had been warned to stay away from Agamemnon's wife, but chose to ignore Hermes' advice. He is punished by Agamemnon's son, Orestes.

The story tells us something of the attitude of the gods towards wrongdoing on earth. It appears that the gods dislike injustice (1.47) and that they think wrongdoers deserve punishment (1.46). They will even warn prospective wrongdoers (1.37) and they will aid their favourites, such as Orestes, to right the injustice from which they are suffering. It begins to appear – and this is the opinion upon which I will build my reading of the *Odyssey* – that Zeus does indeed desire a just world and that he will act through heroes such as Orestes and Odysseus, and through gods such as Athena, to establish this state. In this last sense, Odysseus comes to act, like Athena, almost as an agent of Zeus.

The important story of Agamemnon's house, however, does more than merely emphasize Zeus' desire for justice. It provides a complex of associations which elucidate the condition in which Odysseus, his family, and his court find themselves. Odysseus can be equated with Agamemnon, Telemachus with Orestes (also

1.298–302), and the Suitors as a body with Aegisthus. Penelope is associated with Clytaemnestra and Helen. These equations permeate the poem. They pose pregnant questions. Will Penelope take her Aegisthus (a Suitor) and treat Odysseus as Penelope's cousin, Clytaemnestra, did Agamemnon? If this happens will Telemachus do the right thing and avenge his father as did Orestes? Will Odysseus suffer the fate of Agamemnon?

Telemachus dominates what remains of book 1. The dramatic advantages of beginning on Ithaca with the hero absent and Telemachus and Penelope under threat are great. Their near helplessness, the arrogant violence of the Suitors, demonstrate clearly the need for the return of the hero (and the need for Telemachus to become like Orestes). The tension so created helps drive the narrative. Athena, disguised as Mentes, goes down to Ithaca to encourage the despairing Telemachus: he should summon a general meeting and try to mobilize public opinion against the Suitors; he should go in quest of news of his father, to King Nestor in Pylus and King Menelaus in Sparta (1.156–320). For the first time Telemachus speaks aggressively both to the Suitors and to Penelope (1.328–64). These Suitors show little respect for Odysseus' family or for the gods (1.97–155). They have trampled on the obligations demanded by *xenia* ('guest-friendship'). They have also offended against *philotēs* ('friendliness' or 'loyalty'; Nagy 1979: 241). Both qualities are crucial for the functioning of a civilized society. *Xenia* and *philotēs* also encapsulate the sort of values the poem commends: endurance, self-control, patience, restraint, mercy, gentleness, love of home and wife and family, good breeding, courtliness, honour.

Telemachus leaves Ithaca

In *Odyssey* 2 Telemachus prepares himself for his wanderings. The book falls into two sections. In the first, 2.1–259, Telemachus summons the assembly suggested by Athena at 1.269–76. The assembly is sometimes compared to the divine assembly of book 1 (it could also be compared to that beginning book 5). Assemblies seem to set epic action in motion. So it does here. Telemachus begins the process of maturation that will climax when full reconciliation has been made with his father. For the present, however, we see that Telemachus is not the man his father is: he allows his own weakness at 2.58–79, then at 2.80–1 he ends in tears. The assembly also helps us to understand the Suitors and Penelope. The former become more and more violent as the assembly progresses. They are beginning to earn their fate of book 22. As for Penelope, she, like Odysseus, has the gift of cunning. This is nowhere more evident than in the tale of the shroud at 2.93–110.

In the second half, 2.260–434, Telemachus secretly makes preparations for his journey. Athena, in the form of Mentor, has a ship readied and they leave by night. Telemachus begins to show that he is capable of emulating Orestes and Odysseus and growing towards manhood. This is particularly evident in his proud rejection of Antinous' condescending offer (2.301–20). What it is that Telemachus (and Odysseus) must learn on these travels is embodied in the person of Eurycleia (2.345ff.). In this book she exhibits *philotēs*, and, later, in book 19 she exhibits *xenia* in her treatment of the beggar Odysseus. Eurycleia embodies the values to which the *Odyssey* subscribes: generosity, mercy, gentleness, endurance, self-control, and patience. It is not surprising that she appears at key junctures: at the end of book 1, here, at the departure of Telemachus, and in 19 when Odysseus returns to his palace.

Telemachus, Nestor, and Menelaus

The technique of reenactment is especially prominent in *Odyssey* 3 and 4 when Telemachus visits Nestor and Menelaus. The visit to Nestor at Pylus comes first. Nestor was the oldest and wisest of the Greeks who were at Troy. At Pylus Nestor tells Telemachus stories of the return from Troy of various heroes. Menelaus and Agamemnon are prominent. Menelaus' wanderings parallel those of Odysseus and Telemachus (but Menelaus dallied dangerously long – will Odysseus?). The relevance of Agamemnon should need no emphasis. At the end of this book Telemachus leaves for Sparta, but accompanied by Peisistratus, Nestor's son. Peisistratus is a doublet for Telemachus himself.

Nestor's court is an image in reverse of Odysseus'. His is a paradigm of *xenia* and *philotēs*. Odysseus' court is dominated by hybris and the Suitors. Connections in this book are not limited to Odysseus, Nestor, and their courts. There are analogies, beginning here but strengthened in later books, between Odysseus and Telemachus. For example, both father and son, with Athena's protection, make journeys and both will have difficulties in completing their voyages home. 'Both enter wonderful and wealthy palaces

(Telemachus enters Menelaus' halls, Odysseus those of Alcinous).... Both father and son are at first sunk in introverted pessimism, from which they only gradually emerge' (Rutherford 1985: 138). What is the force of the analogy? The process of maturation which Telemachus is undergoing is mirrored in the development of his father.

In *Odyssey* 4 Telemachus and Peisistratus come to the palace of Menelaus where they are entertained by Menelaus and the now forgiven and almost matronly Helen (on whom see Suzuki 1989) (4.1–305). Next day Menelaus, in response to Telemachus' questions, tells, first, what he thinks will happen to the Suitors, and, second, the long story of his adventures off the coast of Egypt.

Simple parallels are drawn again. Menelaus' court is like that of Nestor: it acts again as a model of *philotēs* and *xenia*, thus providing a measure against which Telemachus and Odysseus must eventually judge their court. Menelaus may be compared to Odysseus (Reinhardt 1960: 94; Rutherford 1985: 138ff.): Menelaus was, apart from Odysseus, the last of the heroes to return home; he lingered for many years in foreign lands; he had to seek divine aid (4.363–81); as Odysseus consults Tiresias in book 11, so here does Menelaus consult Proteus – both seers show the wanderer the way home (Reinhardt 1960: 94). Above all Menelaus dallied too long in search of booty and so arrived back too late to help his brother, Agamemnon (3.313, 4.90–2). When we come to discuss Odysseus and Polyphemus we will see Odysseus tempted in the same way. The role of Helen is also important. The prominence of Penelope at the end of this book, it might also be pointed out, again reinforces comparison. But by this point we have reappraised Helen. Formerly a faithless Clytaemnestra, she is now the embodiment of faithfulness. To which of these figures does Penelope relate?

ODYSSEY 5–8: ODYSSEUS IN PHAEACIA

Odysseus leaves Calypso and meets Nausicaa

Odysseus finally becomes the narrative focus in book 5. He is pictured with Calypso where his resolve to return home is tested. This book is also a fine example of the generic blend so evident and so appealing throughout the Homeric epics. After a divine assembly (5.1–27: often criticized for repeating material from the assembly of book 1; did it once begin the *Odyssey*?) Hermes is sent to instruct

Calypso to let Odysseus go (5.28–115). She does so, but not without attempting to sway Odysseus from his purpose (she offers him immortality) (5.148–227). After accepting Calypso's help in constructing a boat (or a raft) he sails away, for seventeen days (5.228–81). But his scourge, the god Poseidon, destroys his craft in a storm (5.282–332). Odysseus subsequently swims to shore to the land of the Phaeacians (5.333–493).

The tonal and generic blend within book 5 (social comedy and storm scenes) is noteworthy. It is often suggested (Jones 1988: 47) that social comedy or comedy of manners, (Longinus, *On the Sublime* 9.15) is one way of interpreting the interplay between Calypso and Odysseus (as often, comedy masks moral ambiguity). In her attempt to keep Odysseus, her 'circumlocutions and excuses' to Hermes (5.118–44) are both amusing and touching (Jones 1988: 47). Her actions towards Odysseus are marked by the same ambivalence. The contrast between scenes such as these and the storm of the second half of the book could not be greater. Here Poseidon wrecks Odysseus' boat in the most dramatic of incidents.

If, at the end of book 5, Odysseus is tested physically, in books 6–8 he is tested spiritually. Through the testing Odysseus learns and matures (Clarke 1981: 85). The testing is especially evident when, in *Odyssey* 6, he meets Nausicaa who, at the prompting of Athena, is washing clothes and playing ball with her maids on the sea shore (6.1–109). Odysseus, woken by the noise, emerges naked from hiding and begs for Nausicaa's help (6.110–85). She takes pity on him and provides clothes (6.186–250), then instructs him to go to the palace of her father, King Alcinous (6.251–315). Homer hints at Nausicaa's attraction to Odysseus (6.239–46, 275–84) and openly indicates her ripeness for marriage (6.25–35, 282–4). To heighten apprehension (will Odysseus dally with Nausicaa and arrive home too late – like Menelaus?) Homer does not hesitate to make the young woman appealing – to Odysseus and reader alike. But there are real ironies in this encounter. Nausicaa is probably close to the age of Telemachus. It is as if Odysseus were meeting a version of his own child. The irony of sexual attraction felt by Nausicaa for Odysseus is acute.

Odysseus meets Alcinous, Arete, and the Phaeacians

Odysseus is well received by Nausicaa's parents, Alcinous and Arete (7.167ff., 298ff.), especially Arete, the queen (7.133–66 – compare

Fenik 1974: 5–130). He is even offered Nausicaa as a bride (7.311–14). But, to their questions, he responds only with an abbreviated version of his tale (7.241–97). He manages to conceal his identity.

What really matters is the description of Phaeacia (also termed Scheria). The island is a kind of hyper-civilized utopia (7.81–132) whose sense of right and wrong (7.315–18), whose respect for and closeness to the gods (7.92–4, 201–6), and whose *xenia* (whence Odysseus learns the virtue: compare Finley 1978: 83ff.) and *philotēs* are prominent. But this is a magical land. It inhabits a realm half-way between that of the fairy tale places of book 9–12 and the real world of books 1–4 and 12–24 (Fenik 1974: 54; Segal 1962). The interlude acts as a transition between books 1–4 and books 9–12. But Phaeacia represents an extreme. The Phaeacians seem too civilized (7.81–132) and are perhaps not to be trusted (7.17, 32–3). (Their polar opposite is Polyphemus, the wild cannibal of book 9 – see 7.206.) There are always dangers implicit in such extremes. This may account for their strange punishment in book 13. It seems not unlikely, therefore, that Odysseus is expected to learn from the example of the civilized Phaeacians just as, by negative example, he is expected to learn from the wicked Cyclops. The Phaeacia of book 7 may play two roles. It provides Odysseus with a setting in which he begins to learn the virtues which, in books 9–12, he so conspicuously lacks. Phaeacia may also represent a type of civilization which, in its very prosperity, embodies danger.

Odyssey 8 further develops the portrait of Scheria and begins to fill out Odysseus' background. It begins with the Phaeacians meeting in the agora (8.1–45), then entering the palace for a feast where the blind singer Demodocus (an image of the oral poet) sings of the Trojan war (of a quarrel between Odysseus and Achilles) and Odysseus' role in it (8.62–82). The court then moves outdoors where young men show their skill at athletics. Odysseus is reluctant to join in but, when insultingly challenged (8.131–64), does so (these games foreshadow the contest over the bow with the Suitors in book 21) (8.165–233). The athletics (8.104–420) are interrupted by Demodocus' second song (8.266–369: Ares and Aphrodite). Finally they return to the palace where, after gift giving, bathing, and feasting, Demodocus begins his third song (8.499–520: Odysseus and the wooden horse). The climax of all this is Alcinous' question to Odysseus, 'who are you?' (8.535–86). The response subsumes the following four books.

The songs of Demodocus provide a type of cathartic experience for Odysseus. Reliving the past forces him, first, to disclose his identity, and second to emerge from the shell of self-pity, negativism, and self-interest caused by the loss of his fleet and his companions. In book 8 Odysseus emerges from squalor to grandeur (Fenik 1974: 155): the bedraggled shipwreck victim triumphs in the Phaeacian games and, finally, makes known his name and lineage. The regaining of status and the revealing of his identity have a parallel in book 22 where Odysseus reveals himself as master of Ithaca. The first and third songs are of obvious personal significance to Odysseus. Clay (1983) has argued that here we have traces of the real cause of Odysseus' wanderings: the hostility of Athena (Odysseus represented a threat to her power) rather than the wrath of Poseidon. The third song, of Odysseus and the Trojan horse, is more straightforward and patently cathartic. There is also a simple parallel between the horse which reveals its secrets, and Odysseus who will reveal his. The allusion to the destructive raid on Troy may also look forward to the raid on the Ciconians narrated in book 9.

The second song enacts what might happen on Ithaca. If Aphrodite is Penelope, then Ares (an Aegisthus figure) is the Suitors, and Hephaestus Odysseus. Has Penelope become unfaithful with an Ares figure? There may be another side to the song. Odysseus' faithfulness to Penelope is tested in this book when Alcinous offers him Nausicaa in marriage. Does the Ares-Aphrodite story look to a possible future where Odysseus has accepted the blandishments of Alcinous? The force of this complex field of associations is heightened if we realize that for Odysseus the Phaeacian court is everything his Ithacan palace ought to be. Alcinous and Arete are a portrait of how Odysseus and Penelope ought to have lived.

ODYSSEY 9–12: ODYSSEUS' WANDERINGS

Ciconians, Lotus-Eaters, and Cyclops

Odysseus' stature as a heroic figure is for the first time displayed in books 9–12. He begins as the transgressor of the brutal but pastoral Polyphemus, and ends by becoming the ethical individual who survives Thrinacia by heeding the will of the gods. In book 9 Odysseus begins to tell his story. After revealing his name, Odysseus describes how, after the sack of Troy, he set out for Ithaca (9.1–38) with twelve ships (9.159). First he raided the Ciconians in Thrace (9.39–61), then he was blown far off course to the land of the

Lotus-Eaters (9.62–104: is the storm of 9.62–81 punishment for the Ciconian raid?) and to the islands of the Cyclops (9.105–566). Curiosity (9.172–6) and greed (9.228–30 and 9.266–71) led him and his companions into the cave of the Cyclops, Polyphemus, whence he extricated himself by trickery and by blinding the monster (9.307–460). Arrogance led Odysseus to reveal his true name to Polyphemus, who, using this, prayed for vengeance to his father Poseidon (9.461–535).

The events have a dual significance. They provide a measure of the ethical standing of Odysseus. They also reenact or foreshadow other events in the poem. The encounter with the Lotus-Eaters is the simplest. Their beguilements are like those of Phaeacia, or those of Calypso and Circe. Odysseus is tempted but easily resists. He does less well with the Ciconians. Of this raid Thalmann (1984: 170) and Frame (1978: 54) observe that it resembles the original Greek incursion on Troy. Thus there is a minor level of irony: Odysseus is acting out the origins of his separation from Ithaca. The Ciconian raid also looks back to Demodocus' third song in book 8 and to the Egyptian raids of Menelaus (described in books 3 and 4). The attack closely foreshadows the 'Cretan' tales which the disguised Odysseus tells Eumaeus at 14.185ff. (compare also his tales to Antinous at 1.424–44, and to Penelope at 19.261ff.). But the tale also has a moral dimension. We disapprove of Odysseus' and his companions' actions. Odysseus seems too cavalier in the way he carried out his raid (9.40–2) and the companions continued celebrating the sack too long (9.43–6).

Polyphemus, a figure of violence and unreason, is the polar opposite of the Phaeacians and the Lotus-Eaters. He has an obvious parallel in the Suitors. In blinding the monster Odysseus takes proxy and understandable revenge on the Suitors. But other readings are possible. I believe that Odysseus' violence towards the son of Poseidon seems regrettable. It is the product as much of Odysseus' lust for gain and insatiable curiosity as it is the result of Polyphemus' brutal nature. But the pastoral innocence of Polyphemus and his admirable world is easily overlooked. Lines 9.105–35 present us with an almost child-like world that is surely to be admired (Polyphemus is also a vegetarian who is taught to eat meat and to drink alcohol by the worldly Ithacan). Odysseus' intrusion, driven by insatiable curiosity and lust for gain (contrast Telemachus at 15.67–91), disrupts this world (note also his arrogant boasting at 9.502–5; Ajax suffered for this at 4.505). Once captured by the Cyclops, Odysseus has little choice but to act with violence. But the issue is surely this: should he have been there in the first place? I believe that he should not have been. It is his arrogant irruption into this brutal but innocent world that earns Odysseus the punishments which will dog him to the end of book 12 and to the destruction of the last member of the last ship of his fleet.

Aeolus, the Laestrygonians, and Circe

The three adventures described in book 10 (as in book 9 two shorter encounters are followed by a longer one) are also ambivalent. In the first Odysseus and his sailors arrive at the floating island of the god Aeolus (10.1–79). When the time for departure comes Aeolus gives Odysseus a leather bag containing all the winds except the favourable west wind. Curiosity – that of Odysseus' crew on this occasion – proves destructive. The crew open the bag while Odysseus sleeps (10.28–79). The winds rush out and blow the wanderers back to Aeolus' island. The god has by now had enough of them. From Aeolus Odysseus can derive no advantage. But this time at least it was not his curiosity which caused the harm to his companions.

The episode with the cannibalistic Laestrygonians (10.80–132) is sometimes said to be functionalistic – it gets rid of Odysseus' remaining ships. The Laestrygonians are a more populous version of the Cyclops (Frame 1978: 57): violent, eschewing guest-friendship, they show a comparable enthusiasm for the consumption of raw flesh. The havoc the Laestrygonians wreak on Odysseus' sailors (eleven ships are destroyed) enacts Polyphemus' revenge by proxy. Odysseus is forced to abandon all but the crew of his ship to the Laestrygonians (10.126–32). Had he not exercised real caution when first he came to the Laestrygonians his own life would have been forfeit (10.95–7). Yet we are still entitled to question his capacity for correct decision. Why allow eleven of his ships to moor inside the Laestrygonian harbour? If he had not permitted this, departure from the Laestrygonians might have seemed less precipitate, less self-centred (unkingly and unfatherly), and perhaps less uncaring (10.131–2).

Odysseus and his surviving companions sail on to the magical island of Circe (10.133–574). Circe turns some of the sailors into pigs (10.229–43). But Odysseus' cunning proves her master (10.274ff.). After a year's liaison, he asks to leave. Is Circe like Calypso? Both are goddesses and test his loyalty to Penelope. The malevolent aspects of

Circe's character need little stress: she is a witch who drugs animals and transforms men into beasts. Calypso, on the other hand, is less menacing and promises not metamorphosis but immortality. Odysseus' moral leadership is tested in this episode and is found successful. Yet Eurylochus and the companions are wary of Odysseus here, fearing that he may repeat what happened with the Cyclops (see 10.437; Rutherford 1986: 151).

The dead

Odysseus' *catabasis* (descent to the underworld) is the first Greek example of what was a fixed feature of ancient epic (Bowra 1952: 78–84). Some have argued that book 11 is an interpolation. Yet the structure of book 11 seems to be quite deliberate (Jones 1988: 98). It begins (11.1–50) with Odysseus' passage to Hades and his offerings to the shades. After the brief first appearance of his mother (11.84–9) – a Penelope figure – Tiresias appears. His appearance may reenact that of Proteus in book 4. Thus Odysseus' fate is tied in again with that of Agamemnon, this time through his brother, Menelaus. Tiresias' prediction (11.90–151), though less detailed than that of Circe at 12.37ff., explains the wrath of Poseidon.

The pathetic female figure of Anticleia (who forcefully emphasizes the needs of family, 11.181ff.) leads into the impugned catalogue of women (11.225–332). The vision is concluded by the appearance in 'real time' of Arete, and then Alcinous, who urge Odysseus to continue with his tale (11.333–84). The framing of the catalogue by Anticleia and Arete hints at its purpose. Many of the figures in the catalogue were examples of egregious marital infidelity. Penelope's firmness of purpose has frequently been queried through the paradigmatic figures of Clytaemnestra and Nausicaa. The catalogue, therefore, repeats, albeit at too great length, the central theme of fidelity to home and to family.

When the story resumes Odysseus is reliving his Trojan past (compare Demodocus' third song in book 8). Odysseus meets Agamemnon, Achilles, and Ajax (11.385–567). The thematic significance of the meeting with Agamemnon hardly needs emphasizing. His fate and person have served as a warning for Odysseus since the very beginning of the poem. Achilles is concerned for his son, Neoptolemus. Odysseus tells him what he knows: the son has been worthy of his father. Is there an implicit comparison with Telemachus? The final meeting, with Ajax, is inconclusive. The hero is still angry over not having received Achilles' armour. Yet he too is of paradigmatic significance. As Odysseus suffers the wrath of Poseidon upon the sea so does Ajax suffer the wrath of Athena.

The final section of this difficult book describes Odysseus' visions of the punishments and rewards experienced in Hades by various legendary figures (11.568–635). The scene has shifted inconsistently. Formerly over the pit, Odysseus is now in Hades. Yet the themes of this interlude are perfectly consistent with the poem's vision of the justice of Zeus. It is in accord with this vision that Odysseus and his family must learn to act.

Sirens, Scylla and Charybdis, cattle of the Sun, Calypso

Circe provides Odysseus with a résumé of the difficulties he has still to face (12.37–141). When the hero resumes his voyages, therefore, he passes, forewarned, first by the Sirens (12.165–200), then the Wandering Rocks and the monster Scylla and the whirlpool Charybdis (12.201–59). Finally he arrives at Thrinacia (a third long episode after two shorter ones), the island of the cattle of the sun god, Helius (12.260ff.). Odysseus warns his crew not to touch these cattle (12.271–6). But, driven by hunger, the crewmen slaughter some while Odysseus sleeps (12.340–65). Angry Helius complains to Zeus (12.374ff.). After they set sail Odysseus' last ship is destroyed by Zeus' thunderbolt (12.415–19). Odysseus is the only survivor. Clinging to the ship's mast he drifts to Calypso's island.

How should the three episodes be interpreted? The dangers of the Sirens reflect those posed by Calypso, the Lotus-Eaters, Circe, and even the Phaeacians (Reinhardt 1960: 91 notes that Odysseus' landing on Calypso's island at the end of this book recalls the landing on Phaeacia). Odysseus must resist the seductive blandishments of too easy a world. The episode with Scylla and Charybdis also provides evidence of Odysseus' new strength. Warned against empty heroics by the enchantress (12.116–26), Odysseus at first fails to resist the heroic impulse to stand against Scylla (12.226–31). Eventual escape, however, required avoidance of combat.

Thrinacia reemphasizes the theme of the theodicy of Zeus. Reinhardt (1960: 89) usefully compares the warning given Odysseus here to that given Aegisthus at 1.37–9. That the hasty actions of the crew are to be identified with those of Aegisthus may also be made apparent by their destruction having been predicted (1.6–9) near to the context in which Aegisthus is mentioned (1.35ff.). But, finally,

Odysseus stands back from wrongdoing. Odysseus has begun to demonstrate the moral probity evident in books 13–24. Thrinacia marks the beginning of his role as the instrument of the justice of Zeus.

ODYSSEY 13–16: ODYSSEUS AND TELEMACHUS ON ITHACA

Ithaca and Eumaeus

In book 13 the fantastic world of Calypso, of the Phaeacians, and of the fairy-tale creatures encountered in Odysseus' travels vanishes. This book begins the second half of the poem. Here events are firmly rooted in the real world of Ithaca. Odysseus returns to his subjects disguised by Athena as a beggar. While the dénouement – revenge on the Suitors and reunion with Penelope – is yet some distance away, it is clear that, after the circuitous books 1–12, this is imminent.

As for the events described in book 13 there are several which require note. After Odysseus' departure from Scheria and his arrival in Ithaca (13.1–124) there is the strange fate of the Phaeacian ship (13.125–87). Poseidon, the patron god of Scheria, punished his people for helping Odysseus. He turned their ship to stone. Does this punishment represent a further warning of the dangers of over-civilization and of the peril posed by wrathful gods? At any rate, the punishment meted out to the seafaring Phaeacians by the god of the sea Poseidon, though comprehensible, hardly fits with the notions of justice outlined by Zeus at 1.32ff. The irrational cruelty of the gods, like that of Fate itself, is never far from the surface (so 8.570–1 or 14.443–5).

The arrival on Ithaca of Odysseus resembles his arrival on Phaeacia (Rutherford 1985: 140f.). This serves to mark the upturn in his fortunes and a change in heart on the part of Athena (Clay 1983) who, hitherto, has withdrawn herself from the affairs of the hero. Odysseus ceases to be the despondent character of the early Phaeacian books. He has learnt self-restraint and self-control. Gone is the reckless leader; gone too is the depressed, hopeless figure of book 5. Athena provides her favourite with a disguise – not as a means of self-protection, but as a first step towards enacting his revenge (13.386–91 and 13.397–403), as a means of testing and ascertaining the loyalty of his family and subjects (13.330–6).

In book 14 Odysseus begins the testing. Here it is Eumaeus who, after offering shelter (14.1–80), information (14.81–184), and an ear (14.185–359), provides the cajoling Odysseus with a cloak (14.407–522). Thus the listener witnesses the vindication of the claims of *xenia*. The meeting of Odysseus with Eumaeus in his humble but orderly world emphasizes by contrast the chaos in the palace (Austin 1975: 168) where guest-friendship has been so outraged. Eumaeus stands as an exemplar of the sort of behaviour which ought to be practised by the Suitors in Odysseus' court.

A crucial component of Odysseus' disguise are the 'Cretan tales' (14.199–359; they deserve comparison with Odysseus' story to Athena at 13.187–249). Besides their resemblances to Odysseus' (and in some ways Telemachus') own experiences (notice the themes of disinheritance, absence from home, war, privileged exile, deception, shipwreck) the Cretan tales may also look back to the story of the attack on the Ciconians (book 9). This, it has been suggested (Thalmann 1984: 170), reenacted the original Greek attack on Troy. Is Odysseus' story to Eumaeus a variant version of the events which have led him to all of this trouble? In book 9 we were intended to disapprove of the attack on the Ciconians; here the falseness of the tale is another measure of how Odysseus has grown.

Telemachus and Odysseus

The prominence of Telemachus in book 15 (his first appearance since book 4) indicates that reunion with Odysseus cannot be far away. This resulting tension is matched by the constant shifting of the narrative focus: we begin with Telemachus (15.1–300), shift to Odysseus and Eumaeus (15.301–494), and back to Telemachus arriving in Ithaca (15.495–557). Telemachus dominates the narrative. After taking leave of Menelaus (15.44–181), after evading the hospitality of Nestor and rejoining his ship (15.182–221), Telemachus sails for home urged on by Athena (15.222–300). Back in the hut we hear Eumaeus' life-story. The tale – relevant for Odysseus – repeats the themes of betrayal, disinheritance, and exile. The tale is also relevant for Telemachus who, like Eumaeus, might easily suffer such a fate. It is surely significant that almost as Eumaeus' narrative ends the focus shifts to Telemachus and his return to Ithaca.

The climax comes in book 16: Odysseus and Telemachus finally meet (16.154–320). Thus also are resolved many of the issues of the 'Telemacheia' (books 1–4); partial resolution is also provided for the father and son theme which has been apparent throughout the poem – although full reconciliation will require Odysseus' meeting with Laertes (in book 24 but anticipated at 15.352ff.). The meeting of father and son is not without tensions. Even before Eumaeus' departure for the palace (to announce Telemachus' return to Penelope – 16.68–153), it looks as if Odysseus will not doff his disguise (16.1–153), as if he will test his son in the manner to which we have become habituated. After Eumaeus' departure the apparition of Athena (16.156ff. – a most 'psychological' of apparitions) changes this: she transforms Odysseus into his true self (16.172ff.). It has been recently argued that the appearance of Odysseus to Telemachus uses the imagery of divine apparition (16.172–212). Odysseus, that is, appears as a 'symbolic' god (Kearns 1982). If this is the case, Odysseus' role as father and avenger (16.266–320) is offered 'divine' sanction. Odysseus, as a 'god', is an agent of Zeus. Such imagery may provide a moral vindication for Odysseus' proposed action. (Note also that at 17.483–7 Antinous is warned against throwing a stool at Odysseus: he might be a god in disguise.) Homer intends us to feel no sympathy for the bloody end to which the Suitors come. This is reemphasized in final sections of this book. The Suitors, in particular the brutal Antinous and the 'oily' Eurymachus, after learning of the abortive ambush, debate inconclusively on how best to get rid of Telemachus (16.342–408). Penelope enters to confront Antinous: the hypocritical Eurymachus attempts to pacify her (16.409–51). The contrast with the humble but honest Eumaeus and the beggar Odysseus (16.452–81) could not be greater.

ODYSSEY 17–20: PENELOPE'S TEST

Morning

The whole cast is together finally in book 17. Telemachus has returned to face the duplicitous behaviour of the Suitors (17.1–182); Odysseus, still disguised, and Eumaeus follow soon after (17.182ff.); Penelope is patiently enduring with her servants, Eurycleia and Eurynome (17.492ff.). This book (which begins a day ending in book 19) initiates a new movement in the epic which will climax in the destruction of the Suitors, the reunion of Odysseus with Penelope and, eventually, with Laertes, his father. Penelope comes sharply into focus in these books and, it could be argued, undergoes the testing and moral growth experienced by Telemachus and Odysseus.

Besides providing an exciting and satisfying narrative, book 17 yields a particularly interesting sidelight on some of the techniques of the oral poet. This sequence is built around the technique of polarity and analogy, a trait immediately evident on Telemachus' return to the palace. He is met by Penelope and Eurycleia (17.31ff.) who in many ways act as doublets for Odysseus and his retainer, Eumaeus. Penelope questions her son. He responds with the story of his travels (17.107–49). Note how the reference to Nestor (17.108–15) brings back the theme of fathers and sons, one of especial importance given the substance of the previous book. Note too how the reference to Menelaus and Helen (17.116–19) conjures up the theme of the house of Agamemnon. When Odysseus and Eumaeus are nearing the town they meet a goatherd, Melanthius (17.204–60). Melanthius, the first of several characters who attempts to do violence to Odysseus, gives us a foretaste of what is to come. He is Eumaeus' polar opposite. If the latter reflects respect for *xenia* and *philotēs*, the former reflects its opposite.

This use of polarity and analogy extends even to the pathetic *exemplum* of Argus (17.290–327), Odysseus' at least nineteen-year-old hunting dog. From its mound of dung, the decrepit hound recognizes its long-absent master. It wags its tail, lays back its ears, then breathes its last. Devoted to its master, but neglected by Odysseus' unchecked servants, the dog ironically embodies loyalty. The dog, furthermore, stands as an admirable parallel for Odysseus' aged and neglected father, Laertes (15.352ff. and 11.187–96).

The theme of testing is also important. It is above all the Suitors who are tested. Odysseus, still a beggar, does the rounds of his unwanted guests and asks for food. Their reactions will determine their fate. The most violent rejoinder is produced by Antinous who throws a footstool at Odysseus and reviles him (17.411–91). This is an extreme instance of *xenia* disregarded. What are we to make of the final scene of the book, of Penelope requesting Eumaeus to bring to her the disguised beggar (17.492–606)? Suspenseful narration is the simple reply. But are we not meant to link their prospective meeting with Odysseus' testing? Must he not learn, by testing, whether Penelope has remained faithful, like Eumaeus or the decrepit Argus, or whether she has chosen the route of Clytaemnestra?

Evening

The shape of book 18 is triadic. 'Assaults against and abuse of the beggar Odysseus (Irus 18.1–157, Melantho 18.304–345, Eurymachus 18.346–428) frame an important Penelope-scene (18.158–303)' is the summary of Jones (1988: 164). The structure highlights the three elements which call for consideration. First, Odysseus' resolve is given its most severe testing hitherto. Second, there is the theme of *xenia* outraged. Third, there is the perplexing announcement made reluctantly by Penelope implying that she must now face marriage: does she really mean it?

When Odysseus is pressed to fight his fellow beggar, Irus, he is tempted, against his better judgement, to kill the man with one blow. He resists. Killing Irus would ruin his disguise. With Melantho Odysseus is more restrained. The restraint seems to have vanished in the encounter with Eurymachus. Does not Odysseus' sharp tongue get the better of his hard-learned self-discipline (compare Scylla at 12.226–31)? The provocation of Eurymachus was such that, to avoid being harmed, he was forced to cower at the feet of Amphinomus.

The theme of *xenia* outraged is apparent in the actions of Irus, of Melantho, and of Eurymachus. Melantho is a female doublet of the violent Melanthius of the previous book (and thus a polar opposite of Eumaeus and Philoetius). Both treat a guest with contempt; both fail to perceive that it is their real master whom they are maltreating. The cowardly Irus copies Melanthius and Melantho. Melantho's lover Eurymachus also abuses Odysseus – he barely misses striking him with a footstool. His action mirrors that of Antinous who performed the same action in the previous book.

How do we understand Penelope's reluctant announcement that she will now consider marriage with one of the Suitors (18.269–73)? Odysseus thinks that he understands her motives: she is attempting to cajole gifts from the Suitors (18.281–3). Yet there are no indications that she is not in fact serious – her reporting of Odysseus' advice that she should, after Telemachus has come of age, choose and marry anyone she likes seems genuine (18.269–70). In the next book at 19.571–81 she announces that she will marry whomever of the Suitors proves capable of performing the trial with the bow and axes. Are we viewing the testing of Penelope – a testing comparable to that which Odysseus and Telemachus were subject? Just as they were tempted by *atasthaliē*, so now is Penelope being tempted and wavering. One can only assume that, when Odysseus smiles at her gaining presents, he has misread her moral perplexity.

Night

Odyssey 19 is the final part of the day which was begun with the departure from Eumaeus' hut (in book 17) of Telemachus, Odysseus, and Eumaeus. The core of this book is the encounter between Odysseus and his wife, Penelope (19.96–334, 508–604). It is an anticlimax. Why did Odysseus not declare himself to Penelope? An answer may be found in the scene with his old nurse, Eurycleia (19.335–507). Odysseus allows her to wash his feet. She recognizes him by an old scar (the classic discussion is Auerbach 1973). Odysseus' threatens her with death should she make known his presence. His fears are well grounded. There are many Suitors, but only he and Telemachus. How can two dispatch them all? Disclosure of his presence in the palace would mean certain death. We know he can trust Eurycleia, but does he? Odysseus is as uncertain with Penelope. How can he be sure of her? For all he knows she may have become another Clytaemnestra or Melantho. He must, therefore, hide his identity and test her loyalty.

Penelope continues to vacillate on the question of marriage. It is difficult to be sure of her motives (is she at 19.157ff. attempting to justify the wrong decision?). There is more than one possibility. First, at 19.528f., it is apparent that she could marry and depart with one of the Suitors (thus leaving Telemachus to take over the palace). Second, at 19.533, it is implied that she could return to her parents. Third (19.525–7), she could stay on in the palace in the hope that Telemachus might eventually be able to master the situation. None of these possibilities is palatable. To marry a Suitor is distasteful, though expedient. Her parents seem keen for her to marry – rather than come home. And Telemachus' chances on his own do not look good. One thing does seem certain. The possibilities leave the issue of Penelope's culpability particularly vague.

Next morning

The tension and excitement of *Odyssey* 20 are very much the product of its clipped, constantly changing narrative focus. The sequence begins with Odysseus (20.1–55), shifts to Penelope, back to Odysseus, to the exhausted mill woman (20.56–121), to Telemachus and Eurycleia (20.122–62), then to Eumaeus, then Eumaeus and Odysseus, next to Melanthius and Philoetius (20.162–239), then to the Suitors and to Telemachus (20.240–394). This is achieved in a mere 394 lines. The shifting narrative focus intimates that the poem is moving towards its climax. Narrative content mirrors this: the omen in response to the prayers of Odysseus (20.102–4) and the mill woman (20.105ff.), and Theoclymenus' prophecy (20.351ff.), all point towards the imminent destruction of the Suitors.

Odysseus' hard-won self-discipline is tested again in book 20 (Telemachus demonstrates his at 20.263ff. and at 20.304ff.). As he watches his servant girls laugh as they return from their assignations with the Suitors, he finds the desire to kill them hard to suppress (20.1ff.). Later, the malcontent herdsman, Melanthius, insults him again (20.172ff.). Then Ctesippus attempts to injure him by throwing an ox-hoof (20.289ff.). The theatrical, one-sided taunting and the omens produce in the listener a clear-cut conception of who is right and who is wrong. This allows the bloody destruction of the Suitors and of the servant girls to be carried out without recriminations. Since the 'divine apparition' of Odysseus in book 16 his motives and actions have become above reproach. He embodies the theodicy of Zeus. Such confidence (bestowed by Athena at 20.22–55), however, was not easily gained, for it is only at the end of this book that Odysseus seems to have developed full confidence in the resolution he made at 19.582–7, to deal with the Suitors at Penelope's test.

ODYSSEY 21–4: REVENGE AND RECONCILIATION

The test with the bow and revenge

The test is one of the most satisfying sections of the *Odyssey*. Penelope brings out Odysseus' bow and announces the contest (21.1–79). Following Telemachus' feigned failure, the Suitors begin their attempts (21.80–187). In the meantime Odysseus reveals his identity to Eumaeus and Philoetius and gives them their instructions for the slaughter (21.188–244). All the Suitors fail except Antinous, who suggests they put off the contest till the next day (21.245–72). Now comes Odysseus' turn. Against the wishes of the Suitors he succeeds in getting hold of the bow (21.273–379). While Penelope is away from the hall he strings it and shoots through the twelve axes. Then Telemachus takes up his arms and father and son are ready for the conflict (21.380–434). That bloodily fills out all of book 22. All of the Suitors are killed (22.221–389). The disloyal servants are hanged and Melanthius is mutilated (22.390–477).

Homer has prepared us for the death of the Suitors from the beginning of the poem. The Suitors' wickedness may be compared to that of Aegisthus (1.29ff.; notice how, at 22.413–16, the crimes of the Suitors are described in the same way as were those of Aegisthus). The Suitors' destruction, like that of Aegisthus, represents a triumph of good over evil, and the vindication of the theodicy of Zeus. Homer tells us as much at 22.374 and at 22.413–16. Book 16, furthermore, with its peculiar apparition of Odysseus and, later, the omens favourable to him and his companions, gives a plain indication that in this strange, moralistic *aristeia* (compare the climactic combat of Achilles and Hector in the same-numbered book of the *Iliad*) Odysseus' vengeance matches the will of Zeus.

Between Odysseus and the Suitors, notwithstanding this, there are similarities. Odysseus, especially in his treatment of Polyphemus, evinces a type of *atasthalie* to be associated with the Suitors. The moral growth of Odysseus since that low point is remarkable. Odysseus, it is worth reiterating, undergoes much the same 'alienation' and reintegration as do Achilles and Gilgamesh. The destruction of the Suitors represents a high point in Odysseus' moral reconstruction. To question the violence of book 22 (especially that towards the serving women, 22.465–73, and Melanthius, 22.474–7) is not so much to commit anachronism as it is to ignore plain signals given by Homer. The Suitors are evil: they do not act in accordance with the will of Zeus. They deserve punishment: Odysseus, acting in harmony with the will of Zeus, will punish them.

Penelope

The reunion of Penelope and Odysseus provides a moving climax to the poem (23.153–343). It is not, however, without its problems. It has often been claimed (Page 1955) that the narration is clumsy. Why must Penelope go to such lengths to test Odysseus? He has already gained the trust of the rest of his household and has killed off the Suitors.

Three points may be made. First, the scene does read well. Penelope's conflicting emotions are believably depicted and the encounter is drawn out in the leisurely way that both the *Odyssey* and the *Iliad* so often prefer. Second, the testing to which Penelope subjects

Odysseus is comparable to that to which he subjects others. (Penelope explains her motives at 23.209ff.: she has so often feared being deceived by strangers. Even after his bath, reclothing, and touch-up by Athena, Odysseus does not convince her. It is only when he displays knowledge of the marriage bed that he is finally convincing.) Third, although this interlude may appear over-strong to our realistic tastes, we should nonetheless forbear. The exaggerated and the fabulous, into which category this reunion may fit, has been a constant element of the poem – recall Odysseus' supernatural disguise as a beggar, or Athena transformed into Mentor, then into a vulture (3.371–2), or the feat with the axes, or books 9–12.

But the reunion presents another problem. It represents such a climax that anything that follows must appear bathetic (thus 23.344–72: Odysseus preparing to visit his father). Yet, logically, other loose ends need to be tied up. Laertes is one, the reaction of the Suitors' families is another. Both of these points are brought up at 23.344–72. They will receive their exposition in book 24. It is, I suggest, understandable that the narrative commencing 23.297 appears flat and anticlimactic.

Aftermath

In the third century before Christ the Hellenistic scholar Aristarchus asked whether 23.296 was the end of the *Odyssey*. Since then a battle over the authenticity of *Odyssey* 24 has raged unceasingly. The analysts, led above all by Page (1955), dismiss this book as not Homeric. The language, they claim, is unlike that which has preceded, the storytelling is inept, and the episodes irrelevant. The unitarians have desperately attempted to demonstrate the organic relationship of this book to what has preceded (Wender 1978).

Many of the elements and episodes of which *Odyssey* 24 is constituted are of clear thematic relevance to what has gone before. In the first of the three episodes of book 24 Homer introduces a second *catabasis* (24.1–204). There are, within the description of the descent to the underworld of the souls of the Suitors, two subsections: the first, Agamemnon's description of the death of Achilles (24.36–97); the second, Amphimedon's account of how the Suitors met their death (24.121–90). The thematic relevance of Agamemnon is made apparent at once. He is introduced as the victim of Aegisthus (24.19–22). The importance of the motif of the house of Agamemnon has often been mentioned. Agamemnon suffered the squalid death that might have befallen Odysseus had Penelope become like Clytaemnestra, had Telemachus not become like Orestes. The death of Achilles contrasts with that of Agamemnon (24.96–7): it was a glorious death in battle followed by a splendid funeral. This, we may guess, is the fate predicted by analogy for Odysseus and Telemachus. Amphimedon's death, of course, bears a closer resemblance to the death of Agamemnon: squalid, inglorious, it too was caused indirectly by a woman. The relevance of his admiring descriptions of Penelope should also be apparent (24.192–202): she was no Clytaemnestra. This second *catabasis*, therefore, reinvokes the beginnings of the first book and restates some of the major themes of the poem.

Less needs to be said of the second section of the book. Odysseus' testing of his father Laertes (24.205–412) may seem heartless, but so has been most of the testing (Fenik 1974: 47–50). Odysseus wants to make sure that Laertes has not betrayed him. The poem could not have ended without describing Odysseus' encounter with his father. It has been repeatedly foreshadowed, and it has its logical analogue in the reunion of Telemachus and Odysseus.

Much as we might have preferred the poem to end at 24.412 with Odysseus surrounded by his father and son, and by Dolius and his sons, the logic of the battle with the relatives of the Suitors (the third section of this book, 24.413–548) is at once apparent (compare 23.344–72). Orestes avenged the death of his father, Agamemnon. How can Eupeithes not do the same for his son, Antinous? It is back again to fathers and sons. When battle does break out, the focus shifts to Olympus where Athena requests of Zeus that she be allowed to impose peace. Such a request, indeed such a meeting, must look back to the meeting of the gods beginning at 1.26. The poem therefore ends where it had begun.

The real problem in these necessary events is that they are anticlimactic, out of all proportion, and ill-placed. The repositioning of these episodes would obviate much of the awkwardness. (Why not let Laertes and Odysseus meet in book 16? Why not place the *catabasis* before the reunion with Penelope? Or the battle episode: if Odysseus had rushed to confront the Suitors' relatives before the reunion with Penelope, interest would have been sustained.) The real problem with these episodes, I suggest, is their position. But it is not our task to rewrite Homer. Endings are always a problem.

There is no doubting the strength of the poem's final lines (24.533–48). They are an invigorating and almost humorous re-creation of much of the poem. Odysseus, forgetting all that he has learnt, is out for blood. Zeus, king as ever, is horrified and puts an end to things with a thunderbolt. Athena, dispensing wisdom, settles pledges between the factions. There is an air of frivolity to the whole scene. Has anybody learnt anything? Yet the will of Zeus has been vindicated, if tentatively, and the simple values of endurance, self-control, restraint, friendship, and loyalty to family have triumphed – though only just. That is ending enough.

4

APOLLONIUS OF RHODES, *ARGONAUTICA*

ALEXANDRIA AND APOLLONIUS

Intensified by convex mirrors, a wood-fire light shone thirty miles out to sea from the lighthouse at Alexandria. There were steam-powered warning sirens for bad weather. Some claim that the light-house had a lift (Ferguson 1973: 22). A mole three-quarters of a mile long linked the lighthouse's island with the metropolis. Alexandria was a new city. Designed by Deinocrates of Rhodes, commissioned by Alexander the Great, founded in 331 BC, it received traffic from the sea and the Nile. The city was an architect's creation. With streets set in a grid pattern, it was divided into five sectors, each logically designated by a letter of the alphabet. Enclosed by a wall nine miles long were such show-pieces as the palace, Alexander's tomb, the temple of the Muses and of Sarapis, the shrine of Pan, the university and library, the theatre, the zoological gardens, the gymnasium, stadium, and race course (Ferguson 1973: 22–4). There were large Egyptian and Jewish communities. In late antiquity the city included colonies from all over the world.

The Mediterranean in the third century BC had become a Greek lake, as Cary (1962: 195) colourfully puts it, 'but it had ceased to be under unified political control'. After the death of Alexander the Great (323 BC) his empire was split into a number of states. Of these 'Hellenistic' (a term used to describe the Greek world from 323 to 31 BC; see especially Green 1990) kingdoms, three dominated. The Antigonids were regents of Macedonia, ruled Thessaly and the Greek mainland. The Seleucids, resident in Antioch, controlled much of the east, and the southern half of Asia Minor. With their capital in Alexandria, the Ptolemies ruled Egypt, Cyrene, Cyprus, much of Syria, and a series of island ports in the Levant and the Aegean sea.

Under the Ptolemies Alexandria became the most sophisticated and cultured city in the Mediterranean. Living here during the third century BC were a remarkable cluster of writers, scholars, and scientists. This extraordinary intellectual ferment extended even to the non-Greek populations. During the reign of Ptolemy II Philadelphus (283–246 BC), the Old Testament was translated into Greek for Jewish use (the *Septuagint*). At the same time Jewish writers experimented in Greek (see Green 1990: 325) with biblical epic and tragedy (notably Ezekiel: he based a tragedy on Exodus: text and translation: Jacobson 1983). In Alexandria artists, scientists, and scholars seem to have been actively supported and to have been provided with governmental protection from outside interference (Green 1990: 80–91). Much of the intellectual life of Alexandria centred on the library (or Museum). By the time of the death of Ptolemy I Soter (reigned 323–283 BC), intellectual life was supported by a library containing up to 200,000 rolls (Canfora 1988 provides a reconstruction).

Apollonius produced his epic while living at the heart of this extraordinary melting pot. Little is known of his life. He seems to have been born in Alexandria but, because of a sojourn in Rhodes, received the eponymn Rhodius ('of Rhodes'). Perhaps he moved to Rhodes because of the scorn which greeted the first edition of the *Argonautica*. Apollonius may have been a tutor to the young Ptolemy III Euergetes (reigned 246–221 BC) and, perhaps later in life, he may have been librarian at the Alexandrian Museum. But these meagre facts must be treated with caution (compare Lefkowitz 1981). There is no reliable means of dating his epic, the *Argonautica*. It is usually placed at some time after 250 BC. Apollonius wrote a number of other works: epigrammatic poems and poems on the foundations of cities (these poems appear to have contained 'inner' stories or unusual, even rare digressions, often on erotic and metamorphosis-related themes). They have not survived.

BEGINNING THE VOYAGE: IOLCUS, LEMNOS, CYZICUS, HERACLES, AND HYLAS (BOOK 1)

The basis of Apollonius' story was an old one. The first strand of the myth concerns remote Colchis. Phrixus and Helle, son and daughter of Athamas, the king of Boeotia, fled the murderous designs of their stepmother, Ino. Through the assistance of the gods Hermes and Zeus they flew on the back of a golden-fleeced ram. Unfortunately Helle fell off and drowned in the sea – subsequently named the Hellespont. Phrixus reached Colchis where King Aietes, offspring of the sun god Helius, welcomed him and provided his daughter Chalciope as wife. The ram was sacrificed to Zeus and its fleece, placed in the grove of Ares, was set under the guard of a dragon. The second strand of the story concerns mainland Iolcus and its king, Pelias. He gained his throne by excluding his brother Aeson (Jason's father) from regal inheritance. Pelias had received an oracle warning him to beware of the arrival of a man with only one sandal: this was Jason. To avoid the danger Pelias tricked Jason into embarking on a mission to recover the fleece. That is the basis of the myth. Let us see what Apollonius does with this traditional tale.

In *Argonautica* 1 there are five major sections: the catalogue of the Argonauts, Jason's selection as leader and the departure, the sojourn on Lemnos with Hypsipyle, the disastrous events on Cyzicus, and the rape of Hylas and the abandonment of Heracles. These almost self-contained episodes are connected by the theme of the quest for the fleece. There are other elements welding the poem together. Love is of obvious significance (Zanker 1979). Guest-friendship (*xenia*) and its abuse – betrayal – is a constant theme. So too is respect for the gods, especially Zeus. The *aition* is prevalent (an *aition* is a brief tale or explanation concerning the origin of a particular custom – see Zanker 1987: 120ff.). There is also the theme of *amēchanos amplakiē* ('hapless error', 1.1053–4). Events, especially those affecting Jason, are seen to be often motiveless and often uncontrollable. Then, too, there is the character of Jason. He is an atypical epic hero (Klein 1983; but Hunter 1988), perhaps a new type (even an anti-hero: Lawall 1966; compare the male lead in Theocritus, *Idyll* 2). Frequently hapless (see Hadas 1936), morally flawed, prone to depression (Toohey 1990a), and isolated, he is not unlike the 'unaccommodated man' (Reardon 1969: 293), the male protagonist of the Greek novel. His closest parallels are the protagonists of the Alexandrian miniature epic such as Theseus (Catullus 64) or Scylla (the *Ciris*).

The catalogue

Argonautica 1 begins with an invocation of Apollo and, almost at once, sets out the reasons for the expedition (1.1–22). Occasionally the brevity of this scene-setting is criticized. The story of the Argonauts, however, was extremely well known. Lengthy recapitulation would be of interest only to modern readers. The long catalogue of Jason's Argonaut companions provides the real commencement (1.23–233). It is often criticized. Why include a catalogue here? And why, of the fifty-odd individuals mentioned, do twenty-one not appear again? The simplest explanation is that the catalogue provides a first glimpse of the epic's main players. Furthermore, the geographical and genealogical lore of the catalogue would certainly have appealed to contemporary listeners. Solidarity is also significant. The inclusiveness of the catalogue descriptions and listing perhaps emphasizes the unity of the crew. On occasion after occasion the Argonauts are seen to function together with a remarkable consultative unanimity.

Departure

The departure of Jason and the Argonauts is marked by a heightened sense of pathos. As the heroes march from the city (1.234–46) the townsfolk are in awe. But, with the appearance of the women and of Jason's mother, Alcimede, the tone changes (1.247ff.). When the women surrounding Alcimede begin to speak, they suggest that Jason's departure has brought evil upon her and that Jason's father, Aeson, would be better off dead (1.251–9). Jason attempts to assuage their profound grief (1.265–6). His success may be gauged by the extraordinary simile that follows (1.269–77). Alcimede is compared to a young woman who lives a hard life under a cruel stepmother. Her only solace is her old maid. Here we have a very compelling evocation of the theme of powerlessness. Alcimede's speech continues to emphasize the emotion (1.278–91): she does not speak of the dangers her son may face; rather she expects for herself the worst of a future without her only son. This theme is prominent as Jason departs: Iphias, the old priestess of Artemis, kisses Jason's right hand. Powerless Iphias was unable to do more, for she was swept aside by the crowd (and by the heroes' heedless enthusiasm for their quest, 1.311–16 – see Nelis 1991).

Before the Argonauts embark Jason calls an assembly. They must choose a leader (1.317–62). In his specification of the leader's qualities Jason appeals to the notion of group solidarity (1.338–40): the one chosen must be the best man (*aristos*), their leader (*orchamos*), and responsible for the group's quarrels (*neikea*) and agreements (*syn-*

thesiai) with others. The crew at once choose Heracles, who, with equal speed, refuses the position and suggests Jason. The selection of Jason seems to validate the notion of group solidarity. Heracles is no group man. He would have fitted better into the world of Homer. After the ship has been launched (1.363–93) and the rowing seats allocated (1.394–401), the Argonauts sacrifice to Apollo (1.402–47). The seer Idmon shifts the mood back again to that of powerlessness: he predicts from sacrifice that the mission will be successful but that it will bring about his own death. This news, combined with the unwonted burden of responsibility, throws Jason into a mood of deep despondency and helplessness. The angry reaction (1.462–71) of Jason's foil, Idas, is understandable (Lawall 1966: 140; Fränkel 1960). He taunts Jason with cowardice. Idas' taunt would be unexceptionable were it not for the sentiments expressed at 1.467–8. Here he swears that Zeus does not assist him so much as his own sword. The sentiment is irreligious and, judging from Idmon's strong reaction (1.476–84: he outlines the punishment those who dishonour the gods receive), we are meant to disapprove (compare Agamemnon and Chryses in *Iliad* 1). This theme is repeated throughout the poem. Orpheus' song (1.496–511), designed to calm the dispute (1.487–91), celebrates the power of Zeus (Lawall 1966: 141).

Lemnos

Apollonius first fills in the background (1.609–32): how the Lemnian women were betrayed by their husbands; how the outraged women slaughtered their husbands (and, eventually, all male Lemnians to guard against betrayal); how Hypsipyle spared her father, King Thoas. These events are significant in three ways. First, however much the husbands may have deserved punishment, Apollonius denounces their slaughter as *hyperbasiē* (1.609), a synonym for lack of respect for the gods (hybris). Second the sexual infidelity of the Lemnian males parallels that of Jason in Euripides' *Medea*. (Sexual infidelity is a form of betrayal. That theme is echoed elsewhere – think of Medea and her father Aietes, or her brother Apsyrtus, or of Jason and Medea in Corinth.) Third, Medea's actions in Euripides' play (the slaughter of her children) are anticipated in the slaughter of male kin by the Lemnian women.

Hypsipyle thinks the Minyae (the Argonauts) should be bought off with gifts. If they come into the city they may get wind of the slaughter and spread the story (1.657–66). The Lemnian women choose instead to follow the advice of a crafty old servant, Polyxo. Polyxo urges them to invite the Minyae into their city and, for the sake of the future, marry them (1.675–96). Hypsipyle accedes and a messenger, Iphinoe, is sent to invite the crew to the city. The narrative focus shifts to the Argonauts and to Jason's preparations for his departure. There follows a long set-piece (technically entitled an ecphrasis or 'description' – Kurman 1974) detailing Jason's cloak (1.721–68; Lawall 1966: 154–8; Shapiro 1980). The major ecphrasis associated with a major hero in Homer details the shield of Achilles (*Iliad* 18.478–608). In the *Iliad* the ecphrasis preceded a momentous combat. In this poem the ecphrasis precedes a minor amatory dalliance. Is Jason's beautiful cloak a substitute for Achilles' armour – a sign of the new, sexual themes of the *Argonautica* (compare Goldhill 1991: 308ff.)? The image of the cloak becomes a leitmotif of the poem. Hypsipyle gives him one as he leaves Lemnos. Jason wears it when he attempts the trials dictated by Aietes (3.1204–6) and it is given to Apsyrtus just before his murder (4.421–4).

Hypsipyle explains away the disappearance of the husbands (1.793–833). Jason, sucked in and forgetful of his mission, constantly puts off leaving Lemnos (1.853–64). Heracles puts an end to the amatory dalliance. It has been argued that this is the result either of his homosexual preferences (visible perhaps in the episode with Hylas) or of his being more in the Homeric mould: Achilles, this argument maintains, would not have dallied on Lemnos. That Jason does is indicative of the changed attitudes of the hero (Beye 1982: 88–9).

Cyzicus

Jason and his crew set sail from Lemnos by Samothrace to the Propontis where they put to land at the island of the Doliones, who are ruled by the gentle King Cyzicus and his young queen, Cleite (1.936–88). The hospitality (*xenia*) of Cyzicus (1.961–88) contrasts with the conduct of King Pelias, or the suspicious Lemnian women, or King Aietes. *Xenia* is prominent again when the Argonauts moor in the harbour opposite Cyzicus. Here, instead of receiving a welcome, they are attacked by the giants. It takes Heracles and the younger crewmen to put them to rout (1.989–1011).

Jason and Cyzicus are doublets (witness their ages, 1.972–3). The force of the comparison becomes apparent when the Argonauts are blown back to Cyzicus at night. Jason's crew are ignorant of where they have come to land. The inhabitants of Cyzicus assume that these night visitors are hostile. Battle breaks out, King Cyzicus is killed, and the Doliones are put to flight. His young bride, grief-stricken, commits suicide (1.1063–5). Jason is inadvertently responsible for all of the deaths. The themes here are powerlessness (resulting from the accidental killing of Cyzicus) and love (between Cyzicus and Cleite). The love between Cyzicus and Cleite may be contrasted with that between Jason and Hypsipyle and later with that between Jason and Medea. Jason destroys Cyzicus' marriage; he will do this later to his own.

The use of the *aition* is especially prominent in this sequence (Fraser 1972: 628). There are several: how an anchor from the *Argo* came to be enshrined in the temple of Jasonian Athena at Cyzicus; how an altar to Apollo Ecbasius was established; whence came the honours paid by the Cyzicenes to those slain in the battle with the Argonauts; the origin of the legend of the fountain of Cleite; the origin of the annual local custom of grinding meal for dough cakes at the public mill; the establishment of a cult of the Mother Goddess on Mt Dindymum – to which are added a pair of subsidiary *aitia*, the origin of the propitiation of Rhea with the wheel and drum, and the origin of Jason's stream. These *aitia* exhibit the Callimachean poetic to which Apollonius subscribes. They perform, however, a role subsidiary to the major themes (powerlessness, *xenia* and its abuse, love). They increase the depth, variety, and pleasure to be derived from the poetic texture of the *Argonautica*.

Heracles and Hylas

The Argonauts on their voyage from Mt Dindymum are troubled by windless conditions. They are forced to row. Heracles overdoes things and breaks his oar (a rare instance of humour – compare Beye 1982: 95, and Lawall 1966: 123ff.). At the end of the day they put to shore in the land of the Mysians (1.1172–86). While most of the voyagers prepare bedding and food Heracles sets out to find a replacement oar. In his absence Hylas, his handsome young servant, sets out to fetch water. As he arrives at a spring the nymphs have just begun their dance. One spots Hylas, becomes infatuated, and draws him in (1.1207–39). Heracles is alerted by Polyphemus and, distraught, begins the search (1.1240–72). Is Heracles' distress caused by frustrated love or mere grief? Theocritus (*Idyll* 13) makes it clear that Heracles and Hylas are lovers. This is less clear in Apollonius' version. There are hints of love: Heracles' reaction to the disappearance (1.1261–72) bespeaks more than paternal emotions; Hylas' looks (see 1.1229–33) are certainly enticing. But for Heracles this event represents also 'hapless accident' (*amēchanos amplakiē*).

At dawn next morning the wind springs up. Tiphys the pilot urges the crew into the *Argo* and to set sail. They are well away before realizing that Heracles and Polyphemus have been left behind (1.1273–83). (Heracles' disappearance may symbolize the absence of the traditional 'heroic' on the *Argo* – Beye 1982: 97; compare Goldhill 1991: 315ff.) Had Heracles not broken his oar, this would not have been the case. Nor, some years later, might Zetes and Calais have met a sticky end. In the dispute between Telamon and Tiphys (the former urging that they turn back for Heracles, the latter that they press on), the two sons of Boreas intervene in Tiphys' favour (1.1298–1301). Later Heracles murders them for their meddling (1.1302–3). The themes of powerlessness and error are thus continued. Does the theme of betrayal appear as well? Heracles seems to have thought so. It is difficult not to link the decision to abandon Heracles with the actions of the Lemnian males and, proleptically, with Medea's betrayal of her parents (see, for example, 3.741–3). Eventually Jason will betray Medea.

FANTASIZING ABOUT THE DARK AGES: THE ARGONAUTIC LEGEND AND ALEXANDRIAN APOLLONIUS

But we are moving too far too quickly. We need to think a little more about two things – both related. Whence does Apollonius derive his myth and how does it gain its special timbre?

Origins first (I follow Hunter 1989: 12–21). The Argonautic legend was persistently popular – it predates the Trojan legend (it is mentioned at *Odyssey* 11.235–59 and books 9–12 generally seem to depend on the Argonautic saga). The *Iliad* (7.468–9, 21.40–1) and Hesiod's *Theogony* (992–1002) refer to the legend. The myth persisted into the archaic period (the seventh and six centuries BC) (Huxley 1969: 60ff.). Two important fifth-century treatments were by Pindar and Antimachus of Colophon. Pindar's *Fourth Pythian Ode* (462 BC) recounts the oracle delivered to Pelias, Jason's return to

Iolcus, and his arrival in Colchis; the love theme and Medea's betrayal of her parents play an important role. Antimachus wrote a *Lyde* (*c.* 400 BC). The ancient commentators explain that this lost poem was a collection of unhappy love stories serving as a parallel for Antimachus' relationship with Lyde. The tale of Jason and Medea was told in the first book of the *Lyde*.

There were other influences. Ancient travel literature, such as the *Odyssey*, Herodotus, the Ionian logographers, Xenophon, Pherecydes, and Hellanicus, assisted. There were, apparently, some near contemporary versions of the saga (one by Herodorus and another by Apollonius' possible contemporary, Dionysius Scytobrachion). The key influence is Euripides' play, the *Medea*. Apollonius assumes his readers will know the story of this play: how Jason abandons Medea in Corinth for a royal bride; how, driven by a desire for vengeance, Medea murders their children. The characterization of both Jason and Medea is shaped ironically with the events of the Euripidean play in mind.

But such source-criticism blinds us to two obvious points. The first concerns fantasy or romance, the second concerns the characterization of Jason. The *Argonautica* is an utterly romantic creation. Love is the simplest evidence of this (so Lemnos). Yet romance is also built upon nostalgia and sentimentality. The whole concept of sophisticated urban intellectuals recreating a hazy, Dark Ages world of mighty heroes points to this clearly. In a sense, the poem represents an extreme of over-urbanized fantasy.

Apollonius was not naive. The characterization of Jason is startlingly anachronistic. I have outlined the traits of the traditional epic hero: of superior social station, this tall, handsome, muscular person is often a king or leader; he excels in athletic and fighting skills – and has the courage and intelligence to utilize them. Jason is not the possessor of these qualities. Our Jason may be handsome and attractive to women like Hypsipyle, he may also be of superior, albeit down-at-heel, social status, but he is not the equal of Heracles in athletic or fighting skills. Besides, he is too prone to depression and to haplessness in the face of trouble. Jason is a 'new man', an ordinary well-born Alexandrian, more at home in the sophisticated urban world of Apollonius than in the backblocks of northern Greece and the Black Sea.

SAILING IN THE DARK AGES FROM THE BEBRYCIANS TO COLCHIS (BOOK 2)

Our last image of *Argonautica* 1 was of the crew rowing to shore in an unnamed land. Let us pick up the narrative at the beginning of book 2.

Bebrycians

Amycus, king of the Bebrycians, is a real Dark Ages villain. He is full of hybris. He is *hyperopléestatos andrōn*, 'most arrogant of men' (2.4). The events among the Bebrycians (which recapitulate the themes of the battle with the giants) act as a foil to the more ambiguous experiences of the previous book. Amycus' characteristics exhibit themselves through violence (he forces visitors to box with him; he usually kills them) and through his violation of the rules of hospitality (2.5–7), a fault shared by the earth-born giants. Amycus challenges the Minyae (2.11–8) and is taken up by Polydeuces (2.22–4). The fight (2.67–97) is an exciting one. Civilized Polydeuces kills barbaric Amycus (Fränkel 1952; Lawall 1966: 132). The subsequent battle with his followers reaches a similarly satisfying conclusion (2.98–144). Even here Apollonius cannot resist 'hapless error': the Bebrycians spread abroad their troubles (2.135–6); the neighbouring Mariandyni, under their king, Lycus, took advantage of their reduced state to ravage their lands (2.137–44).

Phineus, the Clashing Rocks, and the epiphany of Apollo

In the long episode concerning Phineus (2.178–536) the themes of hybris, powerlessness, love, and chance return. Hybris dominates. Phineus, gifted with foresight by his father Apollo, did not respect Zeus; he told too much of the future (of Zeus' 'sacred will', 2.181–2). The punishment was a lingering old age, blindness, and the Harpies despoiling the food brought by his neighbours (2.181–92). If Phineus had been a villain, he is sufficiently pathetic now to inspire pity. Zetes and Calais, respecting the gods, will drive off the Harpies if Phineus swears this action will not bring down divine wrath (2.244–53).

Phineus, by now a reformed sinner, provides a powerful instance of the powerless (*amḗchanos*) individual. His affliction mirrors the emotional condition which Jason exhibits throughout these first two books and which he exhibits again (2.408–10) on hearing Phineus' predictions concerning the rest of the voyage (2.311–407). Phineus introduces the love theme. When Jason dolefully asks what help they will have to complete their voyage (2.411–18), he replies that there will be Cypris, the goddess of love (2.423–4): that can only refer to Medea. Hybris reappears intertwined with powerlessness and chance in the Paraebius narrative (2.456–97). Paraebius' father had, in his youth, cut down a tree that was beloved of a Hamadryad. He did this despite her entreaties. The Hamadryad cursed Paraebius' father and children. Paraebius consulted Phineus on the curse and was advised to build an altar to the nymph, to make sacrifice and prayer on it. This averted the curse. Paraebius, from gratitude, looked after Phineus.

The description (2.549–610) of the passage between the Clashing Rocks – sometimes termed the 'Symplegades' – is meant to be enjoyed as a stirring piece of narrative. Soon after a remarkable scene transpires on the island Thynias. Late during the night Apollo appears (2.674–84). The Argonauts are awestruck and subsequently perform sacrifice and rites for the god. How seriously are we to take this passage? The strength of its language indicates that we ought to take it very seriously. Are these the poet's real beliefs? If they are, the lines may act as a gloss on the significance of the poem's many traditional depictions of irreligious actions and attitudes (Lawall 1966: 160–1).

The Mariandyni and the deaths of Idmon and Tiphys

Lycus, king of the Mariandyni, and his army ravaged the Bebrycians after the death of the brutal Amycus. Formerly lacking Heracles' help, Lycus found that Amycus and the Bebrycians were making inroads into his territory. But now the Argonauts have set this right. Lycus' gratitude for their help is such that he sends his son Dascylus on the expedition (2.774–810).

What are we to make of Lycus? He is an obvious foil for Amycus: the former embodied hybris and the outraging of *xenia*. Second, his condition prior to the arrival of the Argonauts amongst the Bebrycians was one of powerlessness. Third, Apollonius likes to alternate in his narrative between moods that could be described as antitheses or polar opposites (Hutchinson 1988: 142). After the optimism of this section (best embodied in the sending of Dascylus) follows the emotional devastation of the loss of Idmon and Tiphys. The pathos (chance and helplessness) of the death of the seer Idmon is stressed. Idmon is unexpectedly struck down by a wild boar on his return from Lycus' court (2.815–34). The circumstances of Tiphys' death (2.851–63) are not given comparable emphasis. The helmsman dies after a brief illness. If his death is less pathetic the results are more catastrophic. Tiphys' skill led them through the Clashing Rocks. Jason's reaction can be expected (2.885–93): he is thrown into a state of utter helplessness (again he is *amēchaneōn*, 2.885). The response of the crew (2.894–8) to Jason's outburst (2.885–93) is often remarked upon. Ancaeus volunteers to take over as helmsman. But three others, Erginus, Nauplius, and Euphemus, also volunteer. This response exemplifies the solidarity of the crew.

Further travel

The interest of the next episode (2.899–945) is geographical. Like many comparable passages we can assume it possessed a charm for the Hellenistic audience which we cannot necessarily share. There are elements of thematic significance. The encounter with the ghost of Actor's son, Sthenelus, is one (2.911–29). The pathetic victim of an arrow wound on the way home from his expedition with Heracles, his appearance repeats the theme of helplessness and, to some extent, chance. Sthenelus' death reenacts those of Idmon and Tiphys. He also provides an obvious parallel for the Argonauts. Will they too meet Sthenelus' fate?

The theme of 'love' is picked up in 2.930–1029. This sequence is notable for the number of lands passed which are associated with individuals, usually women, of dubious sexuality: beginning at 2.946 there is Sinope and her well-protected virginity; at 2.966 Melanippe ransoming her sister Hippolyte from the clutches of Heracles; there are Amazons at 2.985; peculiar practices of parturition amongst the Tibareni are evident from 2.1009; beginning 2.1023 the odd mating habits of the Mossynoeci are mentioned.

The sons of Phrixus and Colchis

Upon reaching the island of Aretias (where the Argonauts are forced to chase away feather arrow-shooting birds – 2.1030–89) they meet the sons of Phrixus, who had been shipwrecked on their way to Greece (2.1090–230). Mention of Phrixus (who brought the fleece to Colchis) points to a climax, presumably the proximity to the fleece itself. Soon after taking on board the sons of Phrixus we find the Argonauts putting to shore near their destination (2.1231–85). Phrixus' sons, like Sthenelus, are doublets for Jason and the Argonauts. This becomes especially clear at 3.304–16. They too had been on an expedition to distant parts, an expedition that was somehow to be related to the estate of their father. At 3.597–602 it is made apparent that Aietes, like Pelias, lived in fear of a prophecy concerning trouble from his own family. As Pelias did with Jason, so Aietes does with the sons of Phrixus. Their present ill-fortune offers, therefore, a glimpse of the sort of fate which may await the Argonauts.

CALLIMACHEAN POETICS AND THE EPIC FROM HOMER TO APOLLONIUS

Enough of the narrative has now been seen to enable us to begin to isolate some of the characteristics of this romantic epic. One of its prime traits has been its learning, but it is a learning which, by its romantic recasting of heroic myth, easily becomes ironic. There are specific peculiarities (Hopkinson 1988: 10–11): experiment in form and language (thus the archaic dialect and the strikingly varied tone), allusion, an interest in the erotic, and an approach to myth from an off-beat angle (an elliptical narrative, unusual subject matter, the episodic development of digressions or stories within stories). There is, furthermore, a preference for realism, sentimentality, and romance.

Such characteristics are in marked contrast to those we have observed in Homer. Why the change? The answer cannot easily be formulated, for a history of epic from Homer to Apollonius cannot be written. No epics survive. What there was (fragments: Powell 1970; Lloyd-Jones and Parsons 1983) seems to have been insufficiently remarkable to warrant survival. Perhaps the genre had gone into a decline. The little information we have is not encouraging (Ziegler 1934). There was, for example, a long *Thebaid* of Antimachus (*c.* 400) and, from amongst Apollonius' contemporaries, epics by Rhianus of Crete. The genre seemed also to embrace poems about the foundation of cities (Apollonius wrote them himself) and the chronicles of cities (such as Rhianus' *Messeniaca*, or Euphorion's *Mopsopia*), and about the deeds of living kings (such as those of Simonides of Magnesia), as well as mythological epic. We are forced back again to the scanty comments of the ancient commentators or to reliance on the very little known of contemporary literary criticism and poetic theory (compare Heath 1989). Here the theory and the practice of Apollonius' contemporary, Callimachus, offer considerable assistance (Hutchinson 1988: 85ff.; Zanker 1987).

Poetry in Apollonius' era had ceased to have the public significance it did in the fifth century. As a medium for communication it had been replaced by prose. Hopkinson (1988) suggests that a new audience for poetry developed, one of well-read, private, even learned individuals. For such readers poets like Callimachus above all developed a new type of mannered, miniature epic (see Chapter 6). The Callimachean miniature epic throws traditional epic on its head. It seems to have done this deliberately, having been developed in reaction to what Callimachus may have seen as the moribund praise of the historical epic and the tedium of the long mythological epic. Apollonius' *Argonautica* – as we have just seen – exhibits most of the characteristics of the Callimachean, avant-garde epic (Hutchinson 1988: 85–142), with the exception of brevity. But even this is offset by the narrative's being built up of independent episodes (Levi 1985: 420).

CALLIMACHEAN EPIC: MEDEA AND JASON IN LOVE; JASON REGAINS THE FLEECE (BOOK 3)

Argonautica 3 represents a triumph in the application of Callimachean poetics to large scale epic. It begins with an invocation of Erato (3.1–5), the Muse not of epic but of love poetry – an indication of the timbre of the narrative to follow. The invocation also acts as a marker. As is sometimes observed (Hunter 1989: 95), the poem's tripartite structure (outward voyage – Colchis – homeward voyage) is emphasized by invocations beginning books 1, 3, and 4. But, just as the invocation beginning book 1 introduces books 1 and 2, so this invocation appears to introduce books 3–4. The bipartite structure so produced may match that of Virgil's *Aeneid* (with its 'Odyssean' books 1–6 and its 'Iliadic' books 7–12 – Erato is also invoked at *Aeneid* 7.37).

Hera and Athena visit Aphrodite

In the opening scene (3.6–35) Hera and Athena meet to discuss how the fleece may best be conveyed from Colchis. This is the first time in the epic that gods appear together. The assistance to be rendered by the goddesses is not typical of the older epics. Eros will cause Aietes' daughter, Medea, to fall in love with and assist Jason (3.25–9). Amatory power has been substituted for martial valour (Cypris for

Enyalius, 3.559–60). The love theme of the first two books has been leading to this prospective liaison (Zanker 1979). The visit of Hera and Athena to Aphrodite (3.36–110) may be compared to Thetis' visit to Hephaestus in *Iliad* 18. But the emphases here differ markedly (Lennox 1980). The realistic depiction of Aphrodite at her toilet and of the domestic exchanges between Aphrodite and Eros (3.129ff.), for example, reflect not a heroic world but the middle-class Alexandria of Apollonius.

Embassy to Aietes; Eros shoots at Medea

Jason explains his plans to his comrades at 3.171–93. He will go to Aietes' court in the company of the sons of Phrixus, and Telamon and Augeias to request the fleece. Aietes' palace, as befits the son of the sun and the brother of Circe, is a magical, ominous place (3.210–34). A description of the palace and its living quarters (3.235–48) allows the narrative to pan in naturally on Medea, also particularly on Chalciope, the mother of the sons of Phrixus. It is after Aietes' unelaborated entrance that Eros fulfils his promise and wounds Medea (3.275–98). This description deserves careful consideration (Barkhuizen 1979). What is new is, first, the interest in such psychological states and, second, the precision of the depiction of Medea's paradoxical state of mind.

This is a good place to mention a problem many readers have felt with Medea. In this book she is the innocent victim, a young woman in the thrall of first love. In book 4 she is a scheming, hardened woman. Are the two Medeas consistent (Dyck 1989)? Compare Homer: Achilles is portrayed as an individual who, through testing, matures. Medea (and Jason) develops through testing. Jason's development is a down-hill slide. Medea, having betrayed her family for a man who, throughout book 4, shows no signs of reciprocating her love, undergoes a process of embitterment. Medea is in her teens. Compromised by love for an empty hero, she exhibits increasingly a ruthless determination merely to gain her own way.

It was to be expected that Aietes' reception would not be welcoming once he had understood the purpose of their journey. He reacts angrily (3.367–81 and 3.396–421) to Argus' explanation (3.320–66). He imposes the famous trials upon Jason. Jason accepts (3.427–31), but is sunk into absolute dejection (3.432; compare 3.423).

Medea's anguish; Argonautic designs; Aietes' anger

At 3.443–71 it is all anguish and the contradictions of Medea's emotions. She cannot remove Jason's image from her mind (3.453–8); she fears for his safety (3.459–60), but mourns him as if he were already dead (3.460–1); she hopes he will escape unharmed (3.466) but will know of her sympathy if he does perish. (3.468–70). The theme of betrayal is implicit: Medea is being led to betray her family because of the overpowering emotion she feels for Jason.

Argus suggests that they approach Medea for assistance (3.472–83). Jason agrees (3.484–8) and the decision is submitted to the group. The prospect of recounting the trials imposed by Aietes reduces Jason again to a state of dejection (3.491); the recounting produces much the same response in his companions (3.504). At length Peleus, Jason's foil, volunteers to take his place. He is followed by several others (3.504–20). Argus, perceiving that the group have reached a consensus, interrupts to state that he will approach Medea (3.523–39). The omen (3.540–54) of the dove falling into Jason's lap as it escapes a hawk is interpreted by the seer Mopsus. It indicates that Aphrodite will assist the expedition. Does Jason's acceptance of the assistance of Aphrodite indicate that he is willing to use love as a means of securing Medea's help? Idas, at any rate, will have none of this (3.556–63). Rather like Heracles, he sees no relationship between Cypris (love) and Enyalius (war).

Medea's anguish and her decision

Medea's anguish is partly the result of uncertainty: should she trust the stranger? It also results from the conflict between *aidōs* and *himeros* (desire), 3.653 (Otis 1964: 77–8). The former dictates loyalty to her parents, the latter following Jason. Medea's ambivalence is especially manifest in the dream sequence (3.616–32). She dreams that Jason entered the contest, not for the fleece, but for her. But she fought the bulls in his stead (Hunter 1989: 164 notes the sexual symbolism of fighting bulls). She must decide, her father dictates, whether to award the stranger the fleece. Betraying Aietes' wishes she awards Jason the fleece.

Medea's ambivalence is exhibited in her actions (3.645–64) after the first monologue (3.636–44). She hesitates to leave her room. She casts herself writhing on her bed. Apollonius compares her to a young widowed bride (she is like powerless Cleite). Medea weeps. Finally, on the report of a servant, Chalciope goes to Medea

(3.670ff.). Medea disguises her desire to assist Jason as concern for Chalciope's sons (3.688ff.). Soon her decision has been made – *erretō aidōs* ('hang shame', 3.785), she states. She will betray her parents. Medea herself gives a name to her decision. It is *atē* (3.798).

Jason and Medea meet

Next come Medea's and Jason's preparations and their journey to the temple of Hecate (3.828–947). Medea admits in her monologue (3.891–911) to wrongdoing or 'sin' (3.891–3). Apollonius insists on Medea's guilt.

The meeting between Jason and Medea takes place at 3.956–1147. Medea, confused by love, hands over the charm almost at once (3.1008–25). She provides Jason with directions (3.1026–62). But she cannot restrain herself: pathetically she asks him to remember her when he is home; then strangely she asks him of Ariadne. Ariadne and Theseus were lovers (see Chapter 6). Theseus acts as a parallel for Jason (Hunter 1989: 208; compare 3.997–1007): like Jason, Theseus underwent an ordeal involving a fierce bull, and was assisted by a young woman (Ariadne, also a granddaughter of Helius). Theseus abandoned Ariadne, just as Jason will Medea in Corinth. When Jason does reply to Medea's question concerning Ariadne (3.1096–101) he makes the link between Ariadne and Medea more explicit. He hopes (3.1100–1) that, as Minos, the father of Ariadne, favoured Theseus (by giving his daughter to the hero), so too may Aietes. Jason has begun to fall in love with Medea (3.1077–8). It is not long before he has as good as proposed marriage (3.1120–30). After they part love does not assuage Medea's perception of her own wickedness (3.1161–2).

The contest

The preparations which Jason must make for the contest are, first, to have collected the dragon's teeth from Aietes (3.1173–90), second, to sacrifice a ewe to Hecate (3.1191–224) and, third, to sprinkle himself and his weapons with the water in which Medea's charm has been steeped (3.1246–67). Idas resists Jason to the end. His reaction to Jason's return from the rendezvous is one of barely suppressed anger (3.1169–70). His fury at Jason's magically strengthened weaponry is exhibited openly, if ineffectually (3.1252–5). The support of Cypris (love) is the cause of his wrath. Love's support is brazenly displayed by Jason's wearing Hypsipyle's cloak (3.1204–6) to the sacrifice for

Hecate. But, Idas or no, the result of the contest is a foregone (though exciting) conclusion. Jason yokes the oxen, ploughs the field, and slaughters the earth-born warriors (3.1278–407).

ESCAPE FROM COLCHIS (BOOK 4)

Invocation; Medea flees to the Argonauts; the fleece

The invocation of the Muse (4.1–5) indicates the ambiguity with which we view Medea's position. The poet asks whether her state is the result of *atēs pēma dysimerou* ('woe resulting from ill-desired *atē*') or *phyzan aeikeliēn* ('unseemly panic'). It is love that drives Medea to flee to the Argonauts (4.11–33) (but compare Dyck 1989: 458; Zanker 1979: 64). Apollonius is almost anatomical in his depiction of Medea's physical symptoms: her eyes are filled with fire, her ears ring, her throat is choking, she pulls at her hair, groans, is suicidal. The passage through the darkness (4.34–65) seems almost to enact a bridal procession (Bremer 1987). But it is a grisly procession (Medea's capacity as a sorceress is stressed at 4.50–3) and an ill-omened one. There is no family accompanying Medea, only the moon, sacred to Hecate, Medea's votary (4.57–65), who compares her own frustrated love for Endymion to that of Medea for Jason. When Jason first addresses Medea in the company of the Argonauts the irony could not be greater: he promises her marriage (4.95–8, compare also 4.194–5). Soon afterwards, through Medea (4.145–61), Jason snatches the fleece (4.162–82).

Escape and the murder of Apsyrtus

Aietes and the Colchians react violently. Aietes, in a state of irreligious madness (4.228), commands the Colchians, led by his son Apsyrtus, to pursue Medea (4.228–35). If they cannot bring her back, their punishment will be death. In the meantime the Argonauts have set off up the Danube (4.241–302: for Apollonius it links the Black Sea with the Adriatic). Apsyrtus and his companions, by portage, reach the fancied outlet of the Danube into the Adriatic before the Argonauts (4.303–28). Here they attempt to block egress by manning the islands in the river mouth – all, that is, except two which were sacred to Artemis. The Argonauts land on one of these (4.329–37). Realizing that they are outnumbered, they strike a deal (*synthesiē*) with the Colchians: they will keep the fleece but will leave Medea on the other island with the priests of Artemis; judges later can arbitrate her future (4.338–49). The bargain is a betrayal. Jason had promised marriage (4.350–90).

When Medea confronts Jason he backtracks, claiming that the *synthesiē* will allow him to murder Apsyrtus; that without their leader the remaining Colchians will be easy to deal with (4.395–409); that Medea will be protected. Jason is improvising. Medea takes him at his word and indicates that she will assist (4.411–20). The two prepare gifts for the unfortunate Apsyrtus (4.421–34), the most striking of which is Hypsipyle's cloak. (The irony in the presence at this point of such an emblem of sexuality is pointed. Ariadne is mentioned too.) Medea now lies to the Colchian heralds, telling them she had been carried off by the Argonauts and urges them to arrange for a clandestine meeting with Apsyrtus (4.435–44).

There follows a most extraordinary personal intrusion into the narrative (4.445–51): the narrator denounces the power of love and with it the plan to murder Apsyrtus. The final lines of this passage are perhaps the most striking. As if there could be no doubt as to the significance of Medea's and Jason's intended action, the author provides guidance. The bloody murder of Apsyrtus follows immediately.

Where is Jason's *amēchaniē* now? He lies in wait for Apsyrtus, then cuts him down while Medea shields her gaze (4.452–81). The blood splatters Medea's silvery veil. The divine avenger of such deeds, the Fury (4.476), watches what is taking place. Zeus' disapproval is indicated at 4.558. This scene of extraordinary slaughter provides the acme of a chain of events forming the themes of sin, hybris, betrayal, and love. What next? The Argonauts attack the Colchians accompanying Apsyrtus and slaughter them to a man.

The wrath of Zeus and Circe; Phaeacia

Following the death of Apsyrtus, the Colchians do not persist in pursuing the *Argo*. Hera dissuades them with a display of lightning. The 'Odyssean' progress of the Minyae, however, is thwarted by Zeus' anger at the slaughter of Apsyrtus (compare the wrath of Poseidon in the *Odyssey*). They are blown back to their starting point (4.557–91). The *Argo* itself explains their troubles stating that Jason and Medea must visit Circe's island (Aeaea) to receive purification from the goddess (4.580–91). They receive purification (4.685–717), but when Circe questions her niece, and when Medea responds with all but the death of Apsyrtus (4.718–38), Circe twigs and, though not offering Medea or her companions harm, she sends them away (4.739–52).

Hera once again comes to the rescue. Through the divine messenger Iris, she approaches the immortals Thetis, Hephaestus, and Aeolus requesting that they assist the Argonauts' voyage past Scylla and Charybdis and the Wandering Rocks (4.753ff.: the narrative is becoming particularly Odyssean) and on to the land of the Phaeacians. Thetis' succour is especially important. She and the Nereids literally bear the *Argo* past the dangers. Thetis' presence is noteworthy. She is the separated wife of Peleus, one of the Argonauts (4.842–81). The marriage had been arranged through Hera, the poem explains (4.805–9). Furthermore, Thetis' and Peleus' son, Achilles, is destined after his death to become in Hades the husband of Medea (4.811–15: a pointed comment on the Phaeacian marriage of Jason and Medea?). The relations of Peleus and Thetis foreshadow those of Jason and Medea. Peleus angered Thetis: he thought she intended to murder young Achilles. The parting, precipitated by anger and suspicions of child murder, enacts that time in Corinth when Jason and Medea will part.

The sojourn on Drepane (4.982–1222), the island of the Phaeacians, is upset by the precipitate arrival of a group of Colchians bent on reclaiming Medea (4.1000–10). The king, Alcinous, wishes neither to incur the wrath of Aietes, nor to offend against the customs of guest-friendship (*xenia*) by handing over Medea. Medea's repeated pleas (4.1011–29 and 4.1030–52) for assistance (arguing that she left Colchis from fear, that she is still a virgin, and that Jason must honour his vows – *synthesiai kai orkia*: an echo of 1.338–9) persuade Arete to urge her husband not to turn them away (4.1073–95). The solution is marriage: Alcinous determines that if Medea has shared Jason's bed, she must stay (4.1098–1109). A hasty, compromised (4.1161–6) ceremony is arranged (4.1128–69).

Libya, Crete, and the last adventures

Beached, but in a state of helplessness (4.1261–307), on the shores of North Africa (4.1223–50), the crew are rescued by a night vision given to Jason by the Libyan nymphs (4.1308–79). Following their advice, the Argonauts shoulder the boat and manhandle it across the sands to the Tritonian lake (4.1380–92). What transpires here (in particular the deaths of Canthus and Mopsus – 4.1485–536) may best be seen as the working out, again, of the wrath of Heracles, the testimony of his vengeance for having been abandoned and betrayed amongst the Mysians. (Lawall 1966: 128 believes the episodes here balance those of books 1 and 2; this signals that the end of the poem is close.)

When the Argonauts arrive at the Tritonian lake they go in search of water. Here they happen upon the garden of the Hesperides where the nymphs, after some persuasion, provide them with water (4.1393–460). The very day before Heracles had come to the same place. Here he killed the monstrous snake which protected the silver apples hanging in the trees. He stole these and, in need of water, created a spring (4.1432–49). The Argonauts, wishing to thank Heracles for the life-giving spring, set off after him (4.1458ff.). In this search take place the deaths of Canthus and Mopsus. Their deaths, though indirectly, are the result of the abandonment of Heracles in book 1. Thus the theme of betrayal reappears.

The theme of betrayal is also evident in an implicit comparison of Heracles and Jason. The comparison is forced by the similarities between Jason's and Heracles' exploits. Both remove a valuable object from a tree that is protected by a monstrous snake. Heracles' act was a wanton act of aggression which, as the reaction of the nymphs shows, caused considerable grief and destruction. So too with Jason. At the very least he has deprived Aietes of a daughter and a son. In time his theft of the fleece will result indirectly in the murder of his own children.

If there are hints of Odysseus' ambiguous treatment of Polyphemus in the garden of the Hesperides, there are even more when the Argonauts meet the monster Talos (4.1620–93). Talos, the bronze monster, blocked the Argonauts from landing and seeking supplies (thus forcing comparison with Amycus). Success for the Argonauts seems to hinge upon his destruction. Medea does this in a particularly chilling manner (4.1661–72). Once again civilization triumphs. Medea, aiding Jason, did this to her own father.

The last two episodes of the poem are relatively brief. In the first the Argonauts, trapped on the Cretan sea in a pall of darkness, are rescued by Apollo (4.1694–730). In the second (4.1731–72) Euphemus, after experiencing a prophetic dream, casts a clod into the ocean. From this springs the island of Calliste on which, in later times, his descendants will settle. Neither vignette is remarkable. Closer examination indicates their real function. In the first the heroes are rescued from darkness, in the second one of them creates, magically, a fertile island. Darkness leads to light and fertility, dream leads to reality. This is Apollonius' parting summary of the purport and result of the mission of the Argonauts. That reality is somewhat different, however, is obvious from the juxtaposition of the two final adventures with the story of unfortunate Talos.

The purport of these two stories may be apparent. That they represent a curiously flat manner of concluding the epic is obvious. The same complaint may be levelled at the poet's farewell (4.1773–81). These three sections, coming after the intensity of events amongst the Phaeacians, appear anticlimactic. There is, in the *Argonautica*, only one other comparably disquieting passage, the catalogue with which the poem begins. Perhaps Apollonius had troubles with beginnings and endings.

5

BEGINNING EPIC IN ROME

WAR AND ROMAN EPIC

At the time the Alexandrian savant Apollonius was writing for his learned North African audience Rome was without a literate culture. Yet, within ten or twenty years of when Apollonius may have died, Roman writers had made their first attempts at epic, drama, and comedy. The victory in the first Punic war seems to have provided the impulse. Increased stability at home, a horizon extending beyond Italian borders, a rise in the number of foreigners, especially Greeks (Gruen 1986: 250ff.), visiting Rome, and, particularly, a burgeoning mercantile class represent some of the stimuli for literature created by the aftermath of the conflict. Epic began at Rome in the 240s and 230s BC.

Almost from the beginning the themes of Roman epic are constant. Power and history – rather than the more typically Greek concerns of family, community, and the gods – provide the real focus. Perhaps this is because Roman literature grew in the aftermath of a war. Conte (1986: 144) goes as far as to maintain that there is a 'Latin epic norm'. He believes that the core of the subject matter of Roman epic should accord with the 'supremacy of the state as an embodiment of the public good', and, what is more, it should accord with an 'acceptance of divine will as providential guidance', and with 'the historical ratification of heroic action'. Power and history are necessarily interwoven with notions of the state. This has some relevance for the ideas I have emphasized above. Transgression, alienation, and reintegration with the community, all displayed through the heroic impulse, were key notions within Greek epic. In Rome these themes are tempered by a concern with power, history, and the state. The hero is still prey to the dangers of the heroic impulse, but increasingly he becomes a cipher for the greater drama of the establishment and maintenance of Roman power and the Roman state.

Fragments are all that survive of the earliest examples of Roman epic. Livius Andronicus, Naevius, and Ennius were the first representatives. They have left very little of their poetry. Were they preceded by other, perhaps oral poets? The *Iliad* and the *Odyssey* were oral, hence we are able to posit an earlier oral tradition. I suppose there must have been a comparable tradition at Rome (Hainsworth 1991: 76): yet the evidence is unclear (compare Cole 1969). Latin poetry begins abruptly in 240 BC with a play by Livius Andronicus. Epic began, perhaps soon after, with a translation of the *Odyssey* by the same writer.

LIVIUS ANDRONICUS' TRANSLATION OF THE *ODYSSEY*

Who was Livius? The 'facts' are few: Livius Andronicus (*c.* 284–204 BC) was a Greek from the southern Italian city of Tarentum. When, about 272 BC, the city surrendered to Roman forces, Livius Andronicus may have passed into the possession of a Roman who subsequently took him to Rome. On manumission he may have taken his owner's name. It is also sometimes suggested that, after manumission, Livius Andronicus took to teaching. Perhaps in this capacity he produced the Latin version of Homer's *Odyssey*. After the performance of his comedy and his tragedy in the year 240 BC, he continued with literary composition throughout the rest of his long, famous life.

The *Odyssia* (*Odyssey*) survives in approximately forty-six lines (text: Mariotti 1986; Morel 1975 – whose numeration I follow; translation: Warmington 1936). One line is the usual length of these scraps. Such a small amount of text will not allow us to formulate an accurate evaluation of Livius' accomplishment. There are, however, a few generalizations which may be drawn. Livius' translation was no mere school crib. It represents an interpretation. Through this process of interpretation Livius exhibits himself as a pioneer in the transplanting of Greek concepts into Latin. Here are a few famous examples: for the Greek *Mousa* (Muse – invoked at the outset of traditional epic) he substitutes (fr. 1) the *Camena* (a fountain goddess enshrined outside Rome's Porta Camena), for *Moira* (Fate – fr. 11) *Morta* (Death), and for what seems to be *Mnēmosynē* (Memory –

fr. 23) *Moneta* (the adviser or warner). Elsewhere (fr. 20) he generalizes Homer's originally personal statement; in fr. 22 he translates the marginal comments of a Homeric scholar rather than those of Homer himself (Waszink 1972: 887ff.). Of even greater significance is the solemnity and pathos which Livius injected into his *Odyssia* (Mariotti 1986: 42) – this is particularly evident in his use of archaisms. Greek epic is a particularly clear, even sinuous product. Roman epic, with the exception of Ovid, plays on solemnity, pathos, and gravity. It is as if Livius has set the Roman tone (Williams 1983b: 58).

Was metre a problem? Our ears, schooled on the hexameter, argue that the greatest difficulty under which Livius may have worked – and Naevius after him – was the Saturnian metre. Modern critics are scathing in their estimation of the powers of this measure: there is a 'jerky combination of iambic and trochaic rhythms that broke each line into predictable halves; it was no match for the easy flow of the hexameter. The choice of that metre for epic must have been forced on [him] by Roman conditions' (Williams 1983b: 59). To judge from a pair of Roman sepulchral inscriptions engraved in 298 BC and 259 BC (Williams 1983b: 57), this metre seems to have had some popularity. Does this point to an oral tradition predating Livius (see Cole 1969)? That this tradition was supplanted, however, may reflect historical accident as much as metrical inadequacy. It is easy to be metrically wise after the event.

The transformation of the Greek epic into an acceptable genre for Roman literature is probably Livius' greatest achievement. There are other achievements. The production of an interpretation of a master work of Greek literature is one. Waszink (1972: 889) stresses a critical third. He believes that Livius Andronicus' introduction of Greek gods into a Roman epic context was crucial: 'perhaps because of his Greek background Livius did not realize that he had introduced a completely foreign element into the life of contemporary Roman society.'

THE FIRST PUNIC WAR AND NAEVIUS

The Carthaginians were originally a Phoenician people (hence 'Punic', an adjective implying Phoenician). They had settled in North Africa with Carthage as their capital. This Punic people had become a considerable power: their empire included areas extending on land as far as Gibraltar, and on sea as far as Sicily, Sardinia, and southern Spain. The Carthaginian occupation of Messina (in northeast Sicily) and the threat this posed to the Greek cities of southern Italy (those which were Roman allies) provoked conflict. To prevent Carthage controlling the straits of Messina and threatening the Greek Italian cities, Rome sent forces into Sicily. The upshot was the first Punic war (264–241 BC). Rome did not fare well in the early stages of the conflict. Sea defeat followed upon sea defeat; even a land invasion of North Africa, led by Regulus in 256 BC, was not successful. Victory came finally when the Romans defeated the Carthaginian fleet off the Aegates Islands in 242 BC. The Carthaginians subsequently sued for peace. The results for Rome were dramatic. From this conflict sprang the origins of the Roman empire: first Sardinia was incorporated, then Corsica, and later Sicily. Within Italy the effects were equally dramatic. Rome, with the prestige of its defeat over the Carthaginians and its burgeoning overseas empire, came increasingly to be seen as the leader of the Italian states.

The significance of the Punic wars for the development of Roman self-consciousness cannot be overemphasized. Rome did not become the dominant force within the Mediterranean until some time after the second Punic war (218–201 BC). But what this first victory seems to have done was to provide the Roman people, a culturally and imperially backward group, with some sense of their own power as a collective entity.

Gnaeus Naevius (c. 270–201 BC) wrote his Roman epic about the first Punic war. The poem, unsurprisingly, is named the *Punic War* (text: Strzelecki 1964; Marmorale 1953; Morel 1975; translation: Warmington 1936). This was the first Roman national epic. Beginning with the mythological origins of Rome in Troy it produces a narrative climaxing in the victory of the Romans over the Carthaginians. (The concern with power and with history, twin themes of Roman epic writing, is evident.) Why did Naevius write this poem? The *Punic War*, at its simplest, may have represented an inchoate celebration of the nascent nationhood of Rome.

Who was Naevius? About 270 BC, and, possibly, in Campania, he was born into a lower-class family. Naevius served as a soldier in the first Punic war and seems to have begun to produce plays in Rome in the mid-230s. These were adaptations of Greek originals or plays based upon Roman historical themes. (He may have begun the epic at about the same time.) He is said to have been particularly bold in his attacks on famous Romans, so much so that he was gaoled. He was subsequently exiled, perhaps for continued attacks, to Utica in North Africa. Naevius died there towards the end of the century.

What of the poem itself? About sixty lines comprise its remains, the longest passage is of three lines. The poem was composed originally as an unbroken narrative. It was divided into seven books in the second century BC by C. Octavius Lampadio (Rowell 1947). If the book lengths corresponded roughly to those of the epics of Homer or Virgil (500 to 700 lines per book), the length of the poem may have been somewhere between 3,500 and 5,000 lines. How were these books arranged? It has been suggested (Fraenkel 1935) that the first book of the *Punic War* provided an account of events of the war down to the capture of Agrigentum in 262 BC (Rowell 1947). At Agrigentum was a temple to Jupiter on whose pediment were depicted the foundation legends of Rome. The poem may have provided, beginning in book 1, an ecphrasis of this pediment whose description extended at least until the conclusion of book 3. (Alternatively the Trojan material of these first three books was not an insert, rather it was free-standing (Büchner 1967: 9–25).) Book 2 seems to have concentrated on Aeneas. The storm of Virgil, *Aeneid* 1 and its council of gods may have been derived from here. It is possible that Aeneas' love affair with Dido may also have been described (thus providing an aetiology for the war itself). Book 3 describes Aeneas' arrival in Italy. Anchises dies here. The book may also have contained narratives of the Roman regal period. Books 4–7 tell of the war, and may have outlined the years 260–241 BC, with each book embracing approximately a five year period.

Why did Naevius include this Trojan material within his epic? One attractive theory (Waszink 1972: 906ff. provides a survey) argues that Aeneas is depicted as visiting Carthage and meeting Dido within these books (so, for example, do Strzelecki 1964 and Marmorale 1953 interpret fr. 28 Marmorale). Dido, as Virgil recounts in *Aeneid* 4, fell in love with Aeneas. Although he reciprocated the emotion, his mission to found Rome forced him to leave her. She committed suicide from grief but not without prophesying eternal enmity between the Carthaginians and the Romans. The Trojan material, therefore, provides an *aition* for the Punic war. It is sometimes objected that such a link between the two sections of the poem is too sophisticated for this 'archaic' Roman poet. The criticism seems unnecessarily querulous. The *Punic War* may be a prosy affair, but a belief in the vital continuity of Roman history, that Aeneas, the early kings, and their dilemmas provide prototypes for contemporary leaders and heroes, is a simple idea that is not restricted to Naevius. It is at the heart of the epics of Virgil, Ovid, and Valerius Flaccus.

The vital contribution which Naevius provided for the development of Roman epic has been summed up by Waszink (1972: 921), reproducing a very useful set of observations which were made by Bruno Snell. After stressing the importance of political considerations in Naevius' poem, Waszink states that the poet 'linked together three motifs of Hellenistic poetry: themes concerning foundation legends, history on the large scale . . . and divine machinery'. All of these traits are to be found again in Ennius and Virgil. Naevius, rather than Livius Andronicus, is the first real representative of the Roman epic tradition.

Power, history, and the heroic impulse are of clear importance for Naevius. The heroic impulse may be seen as the motor of historical change and, very likely, of Roman power. Wars such as the Punic and the acts of heroism by men such as Regulus (fr. 42 Marmorale) have forged the Roman nation. Whether this impulse was treated critically – as happens in Homer and Virgil – we cannot know. It seems unlikely. Naevius gives the impression of believing, if not in all politicians, at least in Rome.

THE SECOND PUNIC WAR AND ENNIUS

At the end of the first Punic war the Romans set a series of indemnities upon the Carthaginians and took possession of Corsica and Sardinia. To compensate, Hamilcar, the Carthaginian general, had been consolidating influence in Spain (237–219 BC). His capture of the city of Saguntum, a city allied to Rome in Spain, provided the impetus to renewed war (the second Punic war of 218–201 BC). The early events of the conflict are well known: the tales have often been told of Hannibal and his elephants' crossing of the Pyrenees, the Rhone, and the Alps, and of his fifteen years marauding in Italy (including the near annihilation of the Roman army at Cannae in 216 BC). Hannibal advanced within sight of Rome. But for the lack of Italian allies, he might have captured it. Roman victory was finally achieved by taking the war to Africa (204). Publius Cornelius Scipio (a future patron of Ennius) undertook the action and defeated the Carthaginians at the battle of Zama in 202 BC. The enormity of the invasion and the enormity of the Roman victory cannot be overestimated (further see Chapter 11).

Quintus Ennius (239–169 BC) wrote his *Annales* about the second Punic war. How do the *Annales* (text: Skutsch 1985; translation: Warmington 1935) relate this war? Here is a brief outline of the contents of the fragmentary poem (the fragments amount to not much more than 600 lines – less than a twentieth of the final scope of the eighteen books).

Fifteen books spanning the thousand years 1184/3 to 187/4 BC represented the original ambit of the poem. The fifteen books may have been grouped into triads (I am following Gratwick 1983: 60ff.). The first triad (books 1–3) covers, in book 1, events from the sack of Troy, via Aeneas, Romulus and Remus, to the foundation of Rome. Books 2–3 seem to have narrated the events of the legendary period during which Rome was said to have been ruled by kings (the so called 'Regal period'). The second triad (books 4–6) describes, in book 4, events from the foundation of the republic (510 BC) to the Gallic invasions (390 or 387 BC). Book 5 narrates events down to the end of the Samnite wars (295 BC), book 6 the war against Pyrrhus (281–271 BC). The third triad (books 7–9) deals with, in book 7, events to the invasion of Hannibal (218 BC). Doubtless Ennius gave the first Punic war short shrift because it had already been dealt with by his earlier rival, Naevius. Books 8 and 9 describe the rest of the second Punic war (218–201). The density of narrative detail increases considerably in the fourth (books 10–12) and fifth triads (books 13–15). Within the former, book 10 outlines the war against Philip of Macedon (201–196 BC), while books 11 and 12 carry the narrative down to the commencement of the war against Antiochus III of Syria (191/2 BC). The final triad of the original edition seems to outline events as follows: book 13, the war against Antiochus (191 BC), book 14, Scipio's victory at Magnesia and the naval war (190 BC), book 15, the actions of M. Fulvius Nobilior, Ennius' patron. The final, appended triad (book 16–18) described the events of the Istrian war and ran to 171 BC.

What of the author of the *Annales*? He did not experience such a turbulent career as Naevius. Ennius began life in Rudiae in Calabria – which was a trilingual town. Ennius, therefore, may have spoken Oscan, Greek, and Latin. He arrived at Rome in 204 or 203 after serving in the Roman army during the second Punic war. He was awarded Roman citizenship in 184 BC. Ennius was brought to Rome by the severe Marcus Porcius Cato in whose patronage he remained for some years. Subsequently he became the client of the aristocrat, Marcus Fulvius Nobilior. Fulvius Nobilior, amongst others, was famous for instituting the cult of the Muses in Rome. It is with an invocation to the Muses, not the Camenae like Livius Andronicus, that Ennius begins his epic. The original version of his poem concluded with a narrative of the exploits of Fulvius Nobilior. Ennius also composed tragedies and satires.

Where did Ennius derive the idea for the form of his poem? The title of the poem looks to the records of each year's events (arranged day by day) kept by the Roman priest caste (the *pontifices*). These were instituted, according to legend, by King Numa. According to Jocelyn (1972: 1008–9) the pontifical records covered such matters as the transference of *imperium*, terrifying prodigies, crises in the city food supply, decisions on new religious practices, matters related to the calendar, important funerals, the establishment of colonies, the arrangement of alliances, declarations of war, the levying of troops, and so forth. Many of these matters appear in the *Annales*. Doubtless for much detail Ennius would have consulted other books, perhaps the Greek historians or Roman practitioners such as Fabius Pictor, and also would have used the oral histories of the more prominent families.

Form needs inspiration. The concept for a poem that leapfrogs back from Hannibal to Numa to Troy belongs to Naevius. There were other influences: the 'annalistic' *Chronographiae* of the Hellenistic savant, Eratosthenes, is one; Hellenistic poetry on the foundation of cities (Apollonius) and on the history of peoples represents another (see Chapter 4). Origins, it seems, were in the air during this period. Ennius' old patron, Cato, composed a prose work, the *Origins* (*Origines*) covering much of the ground of Ennius' poem.

Naevius' concept may have been inspiring. The same could not be said for his metre. Turning his back on the Saturnian metre used by Livius and Naevius, Ennius chose the measure utilized by Homer and Apollonius. Henceforth the hexameter was to become the medium for Roman epic. How does Ennius' hexameter compare to that of his Greek predecessors? First, it is clear that Ennius was determined to imitate the 'easy informality' of the Homeric hexameter line. (These comments are drawn from Williams 1968: 684–99.) In Homer the metrical line does not force elaborate patterning onto the structure of sentences (as is the case with Catullus, especially, and with Virgil). Rather the sense flows easily from one line into the next. Second, Ennius, unlike Homer, concentrates on the sense of hearing rather than that of vision. Ennius' concern is consistently on the dignity of language 'reinforced by onomatopoeia, alliteration and assonance, no less than by polysyllabic words' (Williams 1968: 689). Ennius' text 'makes its primary appeal to the ear'.

Ennius' reliance on Greek rather than Roman models produces a critical chestnut. Gratwick (1983: 66ff.) maintains that the choice of hexameter (the metre of Apollonius and Callimachus) demonstrates the Hellenistic (he means, I presume, Alexandrian) timbre of his poetry. Newman (1967, 1986) and Williams (1968: 696) concur: Ennius is a 'Callimachean' (contrast Jocelyn 1972). Two obvious instances of Alexandrian influence are the experimental nature of his language (Williams 1968: 696) and, as mentioned, his reliance on the *Chronographiae* of Eratosthenes (whose learned approach is often said to conform to the canons of Callimachus' taste). There are also widespread, if not frequent, verbal echoes of Callimachus' writings. Two other features are frequently mentioned. First, the dream (fr. I.ii–x Skutsch) with which the *Annales* appear to begin (Ennius tells of a dream encounter with Homer 'who revealed in a discourse on the *natura rerum* that his soul had passed into Ennius' (Skutsch 1985: 147ff.)) is usually taken as a reference to Callimachus. In *Aitia* fr. 2 Callimachus alludes to Hesiod's meeting the Muses on Mt. Helicon. From them he learnt the *natura rerum*. Second, Ennius describes himself at the beginning of the seventh book of the *Annales* as *dicti studiosus* ('keen on the "word"'). The latter designation is felt (Gratwick 1983: 62; Jocelyn 1972: 1013) to be a calque for the Alexandrian *philologos*. Does such a description render Ennius a Roman Callimachus?

What do the *Annales* mean? On the simplest of levels they represent a national encomium. As I have stated above, the vehicle by which the nation has been drawn to its victorious position of power in history is the heroic impulse. Ennius, accordingly, gives the impression of having lauded its appearance in individuals. Like Naevius he lionizes the successful warrior. Ennius' practice may be contrasted with that of the less percipient Cato who, according to Gratwick (1983: 64),

> in the prose *Origines* . . . made a point of referring to officers on active service simply as 'the consul', 'the praetor', without naming them . . . and implicitly asserted the subordination of the individual to the community. . . . Whether conscious or not, this was a reaction against the individualism of Ennius.

The position of Rome's power within history, however, seems to be the crucial concern of the *Annales*. Through the depiction of a series of Roman heroes (culminating in the present) Ennius demonstrates the continuity of Roman history. Ennius' alleged Pythagoreanism may support this conclusion. Pythagoreanism, in which doctrine it is sometimes said Ennius was instructed, believes in the transmigration of souls (or 'metempsychosis'). An instance is provided by Ennius' dream beginning the *Annales*: Homer has transmigrated into the soul of Ennius. The progress of Roman history is ordained, he may have believed, by the metempsychosis of a heroic soul from one generation to the next. If Ennius did believe in this historical continuity he would not be alone. Ovid through Pythagoras in *Metamorphoses* 15 half-seriously puts forward the same theory. Virgil, in *Aeneid* 6, uses the notion of the transmigration of souls as a means of providing a type of continuity for Roman history. Valerius Flaccus' Argonauts, if we follow Jupiter's prediction at *Argonautica* 1.531–60, are the first in a chain of individuals who will climax in Domitianic Rome.

One final question: did Ennius, like Homer, treat the heroic impulse critically? The impression one gains is that he did not. But who can be sure? The poem might appear considerably more like the Homeric or Virgilian epics if we had more of it. Hannibal might be more of an Agamemnon. A comparison with the *Punica* of Silius Italicus (see Chapter 10), which also had the second Punic war as its focus, provides us with an instance of an annalistic poem which also exhibits an interest in the heroic impulse. Silius, however, abandons the theme of moral reconciliation (a development from the misuse to the proper use of the heroic impulse). Instead he divides the process of moral growth between characters: there are heroic villains like Hannibal and admirable heroes like Scipio. Perhaps Silius' model was Ennius.

6

THE ALEXANDRIAN
MINIATURE EPIC

THE LIFE AND TIMES OF A MINOR GENRE

It is not often that we can watch the birth, death, and resurrection of a literary genre. We can do this with a version of the small-scale epic developed in Alexandria at the time of Apollonius. This type of poem (sometimes termed the 'epyllion', or the 'miniature' or even the 'minor' epic) became very popular, not just in Alexandria, but also in Rome. But it did die – some time in the first century of our era. The trouble was that, like the Tasmanian Tiger, it was too specialized. New literary predators and new literary colonists rendered it extinct.

What of the resurrection? That took place with a series of self-conscious revivals as late as the sixteenth and eighteenth centuries (Vessey 1970: 38): from the sixteenth century there are Shakespeare's *Venus and Adonis* (1593) and *Rape of Lucrece* (1594) (Donno 1963), then, much later, Pope's *Rape of the Lock* (Tillyard 1954).

Yet sometimes its very existence is denied (Allen 1940; Vessey 1970; but Hollis 1990). Rather, there were epics of considerably shorter length than those produced by Homer, Apollonius, Naevius, and Ennius (Newman 1986: 31). Short epics had always been composed (Hollis 1990: 25): Hesiod's *Shield of Heracles* or his didactic *Theogony* and *Works and Days* may be typical; from late antiquity many examples survive (Chapter 11). During the Hellenistic period, however, there were at least two identifiable types. The first is simply a narrative on a mythological, sometimes heroic theme told sequentially and without the encumbrance of 'digressions' or multiple stories within the same poem. There was also a second, more eccentric type whose prime trait is the 'digression'. This second type

100

represents a new departure for ancient epic. It is on this second type, therefore, that I intend to concentrate.

As we look at these 'epyllia' we will see that they share a number of traits. Let us catalogue them now. These poems are short, probably not much more than 2,000 lines, and, in many instances, probably not much more than 500 (compare Hollis 1990: 24). There must be at least one digression (Crump 1931: 23; Hollis 1990: 25) within the main story. Typical means of deploying these 'digressions' (Williams 1968: 244) are interweaving, juxtaposition, or treating a series of stories but using some artificial means of linking them. Above all these are emphatically learned, allusive, experimental poems (perhaps most evident in the use of *aitia*) (compare Hopkinson 1988: 10). It may follow, therefore, that their myth stories are often obscure. They also show a curious preference for direct speech (Hollis 1990: 26). In most cases there is a pronounced love theme and, related to this, a strong focus on women (Hollis 1990: 25). Of especial importance is their tendency to concentrate on unheroic and 'morally flawed' characters, often in realistic, even sentimental, settings. This last point needs especial emphasis. It illustrates again the transformation which Alexandrian practice has wrought upon the traditional hero (Zanker 1977). The protagonist of the miniature epic undergoes no 'moral regeneration'. Rather he, frequently she, is left in a quagmire of moral ambiguity. In this aspect the epyllion looks to Apollonius' Jason and forward to the flawed heroes of Lucan and Statius.

BIRTH PAINS: CALLIMACHUS, *HECALE*

A bull had been devastating the countryside around Marathon in Attica. The hero Theseus set out from Athens to deal with the feral pest. On his way to Marathon a rainstorm broke out. He took shelter in the shanty of an old woman named Hecale. Next morning he left to deal with the animal. On his victorious return he found Hecale dead. In gratitude for her hospitality he founded the deme (a 'county') of Hecale and the cult of Zeus Hecaleius. Of this slender tale Apollonius' contemporary, Callimachus, made a poem, the *Hecale*, of between 700 and 1,800 lines (Hollis 1990: 337–40). Approximately 300 discontinuous, often incomplete lines survive. The *Hecale* is the representative Alexandrian miniature epic. It seems to have been this poem which spawned the subgenre.

The poem's deployment of the myth may have run like this (I am adapting Hollis 1990). Hecale and a description of her hospitality began the epic. Following was a description of Theseus' initial arrival in Athens, his father Aegeus' recognition, and his escape from the death planned for him by stepmother Medea. Then, after passage through a storm, Theseus arrives at Hecale's hut. Hecale, entertaining Theseus, describes her life and how she came to be poor. Although she was from a wealthy family, may have married well and had two sons, she lost them all and was reduced to poverty. Theseus' response is not extant. Perhaps he described his own martial triumphs, including his killing of the villain Cercyon who had killed one of Hecale's sons. At some point after this there is an abbreviated outline of Theseus' combat with the bull. Soon after there is an illustration of the celebrations held for his capture of the bull. Then a crow speaks. It tells how she lost her early position as pet of Athena and was reduced to poverty, perhaps as the pet of Hecale. Within the crow's monologue seem to have been digressions concerning Erichthonius and the daughters of Cecrops, Apollo's fiery liaison with Coronis, and a detailed description of country life. In the meantime Hecale has died. The remainder of the poem seems to have narrated her funeral and the posthumous honours instituted for her by Theseus.

Callimachus' account of the legend is anything but conventional. Instead of accenting the combat with the bull, which is the logical climax of the poem, Callimachus highlights a series of digressions related loosely to Hecale (and to the crow). Thus from the encounter with the poverty-stricken, rustic Hecale, emerges a type of low-life realism and of urban sentimentality. The narrative focus shifts away from male and heroic concerns to those of the erotic (note especially the crow's tales) and, of course, those of a woman. We should also note that this poem adapts the *aition*. Indeed, the ostensible purpose of the *Hecale* is to provide two *aitia*: the first for the name of the deme of Hecale (so named by Theseus in gratitude for Hecale's hospitality) and the second for the cult of Zeus Hecaleius (again named in gratitude). The deme and the rite were extant in Callimachus' day. The ironic, recherché intellectualism (or should we say learning?) of all this could hardly be more evident.

How experimental was the *Hecale*? The following characteristics may provide some sort of an answer to the question. The narrative point of view swings dramatically: at times it is that of the poet, at other times of Hecale, then of Theseus, then of the crow. The narrative topics show the same dramatic shift: the *Hecale* engrosses both the mundane poverty of old woman's shack and the dramatic heroism of Theseus' triumph over the bull. Tone oscillates comparably (Hutchinson 1988: 57): the violence of the storm which drove Theseus to Hecale must contrast with the domesticity of her reduced circumstances, the pathos of Hecale's story must contrast with that of Theseus, the banal but fantastic notion of a speaking crow contrasts with its extravagant language. And the actual manner of narration exhibits dramatic variety: narrative, for example, may be allusive, consisting of only the barest mention, it may concentrate on a series of vivid points, or it may entail expansive description.

This catalogue of characteristics may seem tedious. Its importance, however, cannot be stressed enough, for Callimachus' ironic epic throws traditional epic on its head. The product of a world utterly unlike that of Homer, it recasts and reevaluates the heroic (compare Hutchinson 1988: 61–3). Callimachus is unheroic rather than anti-heroic. As Bulloch (1985: 564) acutely notes: 'the *Hecale* . . . was not a *diminution* of the grand themes of tradition, but rather an essential reworking of convention, and the establishing of a new realism.' The significance of Callimachus' innovation for the future of the epic genre, as well as this subgenre, was immense (Newman 1986). First, the revaluation of the heroic makes possible not just Apollonius' Jason or the protagonists of the Roman epyllion, but also the suspect heroes of Roman imperial epic. Second, the play of intellect – which constitutes the real unity of Callimachean poetry – breathes life into a genre that seems to have been nearly moribund (see Chapter 4).

COMPROMISE: THEOCRITUS, *IDYLLS* 13, 22, 24, 25

Meaning or meanings for the *Hecale* remain elusive: the poem is too fragmentary. Yet the labyrinthine texture of the narrative points to a poem that sternly resists 'closure'. I doubt that this can be said of Callimachus' contemporary, Theocritus. The abiding impression of his epyllia is of caution and compromise. The heroic still bulks large. But the ambiguous revaluations of Apollonius and Callimachus are less at issue. Interpretation, therefore, becomes more straightforward.

None of Theocritus' 'narrative idylls' (*Idylls* 13, 22, 24, and 25) is quite what Callimachus produces in the *Hecale*. Take *Idyll* 13 (on Hylas) or 24 (Heracles as a baby). They preserve the playfulness, the interest in female characters, the realism (though this can be exaggerated) of the *Hecale*. Absent, however, is the extreme elaboration most evident in the often violent tonal and technical oscillations of Callimachus' poem. Nor do these poems contain digressions.

Compare *Idyll* 25 (sometimes said not to be real Theocritus (Gutzwiller 1981: 30). An old countryman meets a stranger – Heracles. The old man, after describing their surroundings and explaining to whom the farm belongs, leads Heracles to meet its owner, King Augeas (1–84). This is the first of the three parts of the miniature epic. In the second (85–152), Heracles, in company with Augeas and his son Phyleus, inspects Augeas' cattle and sheep. Heracles rebuffs the attack of the strongest of Helius' twelve bulls. In the third part (153–281), Heracles and Phyleus are walking to an unnamed town. On the way Heracles explains how he tracked and throttled the Nemean lion.

Juxtaposition of the three tales produces an elliptical narrative of the type evident in Callimachus' *Hecale*. The third tale, furthermore, offers a story or digression within a story (Heracles tells it to Phyleus). The poem is nothing if not realistic: lines 1–84 and their emphasis on the rustic's cottage, his dogs, and his way of life bring to mind Hecale's hut. Is the poem experimental? Its unusual adaptation of the digression gives that impression. But, although the timbre of lines 1–84 contrasts strongly with that of 153–281, the poem does not exhibit the same dramatic tonal oscillation. Nor does it evince particular interest in female characters or the erotic; it has no apparent *aition* and its choice of myths is not obscure.

A hymnal prelude to the divine twins, the Dioscuri, Castor and Polydeuces, acts as the first of the four parts of *Idyll* 22 (1–26). Although the poem is a hymn (perhaps it takes its lead from such 'epic' creations as Callimachus' *Hymn to Demeter*) it seems to show many of the characteristics of the Callimachean miniature epic. Its second part (27–134) provides a myth digression. It describes Polydeuces' boxing bout with the Bebrycian King Amycus (see Apollonius, *Argonautica* 2.1–97). In Theocritus' version the Dioscuri, after the *Argo* lands, go off alone to a spring. Here they meet Amycus, who refuses to allow them to drink unless they box with him. The loser is to become the slave to the winner. They do box and Polydeuces wins. The third portion (135–212) narrates a myth concerning the second of the twins, Castor. In this tale the Dioscuri are seen in flight from the sons of Aphareus, Lynceus and Idas. The Dioscuri have made off with the daughters of Leucippus to whom Lynceus and Idas were engaged. A fight eventually takes place and

Castor kills Lynceus. A hymnal epilogue acts as the fourth portion of the poem (213–23).

The generic blending of hymn with epyllion (Hutchinson 1988: 162ff.) is experimental. Experimental too may be the juxtaposition of one story with an honourable ending with another containing a tale that throws heroic ideology into question. The down-to-earth realism of one story provides a dramatic tonal contrast with the more formal, even respectful tale concerning Amycus (killed in Apollonius' version). The focus of this poem is not on women, but in the second half it is by implication erotic.

Theocritus, at least in 22 and 25, is attempting to write Alexandrian miniature epic. A hallmark of the epyllion, as we are beginning to see, is a concern with private or personal emotion. Theocritus' concern is often with the private: thus, for example, Heracles in love (*Idyll* 13 – not really an epyllion). But the heroic is still at the heart of these poems. Notwithstanding Theocritean irony such a consideration ought by now to have been relegated to the mythological handbook.

THE REAL THING: MOSCHUS, *EUROPA*

Moschus was a grammarian and perhaps better understood the rules. Perhaps too he was less cautious. One lasting impression of the Theocritean epyllion is of a poetry willing to take on many of the characteristics adumbrated by Callimachus, but unwilling to take the final step of recasting the heroic. Moschus in his *Europa* took this step (text and translation: Edmonds 1950).

Moschus lived in Sicily (*fl.* 150 BC) and wrote a number of bucolic poems in the style of Theocritus. His only extant and complete poem is the *Europa*. The miniature epic is made up of a series of near static tableaux, perhaps based on contemporary art. They depict the progression of Europa – abducted by Zeus disguised as a beautiful bull – from virgin (7, *parthenos*) to mother (166, *mētēr*). Between these tableaux exist symmetrical links. Here is an outline of the *Europa* (based on Hopkinson 1988: 200):

Tableau 1 Europa in bed (1–27):
    1–15 Europa's prophetic dream matches Zeus' prophetic statement (153–66) with which the poem concludes.
    16–27 Europa reflects on her dream.
Tableau 2 Europa in the meadow (28–62):
    28–36 Europa and her companions gather to pick flowers.

37–62 digression – description of Europa's basket (Io seems to be equated with Europa).

63–107: Zeus changes into a white bull.

Tableau 3 Europa crosses the sea on the bull (108–52).

(note that Europa's speeches at 135–52 and 21–7 frame the poem).

Tableau 4 Europa as mother (153–66).

The *Europa* is short, makes strong use of digression (the basket at 37–62), its concern is erotic, and the narrative proceeds in the main from a female point of view. The poem, too, plays up the sentimental. The elements of the legend receive unusual stress: for example, lines 153–66 seem to view the naming of Europe as too obvious to retell (compare Theseus' encounter with the bull in the *Hecale*). Less obvious characteristics are the learned but ironic timbre (the dialect is Homeric, the subject matter anything but), and the allusiveness (Europa recalls Nausicaa in *Odyssey* 6; the personification of the continents recalls Aeschylus' *Persae* 181–7). Of this work its most recent commentator (Hopkinson 1988: 202) has remarked: 'the whole ethos of the poem – small-scale, Homeric in diction, unhomeric in treatment, ecphrastic, pictorial, pseudo-naive – is, so far as we can judge, typical of the Greek epyllion.' We ought also to stress, however, the absolutely private, even hermetic nature of this poem. (There is no single meaning here.) The *Hecale* made a curt nod to real life through its use of two *aitia*. Theocritus could not altogether wean himself from the heroic public. There is nothing heroic in Moschus and the *aition* (Europa becomes Europe) is virtually ignored.

The *Europa* poses as a light-hearted, but technically adept retelling of a traditional myth tale. Other readings are possible. The *Europa* may be read as an ironic narrative of the circumstances of sexual infatuation, self-delusion, willing seduction, and loss of innocence with an older lover. The bull is the older, experienced lover. Europa's interest in the beast goes beyond mere innocence (so her wiping and kissing the bull's mouth, 95–6, then riding its back, 102–3) and, when finally the bull does carry her off, the protestations, as is to be expected, are not loud (135–52). Seduction and abandonment would have been Europa's fate in Syracuse. In myth it is a different matter: there is a happy ending. She is rewarded with a marriage of sorts (165) and has a continent named after her. Such a reading of the *Europa*, I should add, makes clear one of the most popular themes of the Hellenistic epyllion. This is sexual infatuation.

MATURITY: THE ALEXANDRIAN EPIC AT ROME

The miniature epic reaches a 'maturity' in Rome ninety odd years after Moschus. But, in some respects, it had changed. Wiseman (1974a: 53) argues that what distinguishes the Roman version from poems such as the *Hecale* is 'the obscure and often melodramatic subject-matter of Euphorion'. (Euphorion, a third-century BC resident of Antioch, seems to have specialized in epyllia which focused on love, violence, and melodrama.) To this Euphorionic and Callimachean brew the Romans added, remarkably, the theme of *pietas*.

Parthenius was brought to Italy not long after 73 BC and, according to Clausen (1964), was responsible for importing the Callimachean epic to Rome. Parthenius' only extant work (*Unhappy Love-affairs*, text and translation: Thornley and Gaselee 1960) does not exhibit his poetic abilities. It is a prose collection of outline stories offered to Cornelius Gallus as a quarry for epic or elegiac verse. Even this work, however, provides us with some idea of what his poetic interests may have been. 'What *was* new', maintains Wiseman (1974a: 53) of Parthenius' verse, 'was the recherché erudition of Callimachus coupled with the ... subject-matter of Euphorion.' The types of stories which appealed to both Euphorion and Parthenius may be gauged from one of the love stories taken from Euphorion and appearing in Parthenius' book.

> One treats of Clymenus, who having freely consorted with his daughter Harpalyce, handed her over in marriage to Alastor. Later he changed his mind and took her back. Thereupon Harpalyce killed her brother, set his flesh before her father, and was changed into a bird. Clymenus committed suicide.
>
> (Crowther 1970: 325–6)

The followers of Parthenius seem to have been encouraged by Valerius Cato (born 100–90 BC) who produced two poems of the Callimachean type, a *Lydia* and a *Dictynna* (fragments: Morel 1975). Neither survives. According to Suetonius (*On the Grammarians* 11), Cato had quite a reputation as a teacher. He was especially good with boys showing poetic talent. Wiseman (1974a: 53) believes that he 'made' (whatever that means)

> poets in the schoolroom, and since he was born some time after 96 BC, the boys he steered to poetry were younger than the generation of Cinna and Catullus. With his *Lydia* and his

Dictynna, the learned Cato evidently belonged to the neoteric school of epic, but he was not its *doyen*.

Cinna was a pupil of Parthenius. His *Smyrna* (fragments: Morel 1975) – written perhaps under the influence of Parthenius (Clausen 1964: 191) – seems to have been a key poem in the Roman history of the miniature epic. 'It is likely enough that the publication of Cinna's work was the opening shot of the revolution, and that Catullus' poem on the *Smyrna* [poem 95], with its clear echoes of Calli-machean polemic, hailed the first Roman epic in Callimachus' style' (Wiseman 1974a: 53). The *Smyrna* is a little epic which concerns the daughter (named Smyrna) of the king of Paphos in Cyprus. Aphro-dite punished her with a passion for her father. The gods changed her into a myrrh tree when her father unwittingly made her pregnant. They did not want her punished. Smyrna's child was Adonis, who was born when the tree split open.

HOW MANY MEANINGS CAN AN EPYLLION HAVE? CATULLUS, POEM 64

Against this background (Lyne 1978b) was composed Catullus' Alexandrian miniature epic, poem 64 (text: Quinn 1977; translation: Goold 1983). It represents the earliest and best-preserved example of this type. The poem gives some idea of the enthusiasms of Parthe-nius, Valerius Cato, and Cinna. Even more so it gives some idea of the skein of meanings a poem within this rebarbative subgenre can generate. Written, probably, some time during the early 50s BC, it is one of the most ambitious, if not popular, pieces of the Catullan *oeuvre*. Quinn (1977: 297) believes that it 'served as a demonstration of technical virtuosity and devotion to the poet's craft: it was the sort of poem that might take years to write.'

Two distinct legends interweave to create the poem. The first (the 'outer story') concerns the marriage of Peleus and Thetis, the second (the 'inner story') concerns the elopement of Ariadne and Theseus. The link between the two legends is a bedspread. Covering the marriage bed of Peleus and Thetis it contains embroideries – ec-phraseis – of the events of the 'inner story' concerning Ariadne and Theseus. The poem purports to describe and to moralize on events at the wedding and events as depicted on the bedspread. The thematic connection between the inner and outer stories is not specified.

Here is a tabular scheme of poem 64 (based on Quinn 1977: 298f.):

1–51: the origins of the love of Peleus and Thetis; arrival of the guests at the wedding; the marriage bed.

52–70: the bedspread: Ariadne on the beach deserted by Theseus.

71–115: flashback: why Ariadne was left on the beach; Theseus in Crete (Ariadne's home); Ariadne falls in love with Theseus; the minotaur is killed by Theseus.

116–201: back to Ariadne on the beach (her lament and curse are at 132–201).

202–48: Theseus feels the effect of the curse: his departure from Athens and the farewell of his father, Aegeus; Aegeus perishes.

249–64: back to Ariadne who is rescued by Dionysus (and his worshippers).

265–322: back to the marriage: the mortal guests depart (267–77) and the immortal guests arrive (278–302) including the Fates (303–22).

323–81: song of the Fates (a marriage hymn for Peleus and Thetis; its subject is Achilles, the couple's future son).

384–408: coda: nowadays the gods have abandoned humans.

The poem is determinedly experimental. It repeats many of those thematic and technical characteristics which we observed in the *Hecale*. Formed by a mosaic of digression and flashback it concentrates, like the elliptical *Hecale*, on the unexpected (Ariadne's lament, the death of Aegeus, the Fates and their song) and often glosses over the expected (Dionysus' arrival, Theseus' killing of the minotaur). Catullus' penchant for experiment is not restricted to the interweaving of digressions. Narrative pace is varied by the use of third-personal narrative (expansive or staccato), by direct speech, and by authorial intrusion. The song of the Fates uses a refrain more to be associated with folk song. The epyllion, furthermore, is a profoundly erotic creation. Its central theme is a marriage, and a female character, Ariadne, dominates. The poem's stress on a woman's emotions (note also Thetis and the Fates) exhibits a noteworthy Callimachean characteristic, a stress if not on ordinary life, at least on the real. Ariadne, in her descriptions and monologue, is an intensely vivid creation. Yet, like Hecale, she is a figure of pathos, even sentimentality.

But what does the poem mean? Is it *littérature pure* (Quinn 1969: 68)? Is it a romantic experiment in genre (Jenkyns 1982: 85ff.)? Or is it a trial blending of tonal contraries (Hutchinson 1988: 301ff.)? Is its real theme marriage? Is, therefore, the desertion of Ariadne by her lover, Theseus, an oblique commentary on the disastrous relationship between Catullus and his lover, Lesbia (Putnam 1961)?

In recent years it has been argued that the themes of 'betrayal' (*periurium*) and 'forgetfulness' (of a reprehensible variety) unite the disparate elements of the poem. Consider Ariadne: seduced by the treacherous (*perfidus*) Theseus she is subsequently abandoned on the island of Naxos. Ariadne accuses Theseus of 'forgetting' (58, 123, 135, 248, among others) the covenant (139, 158, for example) made between them. Or Theseus: under the compulsion of Ariadne's curse he forgets the promise he had made to his father Aegeus. Catullus intends us to link the perfidious Theseus with the offspring of the marriage of Peleus and Thetis, Achilles. The link is imprecise. But there is an association of the Greek forces with *periurium* (note line 346). And it is as if betrayal and forgetfulness exemplify an attitude of impiety or irreligiousness of which Achilles also seems guilty. The reference to Polyxena at 368 may imply this (she was sacrificed to Achilles' ghost, at its own request). Impiety, then, provides us with a link between Theseus, Achilles, and the final moralizing section of the poem. Behind the worst of contemporary excesses seem to lurk the notions of betrayal and impiety (386): brothers slaughter brothers; parents and step-parents plot libidinously against their stepchildren; the gods are no longer respected, nor will they visit earth. Where does the wedding of Peleus and Thetis fit? The wedding took place in the Golden Age when the gods still came among humans. They no longer do this because of the treachery of types like Theseus, Achilles, and modern-day Romans. That Catullus saw this Golden Age as a pipe-dream is implied by the fact that the happy marriage of Peleus and Thetis produced such a miserable offspring.

This labyrinthine poem, however, resists such critical certainties. Consider Ariadne again: her emotional monologue runs away with the poem. But what do we make of her (Medea-like) murder of her brother (150–1)? Does this not make her perfidious like Theseus? Does not, then, the plaintive, sentimental persistence of her utterances begin to ring false and even to become oppressive? Contrast Theseus. He may be a villain, but his motives and actions are more varied, more contradictory, and, in their outcome, more tragic. Theseus provides a fertile focus: his actions are sufficiently dynamic to absorb the reader's interest. In this sense Theseus is another Jason or Europa. My point, however, does not relate specifically to either Ariadne or Theseus. Rather it is to indicate the frustrating polysemy of this complex epic. It is as if the smaller the epic became, the more difficult it became to read.

RESISTING INTERPRETATION: VIRGIL, *ECLOGUES* 6

From the period and circle in which Catullus wrote there are references to other epic poems of this type (fragments: Morel 1975). We can only guess at the manner in which these poems were written. Catullus' friend Calvus (see Catullus, poems 14, 50, 53, 96) wrote an *Io* (which mythological character appears in the brief digression of lines 43–62 in Moschus' *Europa*); Cornificius (mentioned in Catullus, poem 38) wrote a *Glaucus* whose subject may have been the fisherman, later turned into a merman, whose beloved Scylla was transformed into a monster (see Virgil, *Eclogue* 6 below); and Caecilius appears to have written a *Magna Mater* (see Catullus, poem 35.18). To what extent these poems concerned themselves with social issues (in the manner of Catullus' coda to 64) is impossible to state. The titles hint that they may have had more in common with Moschus than with Catullus.

Virgil, in his *Eclogue* 6 (written probably in the early 30s), may provide another example of the Catullan formulation of the epyllion. *Eclogue* 6 begins with a long introduction addressing Virgil's friend Varus. Virgil states that he cannot write about great deeds; he must write bucolic poetry, but even this, thanks to its audience, will bring fame to Varus (1–12). Then, following the scene-setting with the hungover satyr (13–30), begins the intriguing 'song of Silenus' (31–84). It is in this section that the Alexandrian influence is most evident (Williams 1968: 243ff.). The arrangement of the 'song' is as follows (Williams 1968: 243ff.):

31–40: creation.
41–2: Pyrrha, Saturn, and Prometheus.
43–4: loss of Hylas.
45–60: the story of Pasiphaë (with mention of the daughters of Proteus).
61: Atalanta.
62–3: the sisters of Phaethon.
64–73: Gallus given the pipes of Hesiod by Linus on mount Helicon.
74–7: Scylla, daughter of Nisus.
78–81: Tereus and Philomela.
82–3: Silenus sang all that Phoebus sang by the River Eurotas.

84–5: Silenus orders the shepherds to drive home the flocks since it is night.

Virgil, like Callimachus, provides a new slant for old material. He does this especially through the interweaving of a variety of stories. The brevity – itself a mark of the tradition – with which each of these tales are treated adds to the novelty of the focus. Rather than spelling the story out (compare the sixteen lines on Pasiphaë with Moschus' 166 on Europa) Virgil offers a 'deft, mobile treatment, in which the main line of the story is totally omitted' (Williams 1968: 246). This interweaving of stories does not just provide the new slant. It also provides the digressive complexity so typical of the Callimachean epic. Like his predecessor, Virgil experiments with form. The interweaving of stories is the most obvious example. There is also the variety with which each story is treated: some receive the barest of detail, some a series of 'vivid points', others a more full exposition; there is also the shift in tone and in the point of view. Another especially Callimachean feature, realism, is to the fore in *Eclogue* 6. Note especially the immediacy of the depiction of Silenus in the scene-setting section (13–30). The poem is resolute in its focus on women. It is also erotic. It is, on most views, a potentially sentimental creation. If it is more so than the *Hecale* and if it omits the heroic altogether, perhaps we can attribute this to the persistent melodramatic timbre of much Roman poetry of this type.

No interpretation for this most baffling of ancient poems will satisfy for long. To facilitate comprehension I offer just one of the many possible. Silenus' song 'contains a high proportion of stories about strange and tragic love: Hylas, Pasiphaë, Atalanta, Scylla, Tereus' (Williams 1968: 247). Even the mention of Apollo (82–3) seems to veil a reference either to the unhappy love story concerning Hyacinthus or Daphne (Knox 1990). The poem presents a variety of mythological stories concerning the effects of destructive passion and, by implication, of art (repeatedly aligned by Virgil – Silenus the lover does the singing – with those forces inimical to the establishment of an ideal Roman world). Contrasted with this world is the orderly public, Roman world of Varus, the poem's addressee. Varus' world (with which the poem begins) is one with which Virgil is in full sympathy but to which he does not always find himself temperamentally drawn. Silenus' world, on the other hand, is shown in all its destructive passion. If it is an unsavoury world, it is the one depicted with the greater charm and affection. Just as the introduction to the poem balances Varus' and Virgil's inclinations, so does the poem balance the passionate world of Silenus and of art with that of Rome. Virgil's ambivalence – his understanding of and fondness for Silenus' realm, and his admiration for the public Roman world of Varus – is something we will see again. In *Georgics* 4 the ideal world of the bees (Varus' Roman world) is balanced against the destructive and passionate world of Orpheus (Silenus' world). In the *Aeneid* the claims and the values of empire (Varus and the bees) are balanced against those of passionate Dido (Silenus and Orpheus).

We ought, however, to be clear: this 'reading' delimits the variety within the texture of *Eclogue* 6. It represents an act of closural violence. (Where does Gallus fit into this scheme?) *Eclogue* 6, even more than Catullus 64, is the most intransigent of poems.

VIRGIL, *GEORGICS* 4: THE 'ARISTAEUS EPYLLION'

Virgil's most famous Alexandrian miniature epic was written some years after *Eclogue* 6. The epyllion concerning Aristaeus (it is often termed the 'Aristaeus epyllion'), occurs within the fourth book of Virgil's *Georgics* (a useful introduction may be found in Wilkinson 1969). This book (most likely written in the early 20s BC) concerns bee lore. Its epic insert represents a new departure. Instead of allowing the epyllion to stand alone, Virgil has incorporated it within a larger, more sequential narrative. The effect is jarring. But the dramatic oscillation from expository didactic to digressive narrative is, if nothing else, in the spirit of Alexandria.

Here is a brief summary of the narrative of *Georgics* 4. After a short preface (lines 1–7) to his patron, Maecenas, the book proper begins. Virgil explains how to locate and to maintain a beehive (8–115). Thereafter begins the well-known digression (116–48) on the expert gardening of the happy old Corycian beekeeper. Then follows (149–227) a remarkable section on the nature of bees: their sense of community (149–218) and their spiritual nature – they participate in the *mens divina* (219–27). Next is advice on the care of bees and the danger of diseases (228–80). Finally Virgil describes how epidemic can destroy a hive and how the bees may be regenerated from the carcass of an ox – termed the 'Bugonia' (281–314). The 'epyllion' forms the second part of the book and provides an *aition*: how Aristaeus came to discover the 'Bugonia'. Here is the structure of the 'Aristaeus epyllion':

315–32: after losing his bees Aristaeus goes to complain to his mother, the river nymph Cyrene.

333–414: Aristaeus and Cyrene meet; she says to capture the sea-god Proteus and force him to tell the truth.

415–52: Proteus is forced to explain to Aristaeus that he must propitiate the spirit of Orpheus, for whose wife's death he shares responsibility.

453–527: Orpheus and Eurydice.

528–58: the eight sacrificed cattle rot to produce a swarm of bees.

The book ends (559–66) with a seal-poem (a *sphragis*) containing Virgil's literary 'signature'.

Even from this sketchy outline the resemblances between the 'Aristaeus epyllion' and the Callimachean epic ought to be obvious. Virgil's story of Aristaeus is itself a digression, but it also contains a digression (concerning Orpheus and Eurydice). The Orpheus and Eurydice story follows the traditional outlines of the tale; its novelty is juxtaposition with the story of Aristaeus. The Aristaeus story, on the other hand, is obscure. Mothers, prematurely dead wives, matrons gone wild in the mountains, decapitation – these are surely Euphorionic or, as it may be, Roman elements. The fascination with the macabre is doubtless the product of the detached and sentimental taste of an urban audience. The steamy atmosphere of the erotic story of Orpheus and Eurydice contrasts with the ordinary, even banal desires of Aristaeus. (He just wants to get his bees back.) Verbal experiment, a Callimachean feature, abounds in the 'Aristaeus epyllion'. There is the shift in point of view from the poet then to Proteus. Dramatic tonal shifts within the outer story and, by comparison, within the inner story are also evident. The actual telling varies its pace from the expansive and graphic to the pointillist.

What is this short Callimachean narrative doing in a poem about the land? Servius, an ancient commentator on Virgil, provides an explanation that satisfies some (Jocelyn 1984). He states (on *Eclogues* 10.1) that the fourth book of the *Georgics* from the middle to the end contained the praises of the poet and statesman Gallus. Gallus (mentioned above at *Eclogues* 6.64–73) was a very close friend of Virgil. He was made first prefect of Egypt after the fall of Alexandria in 30 BC. Perhaps guilty of the over-ambitious prosecution of his vice-regal African office, he was recalled, accused of treason and, in 26, committed suicide. Augustus placed a posthumous ban on his memory. Again at *Georgics* 4.1 Servius informs us that the story of Orpheus was substituted for the praises after the death of Gallus. The veracity of this story has been doubted (Segal 1989: 73–81).

Griffin (1979: 68), in his interpretation of the digression, believes that the society of the bees is to be equated with Roman society: they are 'a powerful image for the traditional Roman state, in its impersonal and collective character'. Virgil deeply admires traditional Roman society. (Its 'patriotism and self-denial . . . are admirable. If Rome had only retained more of such qualities, then the tragedies and disasters of the Civil Wars, and of the end of the first *Georgic*, would never have occurred' (Griffin 1979: 69).) Virgil realizes, however, that like its bee counterpart traditional Roman stability had been gained at a cost ('order is . . . restored, and the poet becomes aware of the cost – a society efficient and admirable, but impersonal and dispassionate' (Griffin 1979: 70)). Orpheus stands as the polar opposite of the orderly society of the bees. His passionate vacillation, then his passionate intransigence produce the destruction of first his wife, then himself. (Aristaeus' own passionate overtures towards Eurydice are equally destructive.) The destruction wrought by Orpheus is to be associated with the disorders and disasters depicted in the first *Georgic* (metaphorically the Civil Wars). It is for these that the society of the bees provides a remedy. But Orpheus is presented by Virgil with remarkable appeal. This seems deliberate. It is as if, through Orpheus, Virgil was attempting to emphasize the limitations of the bee and Roman societies. The reading of Griffin (1979) links neatly with *Eclogue* 6. Mythical digression there emphasized the destructive consequences of unbridled passion. But it did so, as in this poem, with a remarkable sympathy for the victims of passion.

THE DEATH KNELL: OVID'S MINIATURE EPICS

In his ironic epic, the *Metamorphoses*, Ovid takes the epic technique of *Georgics* 4 one step further. Virgil had placed an epyllion within a long sequential narrative. Ovid places an epyllion within an epyllion (Quinn 1979: 73ff.). The effect, while consonant with the Callimachean demand for brevity, paradoxically produces a long epic poem. The interweaving of stories produces a chain-like concatenation of miniature epics which build to form one long poem (Coleman 1971). This is not the place to attempt a demonstration of this point – if in fact so obvious a claim needs demonstration. Rather let me refer to Chapter 8, on Ovid's *Metamorphoses*, where this will be discussed in greater detail. At this juncture, however, I would like to make one observation. Ovid, by his intensive use of the Alexandrian miniature epic, and by his twisting it into *hen poēma diēnekes* (a single, long epic poem), has arguably worked the genre to a standstill. After such virtuoso efforts, it is very difficult to imagine that anything new could be done with the type. In a sense Ovid's *Metamorphoses* may be responsible for the creative eclipse of the epyllion.

RIGOR MORTIS: THE *CIRIS*

The *Ciris*, occasionally but incorrectly attributed to Virgil (Lyne 1978a) or even to his friend Cornelius Gallus, gives ample testimony to the enduring attraction of the Alexandrian miniature epic. That the *Ciris* is not a success may be as much the fault of the author as of Ovid. The poem seems to have been composed late in the first century of our era – or even later still. Perhaps it stems from the epoch of Statius – who, it has been suggested, may himself have been influenced by the epyllion (Bishop 1951). The *Ciris* – which cannot have been alone in its pretensions (Ross 1975: 242) – represents the epyllion on its last legs.

The *Ciris* engrosses the events leading to the transformation into a bird (a *ciris*, whatever that is) of the treacherous Megaran woman, Scylla. Scylla, not to be confused with the monster of *Odyssey* 12 and *Argonautica* 4, was a popular character in the small-scale Alexandrian epic (compare Callimachus, *Hecale* (fr. 90 Hollis), Cornificius' lost *Glaucus*, and Virgil, *Eclogues* 6.74–7). The story of this poem is built upon the legend of Princess Scylla who, as punishment for profaning Juno's temple, fell in love with King Minos. Minos was besieging her home city, Megara. The siege, however, was not succeeding. The city was protected by a magical purple lock of hair on the head of its regent, Nisus. Scylla stole the lock and delivered it to Minos, hoping in this way to gain his affection. It did not work. Minos was so disgusted with Scylla that he tied her to the prow of his ship. Had she not been turned into a *ciris*, she would have drowned. The author of this poem has taken an interesting but minor mythological figure and made her the centre-piece of his small poem. The following outline of the structure of the *Ciris* (based on Lyne 1978a) will give some idea of just how:

1–53: proem; exordium part 1: a *recusatio* for not writing something more elaborate.

54–91: exordium proper: the author attacks certain poets for confusing Scylla the sea monster with Scylla, daughter of Nisus.

92–100: poet asks for new inspiration.

101–28: Megara; its troubles caused by Minos; Nisus' lock.

129–62: (flashback) why Scylla is to be punished.

163–90: Scylla in love.

191–205: apostrophe and mention of metamorphosis (compare 520–41).

206–385: Scylla's nurse, Carme, discovers the problem and encourages her to purloin the lock.

386–458: Scylla cuts the Nisus' lock (386–7); Megara falls to Minos (388) who punishes Scylla (389–458).

459–541: Minos' route home; Scylla's (481–519) and Nisus' metamorphosis (520–41).

The resemblances of the *Ciris* to the Alexandrian miniature epic are marked. The poem's length matches that of Catullus 64. There is a digression (Carme's story of her daughter Britomartis, 294–309) and there is also flashback (129–62). The *Ciris* parades its learning, most noticeably in the introductory sections concerning Scylla's real identity (54–91). The narrative is typically elliptical: the exordia are surprisingly long (1–91), the nurse scene (206–385) is blown out of all proportion, while the actual snipping of Nisus' lock (386–7), which, like Theseus' encounter with the bull in the *Hecale*, ought to have been a high point, is dealt with summarily. What the poem spotlights, at least from line 129 on, is resolutely female and, at that, unstintingly erotic. The poem is sentimental and melodramatic, perhaps in the Euphorionic mode. These resemblances to Alexandrian and Callimachean practice, however, remain at the level of technique. The *Ciris* does not exhibit the same verve or the same originality as its predecessors. It is tempting to agree with Lyne (1978a: 36) when he avers, 'I believe that if more Latin literature survived, we should see that the method of composition of the *Ciris* was approaching that of a cento.'

Lack of originality (bordering on ineptitude) does not render the poem meaningless. The main theme of this poem is *periurium* ('betrayal' – 139), but specifically that within a family (131). The deployment of this topic needs little comment, nor does its relevance for an atavistic, backward-looking society like Rome. Note, however, that the theme of familial betrayal makes more sense of some of the wilder statements of Carme. Why, for example, should she make so much of the notion of incest (237ff.)? The reason for the stress on incest is surely that it is in Roman eyes a betrayal *par excellence* of family solidarity. Religious and sexual dereliction intertwine to provide a focus for the theme of betrayal. The religious subtheme is apparent from the outset: the other Scylla may have been punished for transgressing Venus (77ff.); so does this Scylla transgress Juno at her ceremony (138ff.), to be punished with an incestuous passion; in much the same way Scylla betrays Nisus and is rewarded with metamorphosis. But to take the religious theme too seriously is difficult. In the *Ciris* it seems to lack the ring of conviction. Sexual dereliction is taken more seriously. (This may provide the explanation for the stress on the other Scylla's metamorphosis (77ff.) and for Carme's intrusive reference to her daughter Britomartis (294–309): Britomartis preserved her chastity against the pressing Minos; Scylla would not.) The theme, as we have seen, is a favourite of Virgil and of the neoteric epic writers.

The *Ciris* is an intriguing, if maladroit poem. But, in its ideological clichés, it can disappoint. The *Ciris* dramatizes the hoary old Roman theme, the perversion and betrayal of *pietas*. The maintenance of that virtue was perceived as the key to empire and to social solidity. Catullus' and Virgil's diagnoses were far less confident. The result was a type of polysemy that, we may guess, typified the epyllion at its best.

OBSEQUIES: THE *CULEX*

If the death throes of the Roman version of the Alexandrian miniature epic is marked by clumsy products like the *Ciris*, its obsequies may be read in a light piece traditionally attributed to Virgil, the *Culex*. It has been argued (Ross 1975) that the *Culex* aims to parody neoteric epic narrative technique. The *Culex* may indicate how far the epyllion had come to represent mainstream, clichéd art. The case has been put well by Richardson (1944: 168–9): 'Against just such abuses of art [i.e., those of the *Ciris*] the spritely parody of the *Culex* must have been written, for it mimics with fine humour the flatulence and subjective emotionalism of poetry such as the *Ciris*.'

Before examining the parody it may be as well to summarize, briefly, the contents of the poem. It runs as follows (following Ross 1975): after a proem and an invocation to Apollo and Octavian (1–41), the story proper begins. This divides into four sections. In

118

the first (42–97) a shepherd enters at dawn with his flock, then, while they disperse to rest, the poet reflects on the advantages of the rustic life. In the second section (98–201), after midday, the shepherd settles in a shady grove. As he falls asleep a snake approaches. A mosquito lands on the shepherd and stings him. In irritation the shepherd kills the insect. The blow, however, rouses him. He spots the serpent and dispatches it. In the third section (202–384), evening, the shepherd again settles to sleep. In his dream the mosquito appears: there follows a long description of the gnat's experiences in Hades. The fourth section (385–414) shows us the guilty shepherd attempting to make amends. He established a memorial to the squashed insect.

Amongst the Alexandrian features of the *Culex* are length (approximately the same as Catullus 64) and digressions (in the second section, describing Diana's grove, there is a description of the associated mythological characters; the dream itself is a digression, and within this there are the descriptions of various denizens of Hades). The narrative style is extremely varied: it shifts from invocation, to simple narrative, to praise catalogue, to 'heroic' narrative, then, in the dream section, to the clipped mode of *Eclogue* 6. The tone oscillates accordingly – from down-to-earth realism to the (mock) heroic.

What produces the *Culex*' humour? According to the convincing analysis of Ross (1975), the parody functions on two levels, the technical and, for want of a better word, the situational. The situation described in the *Culex* is unavoidably amusing. We can only laugh at the picture of a heroic mosquito saving a life by giving its own, at its sheer bad luck in being swatted, at its bizarre vision of Hades, at its having a memorial constructed. The parody has also a technical side. Ross (1975: 252) maintains that to parody the epyllion the poet systematically uses Greek forms, archaisms in vocabulary, in inflexion, in grammar, and that 'both the Greek veneer and the stilted resonance of the grand style are carefully calculated for parodic effect, just as are his Alexandrian learning and the broader techniques of his narrative'.

The *Culex* is important for its parody. It demonstrates how hackneyed the Alexandrian miniature epic had become. Inaugurated by Callimachus the miniature epic may have come into being as a reaction to the moribund encomia of the historical epic and the tedious longwindedness of the mythological epic. With the *Culex*

119

the wheel has gone the full turn. The miniature epic occupies the same place within the epical firmament as did the historical and mythological epic in Callimachus' era.

7

VIRGIL, *AENEID*

Discussion to this point has followed closely the unfolding of the stories within each of the epics. In the next two chapters I intend to abandon sequential paraphrase and to pursue an analysis that is based on themes. Why? There are many interpretative paraphrases of the *Aeneid* (particularly Quinn 1968 and Williams 1980a, 1980b). It would, perhaps, be pointless to repeat labours better done by others. As for the *Metamorphoses*, it poses a different problem. Ovid's narrative is labyrinthine, yet it is not hard to follow (Glenn 1986 offers an interpretative paraphrase). What is needed is not paraphrase (which easily becomes as labyrinthine as the narrative itself), but to show how Ovid's 250 odd stories encrypt a limited number of themes and concerns.

LOVE, WAR, AND THE AFTERLIFE OF THE *AENEID*

Love and war – the tension between them has conditioned the afterlife of Virgil's *Aeneid*. Dido or Aeneas, the lover or the general, they represent the two poles between which 2,000 years of readers have swung. The audience has swung more to Dido than to Aeneas. And if the poem lives it may be because of her: there are, for example, almost one hundred operas based upon her romance with Aeneas (Heinrichs 1991). Even Chaucer told her story – not once, but twice (in *The House of Fame* and in the *Legend of Good Women*). Chaucer preferred Dido to Aeneas. Aeneas has had no such privileged post-mortem existence.

Yet war and its resolution have attractions. This (crystallized in the duel between Aeneas and Turnus concluding the epic) has guaranteed the epic a firm place in European sentiment. For hun-

121

dreds of years the *Aeneid* served as an extraordinarily successful ideological vehicle, a vehicle which could work to explain and to justify a colonialism as diverse as that of Germans in Papua and Englishmen in India.

Virgil's *Aeneid* does not achieve an easy reconciliation between the counterclaims of love and war, of Dido and Aeneas. In Aeneas – and he is intended as the focus of the poem – Virgil attempts to create a hero who, while carrying the burden of national destiny, is nonetheless prey to the affections of a Dido. (It is not a question of the personality of a well-rounded national icon.) This lack of reconciliation permeates the epic as a whole. It is not confined to Dido. Aeneas butchers Turnus. Deaf to his opponent's pleas, Aeneas surrenders to a surge of anger and drives in the sword. The unresolved conflict between Aeneas and Turnus spills over into other important areas and ideologies thrown up by the conflict: between anger and self-control; between Rome and the Italians; between colonizing and native peoples; between the state and the individual; between a national optimism and a personal pessimism. The list of polarities, as we will see, is extensive.

Genre too has its influence. If Apollonius' *Argonautica* (see Chapter 4) offers Hypsipyle and Medea as models for Dido's actions, the pervasive presence within the *Aeneid* of Homer's *Iliad* (see Chapter 2) demands a duel between opposing heroes. Can the romantic strands of Alexandrian epic be combined with the robust heroism of eighth-century Greece? There are further difficulties. Homeric gravity is offset by an Alexandrian, near Ovidian levity (or rococo, as Williams 1983a terms it). This may pervade even the most serious of contexts. What are we to make of ships that turn into nymphs? Or baby Camilla who, attached to a spear shaft, is cast across a river?

The relationship between Dido and Aeneas does not succeed. Aeneas surrenders to the claims of a national destiny that will lead to the slaughter of Turnus. (And he does this in a medium that oscillates, more than is often allowed, between seriousness and whimsy.) The unresolved tensions, I believe, are responsible for the extraordinary variety of readings for the *Aeneid*. The *Aeneid* resists simple claims for textual unity. It is as if context provides the unity. History may represent part of this context. The ambiguities of late Republican and early Augustan Rome engendered an attitude which, while striving for 'closure' (Augustus as the apex of historical evolution), cannot easily achieve it. Genre too is part of this context. It resists easy alliances between the seriousness of the Homeric tradition and the ironic observance of Alexandria. Either the *Aeneid* represents a creation which is torn apart by the conflicting claims of context (history and genre), or it is a poem whose final unity resides not within itself, but externally, within the contexts that shaped it. I believe that it is the latter.

VIRGIL'S LIFE AND ITS HISTORICAL CONTEXT

The contradictions between love and war, the private and the public, metaphorically between Dido and Aeneas, or Turnus and Aeneas, have parallels in the little we know of the circumstances of Virgil's life. Let us review a few of the details.

Virgil was born on 15 October 70 BC in a village called Andes near Mantua in northern Italy. He was educated at Cremona, Milan, and then Rome where he prepared for a political and legal career. In 49 BC the Civil War between Caesar and the Republican forces under Pompey broke out (see Chapter 9 for further details). Virgil seems to have abandoned plans for a public life and retired to Naples where he may have studied with the Epicurean philosopher Siro. If we are to detect an ambivalence towards the demands of public life and the state, its origins might as well be here.

Little is known of his life during the remainder of this turbulent decade (during which, first, Caesar fought Pompey, then Antony and Octavian fought Pompey's Republican successors Brutus and Cassius). In 42 BC at Philippi the Republicans were defeated by the forces of the triumvirate, Antony, Octavian, and Lepidus. Tradition has it that, towards the end of the decade, Virgil's father may have been dispossessed of his land. The victorious triumvirate redistributed Italian farmland to their returning veterans.

Yet, in the period following Philippi (42–37 BC), Virgil composed his *Eclogues* (a collection of ten pastoral poems). Surprisingly he had become a member of the literary clique supported by Octavian's friend and adviser, Maecenas. If his father had lost his land (become a metaphorical Dido), then we now find Virgil working for the regime (descended from Aeneas) that deprived him of it. Of course this farm story may be sheer ancient falsehood. Yet it does hint at a compromise that must have confronted almost all of the major writers of this period. It is a compromise that is at the heart of the *Aeneid*.

Let us continue with the mini-biography. During the early years of patronage (37–30 BC) Virgil composed the *Georgics*, a poetic account of Italian farming. Throughout this decade, the erstwhile allies Antony and Octavian (the future Augustus), were in conflict. On 2 September 31 BC at the battle of Actium Octavian finally defeated Antony and Cleopatra. Could Octavian maintain peace? In a sense this must have been the question of the 20s BC. During that decade after Actium it may have seemed possible: with the cessation of civil conflict, with the hoped-for restoration of morality and religion, the new Golden Age of the *pax Romana* would be inaugurated. The *Aeneid* reflects the decade. Composed at Augustus' urging, it was begun in 29 BC and brought to its present state in 19 BC (further polishing was prevented by Virgil's death at Brindisi, on 20 September). The epic is, therefore, a most public and politically engaged creation. And yet there is Dido and, in real life, there is the tale of the emperor's henchmen co-opting Virgil's father's farm. We cannot deny Virgil a history any more than we can deny him a historical context in which to live. Whatever Virgil's political convictions – and they seem utterly conservative and pro-Augustan – the context within which they were formed was far too ambivalent to allow them unambiguous expression.

MYTHOLOGICAL AND GENERIC CONSTRAINTS

Aeneas, we will see, embodies Virgil's vision of empire. He comes to represent a set of values which is abrogated by the conduct of Dido. But these values are not easy. If at times this hero seems to blanch under the demands made of him by Virgil, tradition (another term for context) must share the blame with history and authorial intent.

Legend is the half of it. Aeneas and Troy were intertwined historically at Rome with a variety of national and personal ambitions. This was as true of the era of Naevius (see Chapter 5) as it was of Silius Italicus (see Chapter 10). From its Roman inception the Trojan legend seems to have been of a strongly political cast (Galinsky 1969). The myth was actively revived in the 260s BC, early in the first Punic war. Trojans were chosen as Roman ancestors specifically because they were Greek: Rome, wanting to woo the Sicilian Greeks, stressed their relatedness by pointing to a common Greek ancestry. Virgil's contemporaries, Julius Caesar and Augustus, exploited the legend in a different way. In the late Republic a claim to Trojan lineage offered an individual the patina of tradition. The most influential and aristocratic of Roman houses claimed Trojan ancestry

(Wiseman 1974b). In *Roman Antiquities* 1.85, Dionysius of Halicarnassus, a near contemporary of Virgil, tells us that in his day there were fifty families in Rome of Trojan extraction. Virgil mentions some of these (*Aeneid* 5.117–23). Throughout the century in which Virgil lived (but before he composed the *Aeneid*), there seems to have been considerable Roman enthusiasm for tracing one's origins to Troy (Wiseman 1974b). This enthusiasm was more than merely antiquarian. For men such as Julius Caesar and Augustus, bent on gaining the acceptance of the traditional ruling elite, such a claim was of obvious use. Caesar claimed descent from Aeneas, at least when it suited his political aspirations. The sponsor of the *Aeneid*, Augustus, great-nephew and later adopted son of Julius Caesar, also claimed descent from Aeneas. Julius Caesar and Augustus may well have encouraged the production of at least two of the handbooks devoted to Trojan genealogies (Toohey 1984; compare Syme 1939: 78ff.). A poem such as the *Aeneid* confronts, therefore, a legend that is embedded within the national, political, and popular self-consciousness of Rome. Literary adaptation must inevitably bow to the constraints of this inherited mythical conglomerate.

Genre is the other half. The *Aeneid* is an amalgam of three traditions: the public posture of the historical and annalistic epic; the more sombre habits of the large-scale mythological epic; and the private, ironic tradition of the Alexandrian miniature epic. *Pius Aeneas* must play his part within boundaries of these generic traditions.

Naevius and Ennius render the allure of the annalistic and historical tradition unavoidable (see Chapter 5). Dickson (1932), in a survey of the evidence for lost Augustan epics, found traces of more than twenty-four poems. Seven concerned historical themes. (Closer to Virgil's time there was, for example, Furius Bibaculus' narrative of the exploits of Julius Caesar (fragments: Morel 1975) or Cicero's epic on his consulship (fragments: Morel 1975).) The annalistic and historical epic was of overt nationalistic intent. It aimed to justify, legitimize, even glorify states, cities, peoples, and sometimes individuals. Naevius and Ennius may be typical. Their panoramas of Roman history begin with Aeneas and climax in contemporary conquest. Their influence is typically apparent in the show of heroes in *Aeneid* 6 or the shield of Aeneas in *Aeneid* 8.

Of Dickson's (1932) twenty-four epics, thirteen were composed on mythological themes. Mythological epic, to judge from the

Callimachean posturing of Virgil's contemporaries, had become too pedantic and too longwinded (see Chapter 6). Yet Virgil did compose a mythological poem – an heir to the traditions to be traced back through Livius Andronicus and Apollonius to Homer (Knauer 1964; Gransden 1984, Cairns 1989). Structure provides the simplest indication: the first six books of the *Aeneid* (which describe Aeneas' wanderings) are loosely based on Homer's *Odyssey*; the second six (which describe the battles fought to establish Trojan settlement in Italy) on the *Iliad*.

The *Aeneid*, like the miniature epic, was also Alexandrian (see Chapters 4 and 5). I will have more to say about this later. Here I would like to point only to two features. First, structure: the initial five books of the poem may be described as 'Apollonian' (they present an Aeneas who has much of the indecision and vacuity of Apollonius' hero (Cairns 1989: 195–6 and my Chapter 4); the remainder of the poem is 'Virgilian' (Aeneas becomes a new kind of hero, a decisive, moral figure, an emblem of the Roman people). Second, Alexandria also surfaces in the pervasive and ludic irony which constantly reappears throughout the poem.

Virgil's *Aeneid* exhibits characteristics of each of these traditions. Häußler (1976) justly describes the *Aeneid* as a 'myth-historical' creation. Yet the manner of presentation, as Clausen (1987) and Newman (1986: 104ff.) stress, remains specifically Alexandrian, specifically like that of Apollonius of Rhodes. The challenge facing Virgil was to combine the narrative allure of myth with the ethical and the national concerns of history, but to do this without turning his back on the Alexandrian revolution. Apollonius provided part of the answer. Using this model, Virgil composed a large-scale Alexandrian epic based on mythology. All that was needed to complete the picture was a myth capable of taking the national strain. This came ready-made in the legend of Aeneas.

AENEAS AND THE DEMANDS OF EMPIRE (BOOKS 1, 6, 8, 12)

Aeneas embodies Virgil's vision of empire. The hero is not constrained and motivated so much by a personal sense of honour (like the Homeric hero) as he is by the demands made by a Fate (*fatum*) intent upon the establishment of the Roman empire. We need to look now at those passages in which Aeneas is seen to incorporate imperial destiny and to determine what were the demands made by it.

Aeneid 1

Juno's enmity towards Troy is responsible for the misfortunes suffered by Aeneas in Virgil's epic. Juno is 'Rome's most respected divine antagonist', a paradigm of vindictiveness who is also 'unmanageable and disquieting' (Feeney 1990: 361). Juno's enmity is nowhere more apparent than in the storm scene of *Aeneid* 1. The Trojans are sailing from Sicily on the last leg of their journey to Italy. Juno, obsessed with preventing them reaching their future homeland, approaches the god Aeolus, king of the winds, to encourage him to whip up a storm (1.34–80). He is easily persuaded. The Trojan fleet is scattered (1.81–123). One ship is sunk before Aeneas' eyes and twelve others (of a total of twenty) have disappeared by the time Aeneas and his followers are washed up on the shores of North Africa, near the city of Carthage (1.157–222).

Otis (1964: 227–35) long ago pointed out that the storm scene encapsulates a conflict repeated throughout this poem – frenzy or *furor* attempting to thwart or delay the working out of destiny (*fatum*) and the plan of Jupiter (linked also with *pietas*). In this scene Aeolus embodies *furor*. Neptune, who calms the storm (1.124–56), symbolizes the eventual effects of *fatum* and of the plan of Jupiter. The plan of Jupiter is explained in the next scene, 1.223–304. Here the focus switches abruptly to Olympus where, through Jupiter's prophecy (1.257–96 – produced in response to the complaints of Aeneas' mother, Venus), Virgil spells out what *fatum* has in store for Aeneas and his descendants: he outlines the civilizing and pacific mission of Roman civilization and the Golden Age to be inaugurated by Aeneas. The mission of Aeneas is to inaugurate this process of civilization.

Aeneid 6

The full ramifications of Aeneas' destiny are laid out in book 6. The structure of the book is typically tripartite. The first section describes the preparations for the descent to Hades (6.1–263); the second, the passage through Hades to the fields of the blessed, Elysium (6.264–678); the third, Aeneas' meeting with his father Anchises: here he learns the theory of metempsychosis and of Rome's history to come (6.679–901).

This third section makes clear the imperial message. Anchises (6.679–702) reveals to Aeneas the future generations of Roman heroes. But before outlining these, Anchises details his famous theory of transmigration (6.713–51 and 756–886). The purpose of this speech (a mixture of Orphic, Pythagorean, and Stoic belief) is to explain how the past lives on in the present, how a leader such as Augustus embodies Aeneas, how the progress of Roman history is made constant by the metempsychosis of a heroic soul from one generation to the next.

Anchises points out to Aeneas the souls of famous Romans (6.752–853): the Alban kings, Romulus, Augustus, the Roman kings and many heroes who lived during the Roman Republic. The scene climaxes with the most public of all the poem's utterances, a description of Rome's contribution to history and civilization: first to conquer in war, and then to establish a peace in which the people are ruled in mercy and given the benefits of Roman civilization and settled ways of life (6.851–3; compare 4.229ff.). The pageant of heroes concludes with a description of Marcellus, the son of Octavia, Augustus' sister. (He had married Augustus' daughter Julia and was earmarked as Augustus' successor. He died aged 19 in 23 BC.) The book closes with a remarkably ambiguous description (6.893–8). Virgil states that, leading from Hades, there are two gates, one of horn for the true shades, and the other of ivory, the gate of false dreams. Aeneas and the Sibyl leave by the ivory gate. Does this egress pass judgement on Aeneas' mission?

Aeneid 6 leaves little to Aeneas' imagination. Fulfilment of his destiny now requires a city (Rome) and the cessation of the hostility of Juno. The former is provided in *Aeneid* 8, the latter in 12. Let us look first at Rome.

Aeneid 8 and 12

In book 8 Aeneas visits Pallanteum and its ruler, Evander. The Sibyl had stated he would need the help of a Greek city. Evander was a Greek from Arcadia. In his earlier days he had known Anchises (and in some ways he acts as an Anchises figure). Before the Trojan war he migrated to Italy and founded his city on the Palatine – the site of Augustus' own palace. The visit to Pallanteum allows Virgil the opportunity of showing us and Aeneas the hills and places which the future Rome will occupy (8.280–369). In this way the legendary past of Rome is linked through Aeneas to Augustus and Augustan Rome.

The link between the past and the present is made even more clear in the last section of the book (8.608–731). Here is described the miraculous shield, prepared for Aeneas by Vulcan at the bidding of his wife, Venus. Aeneas' shield reproduces a series of tableaux which have symbolic significance. At the very centre of the shield is the climactic depiction of Augustus' triumph at Actium over Antony and Cleopatra (8.675ff.). Around this are a series of vignettes from Roman history which selectively illustrate (and commend) the key aspects of the Roman character (Williams 1980b: 265–6). As well as playing a symbolic role, these tableaux again emphasize the continuity of the past in the present: how Augustus incorporates Aeneas.

Juno began the action of the *Aeneid*. Cessation of her hostility (reconciliation with the Aeneadae) is necessary if the poem is to reach some form of imperial resolution. This is the cornerstone of the final book.

The divine scene in the clouds at 12.791–842 makes the theme most evident. Here the conflict between Jupiter and his wife (which hostility virtually began the poem's narrative at 1.12–33) is finally resolved: Italian and Trojan will become reconciled by the disappearance or blending of Trojan customs and culture; these will be supplanted by Italian customs. The cornerstone of reconciliation is *clementia* or 'mercy', the policy urged upon Aeneas by his father at 6.853, and embodied by Aeneas when approached by the Latin emissaries at 11.108–19, and urged by Jupiter. Reconciliation on the divine plane requires Juno to follow Jupiter's urging (12.793–806) and to put aside her enmity.

It is now possible to return to the question with which I began this section – what were these 'demands of empire'? The answer should now be apparent. Aeneas' role and, by implication, that of Augustus, was to subject his personal desires to the greater needs of state and empire. The destiny of empire will be assured by Aeneas' willingness to conquer in war, to establish a peace, to rule in mercy, and to endow with the benefits of Roman civilization and stability. That this vision, however powerful, accords ill with the portrait of Dido and with Aeneas' final refusal of *clementia* throws such simple imperial positivism into sharp relief.

HEROISM VERSUS DESTINY: HOMER, AENEAS (BOOKS 2, 10, 12), TURNUS (BOOKS 9, 10), EMPIRE, AND THE HEROIC IMPULSE

Aeneas' comprehension of his mission clashes with Homeric predisposition to heroic impulse. In the first half of the epic Aeneas learns to understand his national role. In the second half he puts it into practice. But he continues to be tested – right up until the end of the poem. And he frequently fails. Turnus' situation is comparable. The most Homeric of Virgilian heroes, he remains a constant prey to the heroic impulse. We could say that generic constraints, expressed through the heroic impulse, pit a Homeric heroism against Virgil's imperial design.

Aeneid 2

Aeneas' response to the heroic impulse provides one telling means of charting the modes by which Homer constrains the portrait of Virgil's hero. *Aeneid* 2 offers the best set of examples. (The book is tripartite: 2.1–249 tell the story of the wooden horse, 2.250–558, the sack of the city and Priam's death, 2.559–804 the escape of Aeneas and his family from Troy. Its doleful purpose, to depict the Trojan disaster, must, however, be balanced against national promise: from the destruction of Troy comes the birth of Roman civilization.)

Let us look at the second section. While Sinon releases the Greeks from the wooden horse, Aeneas has a dream (2.268–97). Hector appears. Troy, he prophesies, will be destroyed. Aeneas' duty is to rescue the gods of Troy from the ashes of the city and to found for them a new home. The implications for Aeneas are considerable. He has a higher cause – he is to become an 'instrument of history'. He must, for the sake of destiny, avoid empty heroics and self-aggrandizing death.

Aeneas is at once tempted by the emptiness of the 'heroic impulse'. After viewing the carnage from the roof of the house of his father Anchises, he rushes to prepare for battle (2.298–369). Disregarding Hector, he surrenders, Achilles-like, to blood lust and to a desire for vengeance: Aeneas and his companions disguise themselves in Greek armour (2.370–401); in the fighting that follows many of his companions are killed (2.402–52). Later in the narrative Aeneas from the roof of the palace helplessly watches the death of Priam (2.506–58). This scene provides a powerful commentary on Aeneas' compulsion towards heroics. Priam, clad in armour, intends to fight. Hecuba, his wife, dissuades him. (Together with their daughters they seek sanctuary at the altar.) Priam's death might have been more dignified had not Polites, one of his sons, run wounded towards him pursued by Pyrrhus. Polites falls dead. Priam's pathetic rejoinder is to attack Pyrrhus. He responds with a fatal sword thrust. Quinn (1968: 6) comments effectively: 'Priam's heroic gesture is not merely futile . . .

but irrelevant – irrelevant to the point of being wrong . . . [a] conditioned response . . . unaware one might, by *enduring*, at any rate do less harm.'

Aeneas' ability to subject himself to the advice of Hector and to resist the heroic impulse is tested again in the third section of *Aeneid* 2. By this point the hero has literally shouldered the burden of destiny – in the figure of his father. Yet he is still easy prey to empty heroics. Aeneas, concerned for his family, is returning home (2.559ff.). He encounters Helen hiding in the temple of Vesta (Goold 1990 believes this interlude is not real Virgil). Will he kill her and avenge the destruction of Troy? Virgil makes it clear (2.575 and 2.588) that Aeneas' desire for vengeance is wrong. By giving way to *ira* and to *furor* Aeneas would become another Pyrrhus. Aeneas resists the impulse and returns home to find his father Anchises sunk in despair. Omens – fire licking around the head of Aeneas' son Ascanius, thunder, and a shooting star – galvanize Anchises and Aeneas (2.671–729). The significance of these signs is apparent: Iulus Ascanius is destined for kingship. Anchises is now willing to leave the burning city. Aeneas' resolve is tested one last time (2.730–95). In the confusion of the leave-taking Creusa, his wife, is lost. Aeneas regresses and, leaving father and son, rushes madly to find her. Her wraith appears to urge him to continue with the mission.

Aeneid 10

The conflict between the heroic impulse and the demands of destiny is marked again in *Aeneid* 10. Some of the most violent fighting of the poem is depicted in this book (notably 10.308ff.). Turnus kills Pallas (10.439–509). Then Aeneas, in an extraordinarily bloodthirsty *aristeia*, wreaks havoc on the battlefield (10.510–605). Aeneas' violence matches that of Achilles after Patroclus' death. Juno becomes so concerned for Turnus' safety that she withdraws him from the field (10.606–88). Aeneas' anger seems to know no appeasement: further enraged by the disappearance of Turnus, he kills Lausus, Mezentius' son (10.769–832), and, soon after, Mezentius himself (10.833–908).

It is difficult to reconcile the rage of Aeneas after Pallas' death (10.510–605) with the advice proffered by Anchises to Aeneas in Hades (6.851–3: 'first . . . establish peace by taming the proud, and secondly . . . offer a settled and civilized way of life in which the people are ruled with mercy' (Williams 1980a: 513)). There is little here of that *misericordia* and *clementia*. In this passage Aeneas exhibits the same lack of control (a surrender to the heroic impulse and to *furor* – 10.545, 565–70, 602–4) to which he almost gave way in *Aeneid* 2. Aeneas boasts over his victims (10.531–6) and, Achilles-like, snares eight young captives to be sacrificed at his slain companion's funeral (10.517–20). The anger and violence, though repulsive, do further the political aim of establishing empire (Aeneas is *pius* at 10.591). Yet Aeneas seems to recognize the personal cost of his anger after he has fought Mezentius' son, Lausus (10.769–832). As he stands with Lausus in his arms, he, the son of Anchises (*Anchisiades* 10.822), seems to comprehend the pathos and futility of the death of this young man (it could be Pallas or Ascanius). With this comprehension he seems to achieve an insight into the violence and waste of his own behaviour and even his own imperial destiny.

Aeneid 12

Or does he? The duel with Turnus provides the best commentary on the strength of Aeneas' insights. When these heroes finally fight (12.887–952) Aeneas quickly gains the upper hand. Turnus pleads for his life, and for a moment at least Aeneas seems to consider the possibility of mercy (*clementia*). But he sees Pallas' belt-buckle on Turnus and, in a fit of rage (recapitulating those of book 10), he kills the suppliant. Aeneas' reaction to the sight of Pallas' buckle may be understandable, but it is not a reaction controlled by a desire for reconciliation. Nor does it demonstrate that attitude of *clementia* urged by Anchises in Hades or by Aeneas himself when approached by the Latin emissaries at 11.108–19. The outcome of the combat seems to cast the possibility of reconciliation, *clementia*, and imperial destiny into doubt. It is as if the generic claims of the heroic impulse have overwhelmed a hero more normally subject to the demands of empire and *pietas*.

Turnus (books 9, 10)

This is probably the best place to say something of Aeneas' main opponent, Turnus. This hero is best thought of as a mirror image, if you like, of an Aeneas of the type left behind in the cinders of Troy in book 2.

Turnus is, like Dido, associated with *furor* from his very first appearance. It is Juno's doing that he becomes so passionately opposed to the Trojans' arrival. She reacts to the sight of the Trojan landfall with anger, bitterness, and resentment (at 7.293–322 she delivers a speech reminiscent of that at the beginning of the poem). By rousing the furies of hell she plans to inflict a maximum of damage on the Trojans before they fulfil their destiny. To do this she summons the demon Allecto who kindles a lust for war (a *furor* or madness) in Amata – and later Turnus (7.323–405). Turnus' complicity in his *furor* is probably not at issue (but Mackie 1991a, 1991b). Although the portrait is not a flattering one (his predisposition to *furor* may be made apparent at 7.406–74; perhaps too his boastfulness, his desire for glory and war, his excessive daring, and his potentiality for violence), we must be clear: the imperial figure of Aeneas must have an opponent, and that figure will, as we have seen, be prone to the influences of the heroic impulse. So it is often remarked (Camps 1969: 35ff.) that Turnus seems to stands for the individualist, Homeric warrior. Turnus' *furor* associates him with those values inimical to empire. That Turnus in the end will demand our sympathies indicates the intransigence of Virgil's model of reconciliation.

In the meantime Turnus will not receive a good press. This is especially apparent during his major appearance, in his *aristeia* of *Aeneid* 9. Part of the purpose of this book is to balance the scales evenly between the Latins and the Aeneadae. The third narrative section achieves this by having Turnus break into the Trojan camp (compare Hector's assault in *Iliad* 12). The long battle description begins with the violent *aristeia* of Turnus (9.503–89), then shifts to young Ascanius who kills the taunting Numanus with an arrow shaft (9.590–671). The remainder of the book is devoted to the battle about the gates of the Trojan camp. Turnus attacks and kills the two strange giants, Pandarus and Bitias, but is eventually driven back by Mnestheus and the Trojans. Had Turnus not been so intent on personal *timē*, had he thought to open the gates rather than indulging in random slaughter, the outcome of his assault on the Trojan camp might have been different. The death of Pallas (10.439–509) reinforces this image of Turnus. Pallas' death alienates us from Turnus (see 10.441–3, 491–2, 495–7, 501–2, 503–5; Otis 1964: 356). This is a hero too prone to violence.

DIDO AND THE DEMANDS OF EMPIRE
(BOOKS 1, 4)
AENEID 1

Dido and Aeneas first meet in book 1 of the *Aeneid* (1.494–656). It is as if we were reading the *Odyssey*. Aeneas wanders, driven by sea storms and the wrath of the gods to a strange land, and arrives to find welcome from a woman. This is like Odysseus arriving in Phaeacia to meet Nausicaa (it is not surprising that at line 1.498 Virgil uses of Dido the same simile Homer had used of Nausicaa – *Odyssey* 6.102f.). Virgil, like Homer, teases us with the prospect of love. The relationship which has been hinted at is soon brought into the open (1.695–756). Now comes the generic affiliation with Apollonius. Here, in a scene closely based on Apollonius, *Argonautica* 3.6ff., Cupid causes Dido to fall in love with Aeneas (who, like Odysseus, begins a long flashback narrative of his wanderings). Venus, wishing to protect her son from Juno's designs, hopes that love will keep him safe at Carthage.

Genre may force Dido's infatuation. (Not just the epic precedent of Apollonius, but also that of Naevius – see Chapter 5.) Yet destiny (Aeneas' *fatum*) demands that we adjudicate the ethical propriety of this affection. The captivation of Dido by love, the poem seems to be trying to say, is not wholly outside her control (Quinn 1968: 135ff.; but Rudd 1990). Dido seems to choose at crucial junctures to ignore shame (*pudor*) and give way to desire (*amor*). The conflict is based upon that of Medea in *Argonautica* 3. Yet here the conflict is formulated in a typically Roman manner: Dido's psychological conflict is between *furor* (madness or frenzy) and *pietas* (like the Greek *aidōs*, this word signifies individuals' recognition of their responsibilities both to gods and to their fellows (Quinn 1968: 111f.)). Opting for love means opting for *furor*. How can we support such a choice?

Dido's infatuation, furthermore, labours under the strain of damning historical metaphor. As the first Carthaginian regent to come into conflict with a Roman general she offers an aetiology for the devastating wars of later history between Rome and the Carthaginians. (Aeneas' final abandonment of Dido leads her to curse him and his race. The fulfilment of the curse was the Punic wars.) Can any Roman support a Carthaginian (Horsfall 1990)?

There is another important historical resonance (Quinn 1968: 152). In more recent history two Roman potentates, Julius Caesar and Marcus Antonius, were led astray by love for a North African –

Cleopatra. The instance of Antony is particularly significant. His affair precipitated the battle of Actium. That naval encounter, on 2 September 31 BC, saw the defeat by Octavian (Augustus after 27 BC) of Antony and Cleopatra. The ostensible purpose of the *Aeneid* is to celebrate this victory (alluded to especially in the long description of Aeneas' shield in *Aeneid* 8). Actium, for Romans in the 20s BC, symbolizes the end of decades of bloody civil war and the establishment of a Roman world order. Aeneas is an exemplar of the forces and powers which led to that victory, a victory which affirmed nationhood, civilization, and peace. How can we sympathize with Dido in the face of all that?

Genre too is weighed against the Carthaginian. This is especially evident in *Aeneid* 4, but the traces are also to be found in book 1. The psychological, empathetic narrative of *Aeneid* 4, its concern with the feminine and the erotic are marked characteristics of Apollonius' *Argonautica* 3 and of the Alexandrian miniature epic. Medea thus becomes the prototype for Dido. Medea, throughout most of the ancient tradition, is portrayed as an odious, unsympathetic person. As we damn the fratricidal matricide, Medea, so, by contagion, may we also condemn Dido.

Aeneid 4

But let us see what Virgil makes of Dido in *Aeneid* 4. This book is devoted wholly to the narrative of Dido and Aeneas' love affair (it divides into five sections: 4.1–89, leading to the consummation, 4.90–172, the consummation, 4.173–278, divine and human reaction, 4.279–449, where Dido and Aeneas clash, and 4.450–705, Dido commits suicide while Aeneas departs). Dido begins the first sequence speaking of her love to her sister Anna. The imagery is all of fire, illness, wounding, frenzy, and madness. The imagery seems to suggest that love is a profoundly destructive passion, a type of *furor*.

The text's ideological rejection of Dido becomes very difficult to sustain. After Anna's cozening reply the narrative switches to Olympus (4.90–128). Venus and Juno haggle over the fates of Dido and Aeneas. (Juno wants to frustrate the foundation of the new Troy, Venus to frustrate her old opponent.) This heartless scene echoes that between Hera, Athena, and Aphrodite beginning *Argonautica* 3. In Apollonius Medea was the loser. Here it is Dido. Virgil makes this plain after the famous cave scene (4.160–72). Sympathy begins to swing in favour of Dido. After the cave scene local reaction was swift (4.173–218). Dido's erstwhile suitor, King Iarbas, was understandably upset. His response is like that of Dido's city: Dido, in love with a foreigner, is neglecting, even spurning her kingdom. The Olympian retort is as unfavourable as that of Carthage. Jupiter sends Mercury to Aeneas (4.219–78). Aeneas must remember his mission and cease from Carthaginian affairs. Aeneas' sense of duty appears pallid in the face of the passionate aberrance of Dido.

The emotional epicentre of *Aeneid* 4 is the encounter between Dido and Aeneas at 4.296–392. Dido's two ardent speeches contrast dramatically with Aeneas' careful, seemingly cold response. Dido's first speech (4.305–30) is a despairing, pathetic affair; her second (4.365–87) is full of hatred and scorn. Aeneas in the centre (4.333–61) remembers his mission. The conflict has its nearest echo in *Argonautica* 4.338ff. There Jason coolly strikes a bargain with the Colchians which will guarantee the safety of the Argonauts. The bargain meant abandoning Medea. Here the resemblance ends. Jason is concerned only for personal advantage; Aeneas has his mission. Increasingly, and despite better judgement, the reader sides with flawed Dido.

Aeneas and Dido do not meet again until book 6. Dido is a ghost then. Here in book 4 she makes one last attempt to influence Aeneas by sending her sister Anna. Wait, she asks, for good weather and for her to become used to the separation before sailing (4.416–49). The plea is ineffectual. Dido sets about planning her own death, but not without an enormous inner struggle (4.450–73). Dido's suicide has a double motive. The first reflects her state of despair: evident in her love, her shame, and her subjection to *furor* (4.522–52). Mercury purports to understand the second motive (4.563–5). Her death is liable to anger the Carthaginians and set them after the Trojans. Such is the extent of her derangement – or so Mercury chooses to warn Aeneas in a dream vision. Aeneas, ever attentive to divine monitions, rouses his crew and sets sail (4.571–83). Aeneas has no choice but to go – but it would, I believe, be churlish to side with Virgil and his Aeneas at this juncture.

So it is with Dido's soliloquy. This, delivered as she watches the Aeneadae sail away, marks one of the most dramatic moments of the epic. In her last words she surveys her life's achievements and, again, curses the Aeneadae. She falls on Aeneas' sword – a tragic, flawed heroine sacrificed to the public values of imperial destiny.

Nothing that transpires after Dido's suicide warrants any change in our sympathies. This is especially the case in the politically correct

Aeneid 6. There, after Aeneas progresses past the dog Cerberus (6.417–25) to limbo, he encounters the shades of those who have perished before their time (babies, the unjustly condemned, suicides, and those who died of love) (6.426–76). His meeting with Dido reaffirms an almost terrifying devotion to duty and destiny – at the expense of great personal cost in happiness (6.450–76). Whose happiness? His own or Dido's?

There is a temptation to maintain that Dido is the closest the *Aeneid* comes to realizing a real epic 'hero'. I have suggested earlier some of the characteristics of this type: the hero is usually of superior social station (and, if male, he will be preeminent in fighting), courage, and, maybe, even intelligence. But, perhaps as a result of a quest or a testing, this hero will undergo some form of moral maturation. After being initially at odds with his human and divine community (misusing the heroic impulse), the hero will develop a deeper understanding of his or her duties towards both groups. Dido conforms to this pattern almost unto maturation. Suicide and despair deprive her of this last stage.

What does all of this tell us? It helps us to perceive how genre (part of the context within which Virgil wrote), if not authorial intent, would have us direct our affections. Despite the ideological barrage directed against the Carthaginian queen, she triumphs in much the same way as do those great but flawed heroes of Homer, Achilles and Odysseus.

VIRGIL'S PRIVATE VOICE

The ideological pendulum has swung away, during the last thirty years, from a positivist interpretation of Aeneas' wars and an implicit condemnation of the dalliance with Dido. The eighteenth- and nineteenth-century *Aeneid* was to be had in the revelation by Jupiter of Rome's greatness (1.257–96), or Anchises' predictions (6.756–853), or the prophetic representations on the shield of Aeneas (8.626–728), or the final promise of Jupiter to Juno (12.830–40). Such episodes extol the greatness of Rome and of the Augustan age. This proud, optimistic, public voice – which strives continuously and sometimes hyperbolically for intensity, elevation, sublimity, and grandeur – is the one nowadays frequently accused of jingoism.

Contemporary critics, in reaction, take one of two courses (Harrison 1990a). Either they stress Virgil's other voice, that plangent and private tone which so sympathizes with the Didos, the victims of

Aeneas' destiny (Parry 1963; Williams 1990; Lyne 1987). Or they (the 'Harvard school' and their followers) reinterpret the character of Aeneas and the intent of the final duel (Putnam 1965; amongst the followers, Boyle 1986): the duel represents a condemnation of Aeneas' behaviour and, through this, the cost of the aspirations of empire and Augustus (so too Bishop 1988). It ought be apparent that I do not believe that the second of these two views is consistent with the evidence presented by the poem. But, to be fair, the ambiguities of that final duel must inevitably pose such a question.

Is Virgil 'most truly himself' when lavishing his melancholy compassion (*misericordia* and *clementia*) on the victims, such as Dido, of Aeneas' mission? The champions of the importance of Virgil's private voice – which school has come to represent critical orthodoxy – believe this is the case. Laocoon, Priam, Polydorus, Dido, Palinurus, Misenus, Pallas, Lausus, Evander, Camilla, and Turnus, they are all offered a sympathy which, at times, fits ill with the vigour of Virgil's public protestations. The proponents of the 'private voice' (like the nineteenth-century critics or the Harvard school) privilege meaning. Much of the force of their *Aeneid* results from its ambivalence, from the tension created between public and private protestations.

How does this happen? Take *Aeneid* 12. How are we to interpret the final duel? Aeneas, as I have already suggested, does not enter this combat in an utterly untarnished manner (he recapitulates the rages of book 10 and 12.441–99). Nor are his actions utterly untarnished: his reaction to the sight of Pallas' buckle may be understandable, but it is not a reaction controlled by a desire for reconciliation. Nor does it demonstrate an attitude of *clementia*. Turnus may be viewed through the same lens. Perhaps for the first time, he begins to demand the lion's share of our sympathy. The more palpably he becomes the victim, the more he gains our sympathies. But we ought not be too confused by facile sympathy. Turnus may witness his world crumble and he may become a truly tragic figure late in this book (note 12.614ff.), yet until this time he remained a most violent and individualist creature. He bends only in the final moments of the duel when he begs Aeneas to spare him (12.931–8) and urges him to 'go no further with his hatred'.

The tension between the private and the public presented by the ending of the *Aeneid* can be seen in two ways: Aeneas' displaying no evocation of either reconciliation or *clementia* is pitted against Turnus' obvious heroism. Not for a minute do we doubt the claims of the public voice (perhaps best represented by the reconciliation earlier in the book between Juno and Jupiter – 12.791–842). But we cannot doubt the claims of the private voice for *clementia* and *misericordia*. There is in the final book of the *Aeneid* no satisfying resolution between the private and the public. That may be Virgil's last word. Virgil does not judge Aeneas when he has him kill his rival. Rather he poses the question: how should these conflicting imperatives be reconciled?

IRREVERENT HUMOUR AND IMPERIAL CONSTRAINTS

So far so good: Virgil's *Aeneid* exhibits a remarkable humanity, a mature and balanced view of the establishment of empire. Although a supporter of the demands of 'destiny', Virgil is a realist and he is honest. Against the public gains are balanced the private losses.

Would that it were this simple. There is, as I have already indicated, a third voice, a ludic, ironic, Alexandrian voice which fits ill with the gravity imposed upon the epic by proponents of the public and the private. To illustrate the effects produced by this Alexandrian voice, I would like to describe briefly the digression (sometimes erroneously described as an epyllion) of *Aeneid* 8 concerning the encounter of the hero Hercules with the monster Cacus (8.184–279 retell the story, 8.280–369 the origins of the related rite).

Hercules is pictured driving back through Italy with the cattle he had removed from the brute Geryon. Evil Cacus stole four bulls and four heifers, then hid them in his cave on the Aventine hill, part of the site of future Rome. (Cacus pulled the cattle backwards by their tails into his cave. This, he hoped, would leave Hercules no trace of their whereabouts.) When the cattle lowed Hercules discovered the cave. He tore away the top of the mountain to reveal the hiding place and, after an almost Ovidian battle, throttled the monster. The local Italians rejoiced in the slaughter and established a rite that, to the time of Virgil, was still enacted.

The tale of Hercules and Cacus has clear importance for the nationalist theme of the *Aeneid*. The legend is an *aition*: it explains the origin of religious ceremonies still practised in Virgil's era. Yet the relevance of the hero at this juncture is striking. Cacus is an out-and-out villain. He symbolizes those forces of disorder which disrupt civilization. Hercules' throttling the monster does the world a good turn. So, we are meant to think, does Aeneas' establishment of the

139

Roman race. Hercules stands as a prototype of Aeneas. His 'Cacus' is the resistance shown by Italians such as Turnus to the fulfilment of his destiny – but also those impediments to destiny such as Dido. Hercules, in many Roman contexts, is also to be associated with the emperor (Bassett 1966; Anderson 1928). Thus we may associate Hercules with Augustus himself (Galinsky 1990). Augustus' Cacus was Mark Antony. Actium, therefore, is perhaps reflected in the conflict between Hercules and Cacus.

What is most striking about this allegory – on first reading – is its utter ethical simplicity. The forces of good – Hercules, Aeneas, Augustus – are lined up against the very embodiment of the forces of evil – Cacus, Turnus, Allecto, Mark Antony, and, by implication, Dido herself. Yet a more attentive reading reveals flaws in this imperial design. Consider the following lines:

> There was a flint pinnacle, sheer on all sides, thrusting up from the cave's ridge, right up in the air, an ideal home for the nests of foul birds. Because it leant left from the ridge towards the river, [Hercules] pressed against it from the left and he shook it and tore it up along with its deep roots; then suddenly he crashed against it. At the blow great heaven rang. The banks leapt apart. The river itself flowed backwards in terror. But the cave and the uncovered kingdom of Cacus showed forth, and the deep shaded cavern opened its doors.

That is Hercules tearing the top off the Aventine hill to display, lurking in his cave beneath, the awful monster Cacus (*Aeneid* 8.233–42). In the lines to follow Hercules pelts the horror with missiles, then, frustrated by Cacus' smoke-screen, he leaps into the gorge of the mountain and throttles the villain. It is pretty stirring material. But how are we intended to interpret such a hyperbolical (and bizarre) piece of description? To take it with complete seriousness is surely impossible. Hercules may be a mythical hero, and he may be capable of superhuman feats, yet we can hardly be expected to believe that events like this can really happen. Worse still: such an easy, and such an unbelievable, triumph makes an absolute mockery of naturalistic portraits of the trials of other heroes (all of whom are also mythical) within the poem. Compare the deaths of Dido, of Nisus and Euryalus, of Pallas, of Lausus, or even of Turnus. Are they not ill-served by the inclusion within the same poem of a combat which is to be taken so lightly? Is not such an instance of extended intellectual irony frivolous? If this passage had appeared in

Ovid's *Metamorphoses*, it would be justly described as humorous, mock epic.

Intellectual irony and humour are a problem for those who insist on the primacy of either the public or the private voice. The seriousness demanded by such readings can allow no easy acceptance of irreverent humour, whimsy, or irony. Such features, however, are persistently characteristic of the poem.

It is as if there were a third voice. Ironic, sometimes playful, it is often learned and often hyperbolic. Williams (1983a: 124ff.) describes this last characteristic as 'Hellenistic rococo' (compare Hardie 1986: 241ff.). It is above all an Alexandrian (and *Aeneid* 8 is a most Alexandrian book) voice which often threatens to disrupt the seriousness of the political and the private voices. This ironic note causes us to question the applicability to life of the poem's moral aims (public or private). This voice reasserts the ludic aspect of poetry. It allows us to establish distance between the lugubrious gravity of the moral message and the simple pleasure caused by encountering this highly wrought literary text. Recognition of this third voice helps to explain the peculiar, often paradoxical effects of passages such as the Hercules and Cacus episode. Perhaps the effect of this third voice may be described as follows: the public voice asserts the primacy of Augustus' peace; the private voice, by so sympathizing with the fates of the victims of the poem, causes us to question any simple political reading; the Alexandrian voice, ludic and ironic, forces reconsideration of the cultural naivety of the public voice, and of the latent solipsism of the private.

Williams (1983a: 28–9 – but in a different context) describes such passages as 'the mannerist fantasy of Hellenistic rococo . . . [which] belongs to the world of mythic unreality'. He cites the description of Mercury in 4.238–55 – especially the description of Mount Atlas ('the mountain is described as if it really were a giant with anthropomorphic features (246–51)') – then compares other passages:

> the storm with which the poem opens is elaborately arranged by Juno in a scene with Aeolus of pure rococo, and it is followed by another scene of equally pure rococo in which Neptune chides the winds, sends them packing, and rides in his grand chariot over the sea to calm it.

Williams (1983a: 124ff.) also refers to the long passage describing the seduction of Vulcan by his wife Venus (8.370–453) and to the 'most incongruous episode in the whole *Aeneid*', the transformation of Aeneas' ships into nymphs (9.77–122).

There are other passages which might be added. There is the fantasy portrait of Neptune riding over the waves with his nymphs (5.816–26); the humorous aspects of the athletic contests in *Aeneid* 5 (5.151–82); the almost comic figure of Charon (6.295–336 and particularly 6.384–416; note the striking contrast with the moving 6.305–14); the unusual description of Pandarus and Bitias as they guard the gate to the Trojan camp (9.672–82); or the bizarre description of the infant Camilla being cast across a river attached by cork bark to an oak spear shaft (11.549–66).

This Alexandrian voice disrupts the gravity associated with the public and private voices. Consider again the transformation of the ships into nymphs and recall that it takes place in what is customarily described as one of the most bloodthirsty of books (Pallas and Lausus die here). The nymphs are not alone. For almost one hundred lines (10.163–259) Virgil indulges in what Quinn (1968: 216) terms 'intellectual irony'. At first it is in the catalogue of the Etruscans: notice particularly the epyllion-like theme of the metamorphosis of love-smitten Cycnus (10.189–93); or the description of the ship which seems to become a centaur (10.195–7); or the ingenious description of Mezentius' foes (10.204–6). Only then is there the ironic description (a foretaste of Ovid's *Metamorphoses*) of Aeneas' meeting with the nymphs into whom his ships have been changed. Just as the conflict between the public and private voices causes us to take stock of the validity of the imperial aim of the poem, so does the Alexandrian voice cause us to establish a distance between the lugubrious moral message of the epic and the simple pleasure of reading.

DID VIRGIL FAIL?

The question (put by Quinn (1972) in another context) takes us right back to love and war, Dido and Aeneas. If by failure is meant the inability to reconcile these opposing forces, then yes, Virgil does fail. In a sense Virgil's narrative implodes. Aeneas' mission demands closure (contemporary jargon for resolution). Repeatedly Virgil seems to be on the brink of providing it. Yet, on most occasions he hesitates: closure is undercut by the conflicting demands of the public, the private, and the Alexandrian voices. The *Aeneid* is perhaps the greatest piece of Roman literature. A small measure of its greatness resides in its lack of closure, in its ability to offer a variety of different poetic worlds to different eras. But I doubt that this was as deliberate as it was reflexive: Virgil, that is, acts as a remarkable prism for the tortured context into which he was born.

The best literature usually ends up by subverting, in part at any rate, the ideology which it purports to recommend. Thus the values which Achilles comes to learn in the final books of the *Iliad* run contrary to the prevailing heroic ideology. The prevailing ideology of the *Aeneid* – seen above all in its public voice – is Augustan. Yet the ideology of the *Aeneid* fails to convince entirely. It is in its vignettes, in its raw poetry (the Alexandrian, poetic voice), and in its humanity (its private voice) that the poem these days gains its popularity. Perhaps we can blame Aeneas for the failure of the public voice. By comparison with the wracked, self-indulgent Achilles, the self-seeking Odysseus, the tawdry Jason, or the tragic Dido, Aeneas is a dull dog. He lacks the more marked capacity for transgression possessed by Achilles and Odysseus, or even Jason. Lacking that capacity and lacking repentance, he fails to evoke in the reader a sense of reconciliation with the poem's ideas. Aeneas comes most to life – and the epic assumes its greatest moral significance – when his *furor* is at its most extreme. It is as if Virgil is unsure whether his hero ought to reflect the corporate values of Roman tradition, or whether he ought reflect the potentially destructive attitudes of excessive individualism.

It is in that very uncertainty, I believe, that much of the undoubted greatness of this epic resides. Context, I have argued, forges the contradictions within the *Aeneid*. Using his unique poetic gifts and his extraordinary sympathy, Virgil seems to have laid himself open to these tensions and allowed them to breathe life into a poem that so easily could have sunk into imperial encomium, maudlin pessimism, or high-handed Alexandrian levity.

8

OVID, *METAMORPHOSES*

In Ovid's epic, the *Metamorphoses*, there are approximately 250 separate stories. An attempt to provide an interpretative paraphrase of that sum would run two risks: confusion and boredom. To avoid such risks I will stick to the promise made at the beginning of the last chapter. My discussion will not follow sequentially Ovid's labyrinthine narrative. It will be arranged topically.

WHY DID HE DIE IN A FRONTIER TOWN?

My temples now are like swan's plumage, and my black hair is stained white with age; old age's weakness and laziness creep up on me; it's difficult now to keep on going. I should be at the end of my troubles, I should be living without fear, I should be enjoying my leisure and hobbies . . . the gods have not decreed it: I have been exiled across land and sea and thrown up on the coast of Sarmatia.

Ovid was about 53 when he wrote these lines from exile in Tomis (*Tristia* 4.8.1–6, 15–16). He was driven from Rome in AD 8. His place of exile (modern Constanza near the mouth of the Danube) was no holiday resort. This is how Ovid describes its winter (*Tristia* 3.10.13–24):

The snow is there all the time. Once fallen, no sun or rain can melt it. The north wind sets it hard and makes it last for ever. One fall comes before another has melted. It can stay like this in some places for two years. The northern storm wind is so strong that it can level high towers and sweep away buildings. [The people of Tomis] keep out the evil cold with skins and stitched trousers. Only their faces are exposed. Their hair often

144

tinkles with hanging ice and their beards gleam white with a covering of frost. Unbottled wine stands up. It keeps the shape of its jar. They don't drink draughts of wine here, but served-up frozen chunks.

The exile could not have been more extreme. In sunny Rome Ovid was well known, moved in the best literary and social circles. Perhaps his life was like those described in the *Amores* or in the *Ars Amatoria* (*Art of Love*). Imagine the effect of year-round snow and skin breeches on the man who had the Muse of tragedy complain (*Amores* 3.1.15–25) at him:

> Can't you put an end to your loving? You're stuck with the same theme. Drunken parties talk about your vile behaviour, and so do street corners all over the place. People often point you out in the street and say: 'There he is, burning up with cruel love.' Don't you realize, you're becoming the talk of the whole city while you go on shamelessly about your activities. It's time to be inspired by something serious, by tragedy. You've hesitated long enough. Begin a big book! You're swamping your talent with trivia. Write an epic!

Why such a fashionable poet – a near parody of the pose of urban life in the fast track – should have ended up in the primitive world of a remote frontier town will never be known. Yet there is no denying this awful exile, and there can be no denying that it colours our reading of his epic, the *Metamorphoses*. It causes us, for better or worse, to look for the subversive.

Let us look first at the little that is known of his life before the exile. (There is not much in it that could be called subversive.) He was born of an equestrian family in 43 BC at Sulmo, a town in central Italy. Provincials went to Rome to build a career. Publius Ovidius Naso was no exception. His ambitious, censorious father sent him to the capital to train for a political and legal career. Things did not go quite as his father had planned. After the usual training in rhetoric and declamation, Ovid came into contact with the leading Roman poets – Propertius, Horace, Tibullus. Poetry attracted him more than a normal 'career' (on all of this, see his *Tristia* 4.10). He tried, albeit half-heartedly, to follow the advice of his father. After travelling abroad and studying in Athens, he began a career. But his father was dead now and had left him money. Ovid, tolerably independent, gave in to the siren call of poetry. This gained him quick success. By

AD 8 he was established as a leading poet. There were already two editions of his successful erotic collection, the *Amores* (perhaps in 20 and 2 BC – he had been reading these publicly aged 18), a tragedy (the *Medea* in 13–8 BC), three books of versified instruction on methods of seduction (the *Ars amatoria*, 2 BC–AD 1), one book on how to avoid seduction (*Remedium amoris* in AD 1 or 2), a handbook on make-up (*De medicamine faciei amoris*, 2–1 BC), a curious Alexandrian account of the Roman calendar entitled the *Fasti* (AD 7–8), and, of course, the *Metamorphoses* (AD 7–8).

He was banished about the time of the publication of the *Metamorphoses*. (The type of banishment was known as *relegatio*. It was subject to later review, and involved no loss of citizenship or confiscation of property.) There is a record of the exile: four books of the *Tristia* (AD 8–12) and the four books of the *Epistulae ex Ponto* (AD 13–16).) Ovid was never recalled. According to Jerome, he died at Tomis in AD 17.

Ovid writes (*Tristia* 4.10.99–100) that the cause of his exile was known to everyone. He says (*Tristia* 2.207–10) that it was brought on by a 'poem and a mistake'. The 'poem' is often thought to have been the manual on seduction, the *Ars amatoria*. The 'mistake' may have been implication in the intrigues of Julia, the emperor's granddaughter. She was banished for adultery at about this time. But there really is no proof for these guesses. We might as well blame the faint praise with which the emperor Augustus is addressed in the finale to the *Metamorphoses*.

ARE THE *METAMORPHOSES* AN EPIC?

The *Metamorphoses* comprises about 250 stories, drawn from Greek and Roman mythology, which supposedly tell of famous transformations. The stories are linked skilfully, but with what often seems to be the most obvious means of association. The transformations exhibit an approximate chronology. They begin with creation and finish in Ovid's own era with the prospective metamorphosis (precisely the deification) of Augustus himself. This is hardly the stuff of Homeric or Virgilian epic. We are entitled, therefore, to query whether the *Metamorphoses* is an epic at all.

An answer is built up slowly. It is a 'yes', but Ovid teases. For the reader who comes to the *Metamorphoses* through Homer and Virgil the frustrating question is constantly forced: what sort of a poem is this? It has the metre of Homer's or Virgil's epics, but the subject

146

matter seems sheer fantasy. For the reader schooled in the ironic opacities of Alexandria (Chapter 6), however, there is instant recognition.

Callimachus' mannered, miniaturized epic is typified by learned elaboration, an elaboration which, through the recasting of heroic myth, easily becomes ironic. We noted specific peculiarities: experiment in form and language, learning and allusion, an approach to myth from an unusual angle, and interest in the erotic that was often tempered with sentimentality. In the hands of some Alexandrian writers (those following Euphorion) this easily became sensational and macabre. This subspecies of epic was particularly fond of digressions or stories within stories. Ovid's *Metamorphoses* exhibits most of these Alexandrian characteristics. And as if this were not enough, Ovid can make his pedigree plain by adapting Callimachean material. Most prominent is the story of the crow and the raven (told at 2.531–632). The crow was one of the most important characters of Callimachus' *Hecale* (Chapter 6).

The *Metamorphoses* reflects not just Callimachus, but also the enthusiasms of Callimachus' era. The versified *Orthigonia* of Boio (or Boios), for example, retold legends concerning transformation into birds. Eratosthenes, better known in the field of ancient geography, wrote a book in prose, the *Catasterismoi*, of tales about transformations into stars. A century later Nicander spread the net wider still. He wrote a five-book hexameter poem called *Heteroioumena* (literally 'Things made otherwise'). Ovid's poem draws on these. But it is also dependent on Roman versions of the Alexandrian miniature epic (Chapter 6). Parthenius may have imported the Callimachean epic to Rome. The subject matter of his only extant work, the *Unhappy Love-affairs*, resembles that of the *Metamorphoses*. So does the *Smyrna* of Cinna, his pupil – Ovid adapts the *Smyrna* in his tale of Myrrha at *Metamorphoses* 10.298–502. From the same period and circle there are other examples: Catullus' friend Calvus wrote an *Io* (the heroine appears in *Metamorphoses* 1); Cornificius wrote a *Glaucus* whose subject was presumably the fisherman later merman whose beloved Scylla was metamorphosized into a sea monster (mentioned in *Metamorphoses* 13–14). Virgil's own *Eclogue* 6 (written probably in the early 30s) may provide another comparison. Inset into Virgil's poem is a long song by the hungover satyr, Silenus (31–85). Silenus' song, an Ovidian collection of stories about strange and tragic love (amongst others Hylas, Pasiphaë, Atalanta, Scylla, Tereus), reflects the content of the *Metamorphoses* (see, especially,

Coleman 1971; Knox 1990, 1986: 9ff.). There is also the *Ciris* whose narrative engrosses the events leading to the transformation into a bird (a *ciris*, whatever that is) of the treacherous Megaran woman, Scylla. All of these Alexandrian poems have been discussed in Chapter 6.

Occasionally it has been suggested that the length of the *Metamorphoses* contravenes Alexandrian poetic theory and its preference for the small-scale poem. Apollonius' epic provides the solution to this impasse (Chapter 4). His large-scale epic conformed to the dictates of brevity by being formed of a number of loosely linked, but nearly independent episodes. Ovid uses the same trick. He builds up his epic by juxtaposing and interweaving a series of discrete tales. It is as if epyllions were placed within epyllions (Quinn 1979: 73ff.). The interweaving of stories produces a chain-like concatenation of miniature epics which build to form one long poem (Coleman 1971). The effect, while consonant with the Callimachean demand for brevity (*deducite*, *Metamorphoses* 1.4), paradoxically produces a long epic poem (*perpetuum carmen*, 1.4).

SHAPING THE IDEAS OF THE *METAMORPHOSES*

The refusal to privilege narrative threads and ideas is at the heart of the Alexandrian tradition. Ovid enthusiastically adopts the practice. To this end he avoids closure – narrative or logical. This shapes the narrative and influences the presentation of favourite themes. Attempts to fix the structure of the *Metamorphoses* are therefore doomed to failure (so the attempts of Otis 1975). The most useful schematization remains that of Crump (1931: 274ff.) and Wilkinson (1955: 148). This is as follows:

Prologue 1.1–4
Introduction: The Creation and Flood 1.5–1.451
Part I: Gods, 1.452–6.420
Part II: Heroes and Heroines, 6.421–11.193
Part III: 'Historical' Personages, 11.194–15.870
Epilogue, 15.871–9.

The lack of a symmetrical structure is apparent. Major divisions do not occur between, but within books. There is no chiastic balance (of the type ABCBA) or parallelism between books of the type with which we have become familiar through Homer and Virgil. Nor does Ovid seem to have made any attempt to produce an equal weight between the major sections of the poem.

Formlessness characterizes the individual book just as much as the poem as a whole. *Metamorphoses* 3 stands out as a particularly impressive instance. Here we can see how Ovid prefers to interweave rather than to demarcate his narrative slices. This sequence, attempting to narrate the early fortunes of Thebes, begins with Cadmus' pursuit of Europa and his foundation of Thebes (3.1–130). The intrusive tale of Actaeon slips in naturally: Actaeon was Cadmus' grandson; his misfortune was a first blight upon this ruler's felicity (3.131–252). Misfortune follows on misfortune as Ovid returns to the main narrative: Cadmus' daughter, Semele, fell pregnant to Jupiter and suffered the fiery consequences (3.253–315). The Theban narrative is again interrupted: Ovid introduces the stories of Tiresias' sex-change (3.316–38) and of Narcissus and Echo (3.339–510). Then back to the chronological sequence: Bacchus, born of Semele, is now grown up; his return to Thebes is met by the scorn of his half-cousin, Pentheus (3.511–81). But before this tale can reach its completion, we hear Acoetes' account of the transformation by Bacchus of a ship's crew (3.582–691). Finally, Ovid returns to tell us what did happen to Pentheus (3.692–733). There is no architecture in all of that. It is as if Ovid 'viewed the construction of the poem as a problem to be worked out on the small scale, in the more or less discrete units that comprise the collection of stories' (Knox 1986: 43).

Architecture is not the only victim of Ovid's narrative. Meaning is devalued by the constant, ironic undercutting of what should be taken seriously (generally Solodow 1988). The 'poetic', Alexandrian voice, occasionally apparent in Virgil (Chapter 7), is pronounced in Ovid. In the *Metamorphoses* Ovid's isolated public and frequent private utterances (which may vary from the humane to the downright cruel) come into conflict with his ludic, Alexandrian stance. The result in no way diminishes the importance of the public or the private, but it does direct attention towards how rather than why the *Metamorphoses* was created. Analysis hitherto has concentrated on attempting to show, through interpretation and critical paraphrase, how the constituent elements of each epic relate to their larger concerns. You cannot do that with Ovid. The *Metamorphoses* lacks a centre. The function of the Ovidian exegete is, while stressing the apparent disunity, to emphasize some of the modes by which Ovid's Alexandrian voice or style (which offers the poem its true unity) becomes manifest. This may offend the reader expecting philosophical profundity (such as Otis 1975; Fränkel 1945). Such a reader may find some consolation in the epic's wry, sometimes humane, and often brutal insights into human nature (Barsby 1978: 36–8). I suspect, however, that such a reader will miss the real source of consolation. That is the poem's polycentricity: lack of narrative and logical closure renders the *Metamorphoses* a most joyfully subversive piece of work.

CREATION, PYTHAGOREANISM, AND AUGUSTUS (BOOKS 1 AND 15): PURPOSE OR PEDIGREE?

Why does Ovid begin a mythological epic with a pseudo-scientific elaboration of the creation of the world (1.6–88)? Part of the answer lies in genre, part in praise. Let us look at genre first.

Ovid is writing an Alexandrian poem. Creation stories form an important element of this influential species (so *Argonautica* 1.496ff., Virgil, *Eclogues* 6.31ff., and *Aeneid* 1.740–6; compare Knox 1986: 12ff.). Comparison with *Eclogue* 6 (discussed in Chapter 6) provides real assistance. Silenus' Alexandrian song began with creation, then, via the flood and the restoration of the human race, focused on the erotic. So, in a roundabout way, does Ovid. After creation, the flood, and the renewal of human life, there is the erotic story of Daphne (1.452–567). It is quite possible that Ovid's Daphne interlude may deliberately echo a reference to Daphne in *Eclogue* 6 (so Knox 1990). If we do not quite have a miniature epic in Ovid's *Metamorphoses* 1, then there are, at least, many of the lineaments of that Callimachean genre: there is considerable generic variety (didactic blended with erotic), the tone is varied (shifting from the humorous to the pathetic and even to the heroic), there are digressions within this story (Mercury's story of Syrinx, for example – 1.689–712), the atmosphere is indiscreetly erotic, the focus feminine, and the tales are psychologically realistic.

But more is going on than mere Alexandrian experiment. By beginning with creation and by linking this with the theme of metamorphosis, Ovid is giving fair indication that he will be writing a poem that, commencing with creation, will trace history down to contemporary times (*ad mea tempora*, 1.4). And this is exactly what he does. Although the chronological progression is tortured by constant flashbacks and wilful inconsistencies (Coleman 1971:

463ff.), there is a clear progression from creation through to the apotheosis of Julius Caesar and the prediction of the apotheosis of his nephew, Augustus (15.745–870). Praise of Augustus remains a focus and is carefully woven into the texture of this first book (note the tempered references of 1.199–205 and 1.557–67).

The account of creation also looks forward to the great Pythagorean speech at 15.60–478. (Creation and Pythagoreanism, therefore, frame the poem.) That digression provides us with a rationale for the theme of metamorphosis: through the flux of history the constant is the human soul changing from one form into another (like Io at 1.568–747, changing from a woman to a cow, back to a woman again, and finally to a goddess). Pythagoras dominates book 15. His doctrines provide a unifying, if ironic, link for the *Metamorphoses* as a whole. I emphasize the word ironic, for Ovid can hardly have believed this material: the strictures, for example, against carnivorism which frame the speech are too outlandish to be taken seriously.

Besides offering a tongue-in-cheek apology for the existence of the *Metamorphoses*, besides offering a frame for the poem by echoing the 'scientific' descriptions of *Metamorphoses* 1, Pythagoras' doctrines place the poem firmly within Roman epic tradition. This is the tradition of Ennius and Virgil. Ennius laid claim to some sort of a belief in Pythagorean metempsychosis (Chapter 5). Such a notion not only allowed him to assert he was Homer *redivivus*, but also to show the heroes of the second Punic wars as soul mates of founding fathers such as Aeneas. Anchises, in Virgil's *Aeneid* 6, offers a real link between the Aeneadae and contemporary Romans, particularly between Aeneas and Augustus. He too does this through a theory of metempsychosis (Chapter 7). Ovid uses metempsychosis in much the same way. The doctrine of universal change (15.176–272), the sections on the rise and fall of cities and the predictions of Rome's greatness (15.418–52) and on the transmigration of souls (15.453–78) provide a clear link between such mythological or nearly mythological heroes as Hercules, Aeneas, Romulus, Julius Caesar, and Augustus.

The doctrines of Pythagoras, therefore, echo a mainstream concern of Roman epic. But, at the same time, Pythagoras declares Ovid's Alexandrian pedigree – just as did the account of creation. How does this happen? Encomium provides one answer. Ennius', Virgil's, and Ovid's theories of metempsychosis are ultimately encomiastic: they provide the link between the mythic past and Roman present. Praise was a traditional aspect of Alexandrian poetry, especially that of Callimachus: Callimachus' *Aitia* concluded by praise of the emperor's wife (the *coma Berenices* – see Parsons 1977 and Knox 1986: 75ff.). Pythagoras' theory of flux, therefore, forces the focus *ad mea tempora* ('to my times') and to history's closure, Emperor Augustus. This encomiastic, Alexandrian conclusion receives further emphasis by what follows – Ovid's personal epilogue. The epilogue may be linked with the Pythagorean theory of flux (Ovid's poetry will remain above the changes wrought by the flux). But it is not uncommon to end a collection with such a vaunt (compare Horace, *Odes* 3.30). The claim is typical of encomiastic poetry. Here (as is often the case in Pindar) self-praise is a rhetorical ploy for enhancing the status of the person to be praised. A great figure (Augustus) needs a great and lasting song. The claim is certainly tongue-in-cheek. But Ovid's claim is typical of the encomium.

GETTING READY FOR THE END: APOTHEOSIS IN BOOKS 9 AND 14; SONG IN 6 AND 11

What are we to make of the brief praise accorded in book 15 to Augustus? From the tale of Aesculapius (15.622–744) Ovid hurries through 250 years to the death and apotheosis of Caesar (15.745–851), then (via 15.807–42) to a prediction of the apotheosis of Augustus (15.852–70). Critics have repeatedly argued that the brevity of Ovid's imperial praise indicates deliberately a personal disaffiliation (Otis 1975: 303–5; Segal 1969). Ovid damns, that is, by faint praise. His ending becomes purposefully anti-Augustan.

Such an interpretation ignores the care with which Ovid prepares the way for Augustus. Consider Hercules. Almost half of book 9 (9.1–323) is devoted to a selective account of his life: his fight with the river god Achelous (9.1–100); his encounter with Nessus and the poisoned cloak (9.101–33); his death (9.134–238) and apotheosis (9.239–72); and finally his birth (9.273–323). We have met Hercules in Apollonius and in Virgil. In *Aeneid* 8 Hercules was identified with the emperor Augustus. Throughout Roman history emperors identified themselves or were associated with Hercules (Nero, Vespasian, Hadrian, Commodus, and Caracalla: Anderson 1928 and my Chapter 10; note that *Metamorphoses* 15.846, of Julius Caesar, echoes 9.272). It is difficult to concur with Galinsky (1975: 252) when he denies the association here of Hercules with Augustus. Horace had made this very identification for Augustus in 24 BC (*Odes* 3.14).

Hercules in book 9, therefore, seems to pave the way for the apotheosis of Julius Caesar and Augustus. Compare *Metamorphoses* 14. Here we have described, in two separate apotheoses, the climax of the trials (outlined in books 13 and 14) of the founder of the Roman race, Aeneas (14.581–608: Venus assists with the deification of Aeneas as well as that of Julius Caesar), and at the conclusion of the book, the climax of the life of the founder of the city of Rome, Romulus (14.805–28 and 829–51). Julius Caesar and Augustus claimed direct descent from Aeneas. Their metamorphoses echo that of Aeneas. That is also true of Romulus. Augustus, in his propaganda wars, was not above manipulating the claim to personal precedent in Romulus (Horace, *Epistles* 2.1.5, *Odes* 4.5.1). Apotheosis is the most successful example of flux in Ovid's metamorphic world. These three metamorphoses – Hercules, Aeneas, and Romulus – prepare the way for that peak for which the narrative strains, the apotheosis of the emperor himself.

But one must be fair. Other interpretations are possible. Many maintain that Ovid deliberately intends to undercut the force of the apotheosis. One such view argues that at crucial junctures within the epic (beginning the middle and last third, for example) Ovid hints at the failure of song, that the capacity of the poet to teach, to ameliorate, and to rectify a world gone awry has been silenced (Leach 1974). We can see this theme in the tale of Arachne at the beginning of book 6. The depictions on the tapestries of Minerva (6.70–102) and Arachne (6.103–28) seem to contrast two forms of art: Minerva's web shows the power of Jupiter and then four scenes reflecting the punishments visited upon mortals who challenge the power of the gods (two of these tales involve metamorphosis). Arachne pictures love between gods and humans (the ubiquitous Europa begins the catalogue). Does Minerva's art represent the more austere classical type (the Virgilian), Arachne's the Alexandrian (the Ovidian)? Certainly Arachne's episodic themes mirror some of the motifs of *Metamorphoses* 1–5: the relations between gods and humans, but specifically the loves of the gods with humans. Does Arachne's being silenced make a statement of the power of Ovid's verse to affect the larger world? The same line of argument may be pursued in book 11 (and back to Pygmalion in 10.243ff. – see Segal 1989: 85ff.). This too begins with an evocation of art and its silencing: Orpheus, the quintessential image for the poet (Segal 1989), perishes (11.1–84). His death, furthermore, seems to mark an important turning point in the poem (Crump 1931: 274). It shifts at 11.194

(after the song of Midas – 11.85–193) from heroes and heroines, from a world of myth, to an increasingly 'historical' world that will climax with the emperor Augustus. The change is ushered in by the telling of the first foundation and destruction of Troy (11.194–220). Does the silencing of Orpheus point to the powerlessness of poetry (Ovid's own enterprise)? Does his silencing undercut the encomiastic movement *ad mea tempora* and to Augustus? It is only fair to point out, however, that the sentimental, even macabre story of the death of Orpheus is followed by the happy reunion in Hades of Orpheus with his wife, Eurydice (11.61–6).

Let us return to Augustus and to book 15. The problem, I suspect, is larger than the emperor. It is not merely the passage on Augustus that does not wholly work. As a conclusion for the *Metamorphoses*, book 15 is not a complete success. The long digression on the doctrines of Pythagoras, for example, is clever, thematically apropos, and, in its way, humorous. Intent, however, does not mitigate dullness. The same could be said of the narrative of the metamorphosis and apotheosis of Julius Caesar: though well prepared for by previous metamorphoses and apotheoses, by the promise of the poem to narrate the entirety of history, Caesar's transformation lacks verve and humour. But perhaps endings are never easy. Compare the conclusion of the *Odyssey* (or of the *Argonautica*). The thematic relevance of *Odyssey* 24 was apparent. The narrative interest was limited. The same point could be made of *Metamorphoses* 15. The book and particularly its conclusion fail precisely because they violate the polycentric, open-ended narrative of the whole. Ovid's epic does not privilege narrative or ideas. When it does with Augustus, the warning bells ring.

LOVE AND METAMORPHOSIS

Love in the *Metamorphoses* is inextricably intertwined with creation, Pythagoreanism, and apotheosis. Love seems to be the motor force not merely of creation but of the flux in the world at large. If Ovid's poem has one over-riding theme, it is to demonstrate the power of love. Consider the theme of apotheosis. Almost half of book 9 (9.1–323) is devoted to a selective account of Hercules' life. The climax is Hercules' apotheosis. Apotheosis results from frustrated love. Deianira, to win back the love of her straying husband, Hercules, unwittingly made him the gift of the cloak poisoned by Nessus. It caused his death. Such is the power of the depiction of

Deianira that it seems to influence other sections within this book. Frustrated love is at issue in the debate with Achelous over Hercules' parentage. It is, also, in the sad tale of Dryope cut off from her husband and child by arboreal metamorphosis (9.324–93); or in the remarkable tales of Byblis (9.454–665: she longs vainly for an incestuous union with her twin brother Caunus) and of homosexual Iphis (9.666–797: brought up in disguise as a boy, she was betrothed to and fell in love with the unsuspecting Ianthe).

What of apotheosis in book 14? It would be unfair to point out that it is Venus herself who accomplishes the mechanics of Aeneas' apotheosis. Better to indicate the context within which the apotheoses of Aeneas and Romulus are deployed. Here is a brief summary of the book's contents. Beginning with Scylla and Glaucus (14.1–74), the narrative shifts to Aeneas' wanderings (14.75–222), to tales of Ulysses, Circe, and related love stories (14.224–440), then, via Aeneas' trials in Italy and his death (14.441–608), to the love story of Pomona and Vertumnus (14.623–771), and finally to early Roman legends and the apotheosis of Romulus (14.772–851). Erotic narrative plays a vital role within the book (but it is a bitter, corrupted love). Scylla (14.1–74) is punished for a type of sexual corruption (the fastidiousness that causes her to reject Glaucus). A second instance of sexual corruption is the Sibyl's treatment at the hands of Phoebus (14.130–53); so too Circe's malevolent treatment of the two lovers, Picus and Canens (14.320–434). Finally there is the fable of Pomona and Vertumnus (14.623–771). Its happy ending is balanced against the inset tale of frustrated love, of Anaxarete and Iphis (14.698–764). Apotheosis, therefore, is intertwined with erotic tales of corrupt love.

Love acts as the motor force for much of the action of the *Metamorphoses*. But we must be clear. Ovid will have no truck with privileged themes, even love. (Love, in fact, ceases to be as crucial after the first eleven books of the epic.) It is also 'decentred' in another way. Ovid is concerned not merely with the predictable, erotic love that is. He is also interested in paternal, maternal, conjugal, and even filial love. No one dominates. The catholicity is most evident in *Metamorphoses* 8.

This section provides a set of variations focused on love – sexual, paternal, and conjugal. The tale of Scylla (encountered already in the pseudo-Virgilian *Ciris*) is a chilling depiction of the power of love. A passion for Minos destroyed Scylla; it also destroyed her father, Nisus (8.6–151). Paternal love is the focus of the Daedalus interlude

(8.159–235): neither advice nor wax and feather wings proved adequate protection for Icarus when he flew too close to the sun. Daedalus inadvertently destroyed his son. Scylla uncaringly destroyed her father. The tale of Meleager inverts the pattern. Unfortunate Meleager (8.260–546), who loses his life because of the animosity of his own mother, suffers from the perversion of parental love. Nisus, to make the comparison, suffered from perverse filial love; Icarus suffered an excess of parental love. The theme carries on into the story of gluttonous Erysichthon's selling his daughter for food (8.738–878). Old Baucis and Philemon (8.618–724 – the episode descends from Callimachus' *Hecale*) exemplify piety (contrast the impious Erysichthon). But, in their desire to die together, they embody conjugal love – despite Ovid's habitual humour. Conjugal love is persistently idealized in the *Metamorphoses*. These amatory variations may be represented schematically:

Scylla: the betrayal of paternal love
Daedalus: paternal love frustrated
Meleager: maternal love perverted
Philemon and Baucis: conjugal love rewarded
Erysichthon: paternal love perverted

OVID'S OTHER INTERESTS

The *Metamorphoses* is not all creation, Pythagoreanism, apotheosis, and love. Ovid has other interests. In fact Ovid is at his least successful when he limits his concerns. Offences against the gods and their cruel, violent, often irrational reactions are often described. Such themes are especially prominent within the first six books.

It begins early. There is Lycaon punished for trying to feed Jupiter a cooked meal of human remains (1.163–252). Pyrrha and Deucalion seem to provide a counter-image (1.313–415). The theme is more important still in *Metamorphoses* 2. We see Phaethon extracting his destructive pledge from his father, Apollo (2.1–328), Callisto falling foul of Diana (2.401–507), Ocyrhoe transformed (2.633–75), Battus punished by Mercury (2.676–707), and the jealous Aglauros punished, again, by Mercury (2.708–832). All, in more or less culpable ways, fall foul of the gods. Notice, however, that their guilt is offset by a concern with the violence and cruelty of the gods: thus is poor mortal Europa carried off by Jove disguised as a bull (2.833–75), or Callisto or Coronis. In book 3 the same emphases are to the fore: the tales of Cadmus, Semele, Tiresias, Bacchus, Acoetes, and

Pentheus all illustrate the future awaiting those who offend or revere the gods.

Hybris, to use the Greek term, illustrates a weakness of Ovidian narrative. Book 3 makes this especially prominent. One of the least satisfactory aspects of this book is that behind the glossy patina of narrative exists a paucity, not of ideas, but of affective insight. Narrative brio is perhaps sufficient to carry the first 1,600 odd lines of the epic. The reader soon begins to look for more. However amusing or horrific are the stories of Cadmus, Semele, Tiresias, Bacchus, and Pentheus, the issues and characterizations do not go deep. The instance of Bacchus and Pentheus illustrates this frustrating tendency. The fable is predictably black and white. Pentheus is the sinner, Bacchus the slightly malevolent but wronged god.

The catalogue may be continued into books 4 and 5. Gods and humans remain the narrative focus. Transgression against the gods plays an important part. The tale of the daughters of Minyas is one instance (4.1–54 and 4.389–415), that of Athamas and Ino another (4.416–542). Or book 5: here Pyreneus is punished for contemplating violence on the Muses (5.249–93); the nine daughters of Pierus and Euippe are transformed into magpies for challenging the Muses in song (5.662–78); Lyncus is transformed into a lynx for challenging Triptolemus (5.642–61).

There are other themes. These are especially prominent in the last third of the epic. From book 12 through to the end of the *Metamorphoses* the narrative becomes more strictly chronological. Crump (1931: 274) has divided this third section into three: stories associated with Troy, 11.194–13.622, stories associated with Aeneas, 13.623–14.608, and finally those associated with Alba and Rome, 14.608–15.879. The thematic concerns shift accordingly. We find in book 12 a move from love to the no less potent concerns of war and violence. This is evident from the outset: the savagery of war is emphasized in the description of the expedition to Troy (12.1–63), its consequences through reference to the fate of Agamemnon's daughter, Iphigenia. The centre-piece of this book, a generic *tour de force*, is the description of the battle between the Lapiths and the Centaurs (12.210–535). The graphic brutality of this combat makes its importance plain. War, violence, and their consequences also colour the depictions of Achilles and Hercules. In the combat with Cycnus (12.70–145), Achilles embodies violence and deflects sympathy towards the victim, Cycnus. In the final scene of the book this situation is reversed. Achilles must cope with the wrath of a god, Neptune. The result is his death (12.580–628). Hercules (12.536–78) is also depicted in an ambiguous light – as the ravager of Nestor's homeland. Despite these new themes and the more straightforward (less Alexandrian) narrative, the habitual irony is maintained. The account of the death of Caeneus is evidence enough (Galinsky 1975: 177f.).

War and violence matter for book 13, but they are blended with themes of amorality, trickery, and lust for material gain. These vices are associated with the Greeks. This is, doubtless, the product of Roman identification with the Trojans, their racial forebears, and of Roman desire to exculpate them from disagreeable attributes (compare Galinsky 1975: 253).

In the long opening section (13.1–383) there is the debate between Ajax and Ulysses. They are contending for possession of Achilles' armour. Ajax' claim is based on martial superiority. Ulysses' on eloquence, craftiness, and an ability to manipulate people and circumstances. Ulysses is amoral. He is also destructive. The death of Iphigenia (13.181–95) is evidence. So is the suicide of Ajax. Ulysses' personal qualities are linked with the fall of Troy: his bringing Philoctetes to the Troad signalled the end of Priam's city. The results of his abilities are also recognizable in the fates of the victims of its destruction (13.399ff.): Polydorus (13.429–38), destroyed by Polymestor's desire for gain, Polyxena (13.445ff.) also destroyed by concupiscence (that of Achilles), and Hecuba transformed into a dog after attacking Polydorus' murderer, Polymestor.

What are we to make of the two 'love stories' with which the book concludes (13.738–897: Acis and Galatea; 13.898–968: Scylla and Glaucus)? Though reminiscent of the interests of books 6–11, they do preserve the themes of violence prevalent in this and the book preceding: the Cyclops, despite an almost bucolic lament, is hardly a pacific figure; nor, after her transformation, could Scylla be viewed as pacific. The prime function of these tales is to provide a respite from the intensity of the preceding Trojan sagas.

CRUEL HUMOUR AND AFFECTIVE INSIGHT

Pandion of Athens had given his daughter, Procne, in marriage to King Tereus of Thrace (6.424–674). Procne, lonely for her sister Philomela, persuaded Tereus to coax her to visit Thrace. Tereus, after falling violently in love with the sister, raped her (in a hut deep in the woods) on their return to Thrace. To prevent disclosure he cut out her tongue. To his wife, Tereus claimed that Philomela had perished. But Philomela managed to embroider her woes on a tapestry. This she smuggled to her sister. Alerted to the truth Procne rescued Philomela, murdered her own son, Itys, then made a stew of him for Tereus. Tereus understood what he had eaten when his son's head bobbed in the casserole. How did it all end? As Tereus rushed to take vengeance on the sisters they were transformed into birds. Procne became a swallow, and Philomela a nightingale. Tereus became a long-billed hoopoe. He is pursuing the swallow and the nightingale to this day.

Quinn (1979: 79) calls Ovid's account a tragicomedy. It is in the blend of horror, tragedy, the macabre, and the comic that the peculiar timbre of this tale resides. The horror of the situation is regularly undercut by ironic, cynical reflections such as 6.467–8, 471, 570 or passages such as 6.486–93 and 6.511–14. Descriptions such as Tereus' mutilation of Philomela (6.549–62: the severed tongue is noteworthy) are as ironic as macabre. The tale ultimately looks forward to the concerns of Silver Latin literature: cruelty and the macabre are particularly a feature of the epic writing of Lucan and Statius (Quinn 1979: 81).

Yet the kernel of the tale of Procne, Tereus, and Philomela is real life. Pick up a tabloid newspaper and you will read such a story twice every week. Real life, however, normally stops short of sliced off tongues, incarceration in forests, casseroled children, and metamorphosis. Ovid's additions to the 'real life kernel' do not, I suppose, violate a metaphorical sense of reality. But their very extravagance introduces an element of fantasy and of heartless humour that allows us to distance the art of the *Metamorphoses* from life. It is yet another example of Ovid's refusal to privilege meaning. Perhaps this is another instance of Ovid's ludic, Alexandrian legacy. It is Ovid at his most compelling.

Narcissus and Echo have much in common with Procne, Tereus, and Philomela. They provide another specimen of this Ovidian trait. The nymph Echo fell in love with the handsome young Narcissus. He fastidiously rejected her love. She became grief-stricken (3.395), anxious, and insomniac (3.396), was unwilling or unable to eat (3.397), and pined away to a mere voice. Hence the term, echo. Narcissus faced punishment (3.406) for his heartless behaviour. He caught sight of his own reflection in a pool and fell in love with it (3.407ff.). Like Echo he became weak (3.469, 488–9), unable to eat (3.437), and gradually starved to death. Subsequently he was transformed into the flower bearing his name. Despite Knox (1986: 22) there is little, if any, evidence for depressive lovesickness of this type in the literature of Augustan Rome. Indeed there is little evidence in literature for this condition before Ovid: the portrait of Narcissus is one of the very first unambiguous examples in Western literature of a syndrome (love-melancholy) which we nowadays take for granted. It is at the depiction of this type of emotion that Ovid excels.

Real psychological veracity would have stopped short of Echo's and Narcissus' metamorphoses. But Ovid's 'realism' operates on the level of metaphor. It is this type of metaphor which, we see again and again, provides this sort of account with its typical timbre. The fates, or at least the modes of death, of Narcissus and Echo are granted such detail, and are so extravagant, that their reality is not quite undermined, but tempered, at least, with a humour that is all pervasive and intentional.

Many stories within the *Metamorphoses* might be compared. In them Ovid strikes a real nerve. Here he is at his best: curiously modern and, despite the irony, compelling in a way that is rarely matched by ancient literature. Compare the story of Ino and Athamas (4.416–542) with that of Pyramus and Thisbe (4.55–166). The former, as a piece of narrative art, is a grotesque *tour de force*: there is the bizarre description of Hades, the overblown description of the onslaught of Tisiphone, the typical cruelty of Juno, Athamas' compelling madness, and Ino's doleful leap – and all of this constantly undercut by typically Ovidian irony. But there is no depth here. Knox (1986: 36–7) stresses that Pyramus and Thisbe are variants of the elegiac type. Yet the sentimental ambience of their tale is something foreign to Roman elegiac poetry. The plangent, separated young lovers, at first forced to speak through a chink in the wall, then separated by accident and mistaken death, and finally by suicide, are touching (despite such bizarre jokes as 4.122ff.). The account of Pyramus and Thisbe, in timbre at least, is very like the pathetic tale of Ceyx and Alcyone (11.410–748). Ceyx, on a sea voyage to Delphi, was drowned. His distraught wife Alcyone discovered his drowned body by the shore. As she leant to reach for it she was transformed into the halcyon bird. Her dead husband was reanimated also as a bird, the halcyon.

ALEXANDRIAN PACKAGING

We should return to Alexandria. If we do not quite have a miniature epic in Ovid's *Metamorphoses*, then there are, at least, many of the lineaments of that Callimachean genre: generic and tonal variety, digressions within digressions, obsession with the erotic and with female emotions, psychological realism and sentimentality. The system of poetic preference, often termed 'Alexandrian', pervades the whole of the *Metamorphoses*. I have already spoken of some aspects of this Alexandrian packaging (digressions, the erotic, the female, realism, sentimentality). There remains generic and tonal variety – an especially Ovidian characteristic.

Think of the oscillation within book 2: the moral tale of Phaethon dovetails into the acute, but pathetic psychological story of Callisto; this is followed by the humorous folk tale-like story of the raven and the crow (2.531–632). Then follows the allusive retelling of the fate of Ocyrhoe, the humorous account of Battus, another simple moral fable (of the harm wrought by jealousy on Aglauros), and finally the ironic, ambiguous Europa legend. Or book 3: there is a movement from mock epic (so Cadmus, 3.1–130), to a sexually charged psychological tale of the type to be seen in the traditional miniature epic (Diana and Actaeon, 3.138–255); the recounting of Tiresias' sex change (3.316–38) is almost bawdy, while the profoundly erotic tale of Narcissus and Echo is sentimental in the extreme (3.339–510); the story of Pentheus and Bacchus echoes Greek tragedy (3.582–691). The examples could be continued. But it would serve only to reemphasize my simple point.

Another important aspect of Ovid's Alexandrian packaging is the inclusion of passages which comment directly or indirectly on the nature of poetic composition. Callimachus did this famously in the preface to his *Aitia*, in the epistle to the Telechines, or the epilogue of the *Hymn to Apollo*. I have already indicated two passages of the *Metamorphoses* which seem to allude to the nature of poetic composition. These were in book 6 (the tale of the spinning contest between Arachne and Minerva) and book 11 (the account of Orpheus' death). Of comparable importance are the opening and closing lines of the *Metamorphoses* as a whole. The former, amongst other things, produces a justification for Ovid's decision to produce a chain-like concatenation of miniature epics building into one long poem. The latter – Ovid's personal epilogue – reinforces the notion of Pythagorean flux (Ovid's poetry will remain above the changes wrought by the flux) and provides a type of self-praise designed to enhance the status of the person at the conclusion of the poem – Augustus.

Orpheus and his song embrace the bulk of book 10 (10.143–739). This is after the death of Eurydice. Knox (1986: 48–64) believes that

Orpheus' song is of considerable significance as an instance of Ovid's poetic preferences (Orpheus is 'the perfect singer' – compare Segal 1989). It demonstrates Ovid's adherence to Alexandria, to the Roman miniature epic, and to the themes of love elegy (in which genre Ovid made his poetic start).

Orpheus' song (contrast Virgil's *Georgics* 4) is an amalgam of the tales of Ganymede, then Hyacinthus (10.155–219), Cerastae and Propoetides (10.220–42), Pygmalion (10.243–97), Myrrha (10.298–502), Venus and Adonis (10.503–739), and Atalanta and Hippomenes (10.560–707). It begins (10.148–54) with elements of didactic epic, something much favoured in Alexandrian epic; the subsequent tale of Adonis and Hyacinthus echoes elegy: Apollo is the sort of elegiac lover 'who is willing to serve in the hunting retinue of his beloved' (Knox 1986: 52). The infatuation of Pygmalion for his statue is described in a manner that might have come from one of Propertius' poems, while the story of Myrrha is based on the neoteric (Alexandrian) miniature epic *Smyrna*, written by Catullus' friend Helvius Cinna. (Ovid's main variation to this story seems to have been to portray Myrrha's problem as psychologically motivated rather than caused by Aphrodite.) In the story of Venus and Adonis Ovid seems also to have used, especially, elegiac motives (for example the elegiac *topos* of the older woman taken with a younger lover). Knox also notes echoes of Propertius and, possibly, Cornelius Gallus. Similarly in the account of Atalanta and Hippomenes he sees an adaptation of neoteric epyllion and love elegy. Knox (1986: 62) believes that 'we have seen that material familiar from neoteric and elegiac poetry has been diverted into new settings, while the singer ostentatiously demonstrates independence in his treatment of details of the plot' and that in Orpheus' song of consolation there is 'a characteristic display of Ovidian wit. It is after all just the sort of poem Ovid wrote.'

There may also be a trace of this self-conscious personal reflexion in the expansive portrayal of Medea in *Metamorphoses* 7.1–403. Ovid had already written on her: there was his successful tragedy of 13–8 BC, *Medea*, and the twelfth epistle of the *Heroides*. The version of the *Metamorphoses* combines, in 403 lines, the events of Apollonius' *Argonautica* and Euripides' *Medea*. It is interesting that Ovid's long version falls close to the centre of the *Metamorphoses*. I wonder if this prominent position is not conditioned by the success of his tragedy?

The story begins in a rhetorical manner with an enormous speech from the love-struck Medea (7.11–71, compare 7.193–219). This attempts unsuccessfully to dramatize her inner conflict between *ratio* and *cupido* (by now a predictable Medean cliché). The excess of paradox and rhetorical question combined with glib lines such as 20–1 flatten what becomes a dull speech unrelieved by irony or insight. Does his own *Medea* intrude here? Galinsky (1975: 64) rightly castigates the banal, abstract summary that follows the speech (7.72–3). Ovid seems intent on treating emotions in a simplistic manner and, in this version, is little interested in his protagonists. It is therefore with some relief that we turn to the 'heroic' description of Jason's trials (7.100–58). But, once this is over, Ovid begins again to over-simplify: Jason, for example, addresses Medea as 'wife' (1.172), something Apollonius deliberately kept imprecise. The legal term makes both their subsequent guilts more obvious and more easily managed: Jason's as wife-deserter, Medea's as child-killer.

Subsequent elements of the story (such as the rejuvenation of Aeson, 7.159ff.) are hardly gratuitous, but, in this psychologically fraught legend, seem beside the point. Presentation is Alexandrian (the telling of a traditional tale from a new angle – the *Ciris* recommends comparison), but the change in focus emasculates. The same objection may be levelled against the guileful killing of Pelias (7.297–349). It overshadows the murder of her children (7.396–7). Such is Ovid's indifference to psychological causality in these two digressions that he does not bother to outline how the innocent girl of the first hundred lines becomes a scheming witch. In the final section (7.350–403: Medea's flight) Ovid's lack of commitment has worried critics ('Ovid is even less interested in Medea as a dramatic character', remarks Galinsky (1975: 66), 'as she soars through the air, Ovid uses the opportunity to give us a tour of the eastern Mediterranean and to allude to fifteen metamorphosis myths which are localized there'). Perhaps the real significance of this narrative is to be found in its self-reflexive nature. While pointedly alluding to the success of his youth, Ovid is demonstrating how Medea should be treated in this ironic, Alexandrian world. The account, therefore, becomes another ironic *tour de force* of poetic self-correction.

BACK IN TOMIS

Why did Ovid die in a frontier town? We will never know the real answer, but I wonder if some of the characteristics of the *Meta-*

morphoses do not provide a few unexpected clues. I have stressed such notions as the enthusiastic lack of narrative and logical closure, the wilful formlessness and polycentricity of the epic (there is no single focus), its unwillingness to privilege particular themes, and its catholicity. There is also the constant irony and the Alexandrian or 'ludic' voice which comes into conflict with Ovid's public concerns. (The tension forces attention towards how rather than why the *Metamorphoses* were created.) What do these notions have to do with Tomis? Contrast the public, political world for which Ovid's father intended him. There 'closure' – jargon for language or action which feigns or claims to have the answers – represents the language of political dissimulation. A political actor may offer the spurious suggestion that she or he has the 'answer', that their political presence in some way represents the *telos*, the logical end of historical evolution. Such claims are usually mendacious and, far from humbug, they may become positively lethal. Augustus may not have been 'positively lethal' but he did pose as a historical *telos*. On the surface of things Ovid's epic encourages us to collude with such claims.

Or does it? Here I am not speaking of intent. Ovid probably thought he was praising Augustus. Rather, the lack of closure, the decentred universe of the *Metamorphoses*, provide a compelling and joyful antidote to the sterilities of political and historical determinism (closure). In that sense the *Metamorphoses* is a most profoundly subversive piece of work. Could Augustus have missed this?

> Now I have finished my task. Not Jupiter's anger, not fire, sword, nor ravenous time can remove it. Let that day (the one that has no power except over my life), let that day end the span of my uncertain years. Yet in my better part I'll be borne immortal above the high stars. My renown will not die. Wherever Roman power spreads over conquered nations, I'll be on everyone's lips. I'll live on, famous through all time – if poets' predictions have any truth.

This is how Ovid finishes the *Metamorphoses* (15.871–9). I have suggested that these lines are encomiastic. But we read the poem from history. We cannot pretend not to know that Ovid was exiled, any more than we can forget that Augustus was emperor and that he ordered the exile. Ovid has claimed apotheosis. So did Julius Caesar and Augustus. Poetry, this poem, comes into an ironic contest with political life. Both will live winking down on us for ever. But I wonder if Ovid's star is not the brighter. And I wonder if Ovid did not realize this. Many more people have heard of Ovid and the *Metamorphoses* than have ever heard of the emperor Augustus and his *Res gestae*. I suspect it will stay that way. But that is a piece of knowledge which we have now. Ovid did not. Poetic immortality cannot have made Tomis in January any the more palatable.

9

LUCAN, THE *CIVIL WAR*

FREEDOM, DEGENERATION, AND THE STRAITJACKET OF IDEAS

Lucan's *Civil War* is the most unpalatable of the ancient epics for many modern readers. Monochromatic characterization, obsession with the macabre, with the sentimental, with the pathetic, a strident authorial voice, an ever-present tendency to exaggerate, an opportunistic historical amnesia – none of these traits has endeared Lucan's poem to an audience schooled on the opacities and restraint of the Virgilian epic. Yet the strident libertarian strain has its appeal.

The *Civil War* has often been interpreted as a commentary on the lethal nature of imperial whimsy, imperial ambition, and 'the unchecked rule of the state by a single individual' (Martindale 1986: 197). It laments, through a partisan recounting of the Civil War between Pompey and Julius Caesar, the collapse of the Roman Republic. Condemnation of the victorious dictator, Julius Caesar, is everywhere manifest. 'Lucan', Martindale continues, 'writes to commend *libertas*, freedom, conceived of both politically as the Republic overthrown by the Caesars and spiritually as the inner freedom of mind that can be obtained in any circumstance by the Stoic sage.'

The key theme is degeneration. Imperial Rome has degenerated from the freedom of the Republic and its ideals. Lucan attributes Rome's degeneration to a lack of Stoic ethical gumption. Romans ought to exhibit self-control, endurance, loyalty, bravery, and calm in adversity. Instead they have become weakened by unbridled greed and ambition. Lucan likes to suggest that such degeneration will cause divine punishment: the gods have punished Rome as

166

indeed they will punish the instrument of Rome's ruin, Caesar. The very cosmos disintegrates (Lapidge 1979).

Lucan concentrates on an idea more than on individuals or events. Loss of freedom and degeneration become an obsessive focus. The *Civil War* is an epic of ideas. 'Theme', argues Charles Martindale (1986: 202–3), 'has overtaken the creation of character . . . and sheer story telling, as the poet's dominant concern . . . the poet is more open about his ideas and the reader is simply not allowed to escape the meaning of the story.' The battle between Caesar and Pompey becomes a battle for liberty itself.

The dominance of ideas produces unexpected characteristics. Facts may be twisted or embellished to measure against preconceptions. Authorial intervention becomes common. Characters, because they embody ideas, become stereotypical. In Homer and Virgil narrative concentrates upon a central hero and on his gradual perception of his responsibilities within a larger community. In Lucan there is a deliberate blurring of heroic focus between three characters, Caesar, Pompey, and Cato. The ideas of the *Civil War* are divided between the three. Caesar illustrates ruthless immorality, Pompey the deleterious effects of moral vacuity (Pompey is a descendant of Apollonius' Jason and the heroes of the Roman epyllion), Cato the moral ideal of the Stoic sainthood. Because these individuals carry the weight of ideas, they can be allowed no moral development. Nor can any one character dominate the narrative. Their personal qualities, taken individually, represent an inadequate depiction of the ideas Lucan demands of his history. For the full picture they must be taken as an ensemble.

PERFORMING THE *CIVIL WAR*

Thought, characterization, voice, and narrative pace are defined by Lucan's *idée fixe*. The verbal texture, however, is usually attributed to the time, its educational system, and the means by which poems of this era were first aired. To take the last point first: Lucan's poetry was first delivered orally at a 'declamation'. It is sometimes argued that Lucan's poem is designed for an auditorium audience (Mayer 1981: 10ff.). This is reflected in Lucan's hexameter: its avoidance of elision and the regularity of its placement of the caesura produce what is often denounced as slick. Metrical nicety is not something a listening audience is liable easily to absorb. Diction too – built upon a small vocabulary with infrequent coinages, exhibiting infrequent allusion to earlier poets, and, after books 1–3, showing little care in the production of traditional word patterns – may have been affected by hasty declamation (Mayer 1981: 10ff.).

Education and the era were potent influences. The study of rhetoric dominated the secondary school curriculum. Yet the imperial system of government debarred the gifted orator from practising his talents in a practical manner. Rhetoric increasingly sought outlet in the composition of forced exercises. Such 'artificiality' exerted a formidable hold on the contemporary literary imagination. This may be reflected in the many, often artificial speeches in this poem, the hyperbole, the use of pointed aphorism, the apostrophe, and the moralizing (MacL. Currie 1985). Williams (1978: 267–8) very neatly explains some of the rhetorical features not just of Lucan's poem but of Silver Latin in general:

> The poet . . . became assimilated to the orator, and, since the function of both was to entertain an audience, particularly by generating emotion that would move them, measurement of the emotion so generated became a measure of the quality of the composition.

THE COURT POET (BOOKS 1–3)

Nero seems to have encouraged the composition of the first three books of Lucan's *Civil War*. We may imagine that the performance of these books took place before an admiring emperor. It is unimaginable, however, that Lucan's ardent Republicanism and his enthusiasm for political freedom would not have been coloured by such constraints: thus, we will see, emerges the paradox of the proem. Be that as it may, the passionate concern with freedom deconstructs any such simple encomiastic intent. The tensions so generated (between the poem's aim and its audience) produce the impression of an utterly compromised vision. Such passionate compromise is one of the many strengths of the *Civil War*.

Let us look in a little detail at these first three books. Paraphrase and interpretation offer the simplest means of 'construing' the narrative and its obsessions. They may also offer the most economical means for bringing out the characteristics which I have been discussing.

Caesar (book 1)

Rather than launching *in medias res*, like Homer or Virgil, Lucan commences his epic with a long introduction (1.1–182) which, after outlining the subject of the poem (1.1–7), upbraids Rome's citizenry for allowing the war to take place (1.8–32). The long, flattering address to Nero (1.33–66) extends the introduction even further. For the modern ear the praise is excessively sycophantic and ill fits with Republican sympathies. It points to a peculiar quality in Lucan's posture: how does a champion of the Republic compose for the most autocratic and homicidal of regents?

The introduction continues to outline the general causes of the Civil War (1.67–97): first, the decline of all that is great (1.67–82; degeneration is given first billing), and second, the first triumvirate (1.82–97). Then the specific causes of the Civil War: the deaths of Crassus in 53 BC (1.98–111) and of Julia in 54 (1.111–20); there was also the rivalry between Pompey and Caesar (1.120–8). Pompey and Caesar are compared at 1.129–57. The contrast is basic to the poem. Pompey is identified with the Republic – a formerly powerful and great body that has now become heavy and torpid with old age. Caesar, enemy of the Republic, is a demon of amoral energy. Lucan's character-drawing allows no shades of grey: Caesar is evil; Pompey the embodiment of lassitude and indecision. Ideas also form the basis of the last section of this introduction. In 1.158–82 Lucan outlines the key to Republican corruption: Rome has been waylaid by an excess of 'luxury' produced by its foreign conquests.

Narrative begins at 1.183. Caesar is about to cross the Rubicon (1.183–227). From this action will follow the downfall of the Republic. The theme which dominates this second section of the book is that of irreligion and hybris. Caesar is the sinner (his nemesis would presumably have taken place at the end of book 16). Paradoxically Caesar, the darling of fortune, is also the instrument of the gods' vengeance: the Civil War and the enslavement of Rome are punishment for moral vacuity. After the Rubicon Caesar captures Ariminum (1.228–61) and is met almost at once by the expelled tribunes and Curio (1.261–95). Curio is an especially evil creature: in the most general of senses he may be seen as a manifestation of Caesar's own evil (compare Ahl 1976: 88–9). At Ariminum Caesar addresses his soldiers (1.296–356) and is answered by the irreligious (1.379–80) centurion Laelius (1.356–91). In Caesar's speech the extent of his hostility to Rome becomes clear. He is identified, metaphorically, with the Carthaginian Hannibal (Ahl 1976: 107ff.).

Caesar's summoning of his forces from Gaul (1.392–465) ushers in an almost Alexandrian geographical excursus. The description of the various now freed regions of Gaul, of Gallic practices and geography has been termed irrelevant digression (Haskins 1887: lxxiv). The relationship of this type of digression to the Alexandrian *Argonautica* – whose influence is repeatedly present in the *Civil War* – is manifest. But Lucan's Alexandrianism is overlaid by moralizing. It is not enough merely to describe Gaul. Lucan suggests that as Rome is about to become enslaved, so the Gauls are about to become free.

Gaul also provides a means for shifting focus to Rome to portray Caesar's effect on its inhabitants (1.466–522): there is, in the description, panic, powerlessness, sentimentality, and pathos. The timbre, if not the actual details, seem especially indebted to Apollonius and to Ovid. This theme of powerlessness is particularly important. Lucan drives the point home by shifting the focus to religious matters. He describes the expiatory rites and ill-omened sacrifice of Arruns (1.584–638). Later the coming disasters are foretold by the astrologer Figulus, and by a frenzied matron (1.639–95).

Pompey and Cato (book 2)

Book 1 sets the scene: Caesar's whirlwind march on Rome and the reaction there. It also makes plain what sort of person is Caesar. In book 2 there are Caesar's opponents: Caesar's nemesis, Brutus, unworldly Cato, and Pompey – past his prime and too willing to slaughter his fellow Romans.

Panic at Rome, the concluding subject of the previous book, becomes Lucan's focus – but only after brief remonstration with the gods for allowing knowledge of the future (2.1–15). The theme of powerlessness is again prominent: Lucan outlines the lamentations of the Roman matrons (2.28–42) and of the Roman men (2.43–66). If Lucan's subsequent Caesarean parallels are anything to go by (Marius at 2.67–88, driven by Caesarean energy and villainy, is an instrument of divine hatred; Sulla, at 2.134–220, is little better), Rome's remaining population are justified in their reaction. The bloody description of the results of Marius' and Sulla's occupations represents a chilling prophecy of what might happen when Caesar assumes control.

The alternative to Caesar and Pompey appears at 2.234–391. This is Cato and he is introduced through Caesar's future assassin, Brutus. Brutus has come to consult him (2.234–84). Should he fight or remain neutral? Cato's reply (2.284–325): civil war is the worst of evils. But who could sit by when such catastrophes are about to befall Rome? The blame, Cato continues, should be referred to the gods for including Cato amongst the guilty. Neither Stoic detachment nor neutrality is possible. Cato will join with the Pompeians. His reaction, compromised but honourable, may be taken as Lucan's own solution to the conflict between Stoicism and participation in a morally base conflict. But Lucan cannot leave the pious Cato alone. Marcia, Cato's former wife, returns to his house and, now that her second husband is dead, requests remarriage (2.326–49). Her request is granted. Cato's sainthood (he neither shaves for the marriage ceremony nor consummates it afterwards) may be guaranteed through this bizarre ceremony, but not his reality (Johnson 1987: 43).

The tonal, even generic shift which follows is worth emphasizing. Lucan describes Pompey retiring to Capua (2.392–8). The retreat introduces a brief description of some of the geography of Italy (2.399–438), the Apennine Mountains and the rivers. The contrast could not be more stark. The precedent for this type of learned diversion is 1.392–465 (the geography of Gaul). The technique is ultimately Alexandrian.

Caesar becomes again the centre of the narrative. As Caesar overruns northern Italy (2.439–77), opposition is minimal. The opposition of Domitius at Corfinium is particularly telling. The Pompeian is betrayed by his soldiers but set free by Caesar (2.478–525.) Caesar's *clementia* was legendary. Lucan does what he can to play this down. It would have been better, he editorializes, if Domitius had perished.

Pompey enters the narrative in person for the first time at 2.526ff. (he addresses his troops at 2.526–595 and retires to Brundisium; at 2.628–49 he dispatches his son to rouse the eastern nations). What do we make of him? He is old now, prone to hesitation, to inaction, to vanity, and not above political intrigue. Lucan approves of Pompey's willingness to defend the Republic, but he does not approve of his fratricidal means.

Caesar marches on Rome (book 3)

A vision to Pompey of his first wife, Julia (3.1–35), begins this book. Julia was the daughter of Caesar and marriage to Pompey was to cement good relations. Her untimely death in 54 BC is designated in book 1 as a major cause of the rift between Pompey and Caesar (1.111–20). The scene is grotesque: Julia threatens to disturb Pompey's nights with visions; this will spoil his new relationship with Cornelia. Her function, however, is primarily to emphasize the wickedness of civil war. How could Pompey embark on a war with his former father-in-law? Pompey ignores the omen and beaches his men at Epirus (3.36–45).

Caesar and the Roman response to his advance occupy the second section (3.46–168). Pompey has abandoned Rome. Caesar moves to fill the void. After securing the corn supply, Caesar marches on Rome (3.71–97). Caesar's condemnation of Pompey's stewardship of the city (3.95–7) seems to reflect that of Lucan. The response of the Roman Senate to Caesar's arrival is servile. The Senate seem overwhelmed by that same sense of *amēchaniē* as when news was announced of Caesar's crossing the Rubicon. As Caesar reaches Rome and attempts to enter and plunder the Roman treasury, the tribune Metellus endeavours to prevent its opening (3.112–43). He is induced by the former consul, Cotta, to give way (3.143–68). A number of themes interact: the powerlessness of Cotta and Metellus; a too compliant servility on the part of the Romans. The theme of degeneration – how could the once mighty Rome so readily allow itself to be pillaged? and the theme of hybris – Caesar is as guilty of sacrilege as he is of the destruction of tradition.

Following the catalogue of Pompey's forces (3.169–297), there is the bloody and protracted siege of Marseilles. It dominates the remainder of this book. This and its aftermath foreshadow what may yet happen to Rome, should it choose to resist Caesar's advances. There is more involved. The resistance of the Massilian citizens (3.298–355) reflects the type of response which Lucan would have hoped for of Rome. Thus heroic resistance against the tyrant is left to a provincial city, and one of Greeks at that. As for the siege itself, it begins with a remarkable event. Short of material for his siege apparatuses, Caesar orders the felling of a wood sacred to the Druids (3.399–452). This is indicative of Caesar's self-confident irreligiosity. But it is as if he were above mere divine shrines. Such is the support of the divine and of fortune for his undertaking that he

172

can defy nature and local divinity. His self-confidence was so great that he left the actual siege operation to his legate (3.453–96) and set off for Spain.

The real action of the siege takes place on the arrival of Decimus Brutus with the Roman fleet: there follows a remarkably vivid naval battle and victory for Brutus (3.509–762). Battle scenes are typical of all epic, but Lucan does add his own, or his age's, particular touches. He stresses the bizarre, the macabre, and some of his descriptions of death border on the comic (Argus at 3.723–51 stands out). Most of the fatalities, it is worth adding, are Massilian – perhaps to emphasize the enormity of Caesar's villainous brutality and to stress the heroism of the Greek defenders?

A COMPROMISED LIFE

Then he [Nero] ordered death for Annaeus Lucan. When, because of loss of blood, he felt his feet and hands going cold, and life gradually leaving his extremities (though his heart was still warm, and his brain clear), Lucan remembered the poem he had written in which a wounded soldier died a similar death. He recited the verses. That was his last utterance.

As we can see, the patronage extended to the court poet of *Civil War* 1–3 did not last. Nero banned Lucan's work (Haskins 1887: xxvii–xxix; Dilke 1972: 74–8). Lucan seems to have been incensed by the interdiction. Perhaps it led to the circumstances of his death described above (at Tacitus, *Annals* 15.70). How did it happen that the court poet of *Civil War* 1–3 fell so foul of the regent so lavishly praised in the proem to book 1?

The Republican poet had conspired against Nero with a group gathered about Calpurnius Piso. The conspirators intended to assassinate Nero and to appoint a new emperor. The plot backfired. Amongst others Lucan and his two uncles were condemned to death. The nobility of the intent, however, was compromised by reality – not unlike the *Civil War*. In Suetonius' life of Lucan and in Tacitus (*Annals* 15.56) it is said that after his arrest Lucan denounced his mother, Acilia, in the expectation of gaining pardon (but Getty 1940). Lucan hoped this might evoke fellow-feeling in the matricide, Nero. Acilia was neither pardoned nor punished. The sorry fable does not end here. Lucan's father, Mela, in pursuit of his dead son's personal fortune, was falsely implicated in the Pisonian conspiracy by one of Lucan's friends. At the urging of Nero, Mela took his own life. Lucan's uncles, Seneca and Gallio, perished in the same circumstances. The only glimmer of light in this black landscape appears with Lucan's stage-managed death.

Lucan's short, sordid, but tragic life adds allure to his poem. The trajectory of his rise was as sharp as his fall. During the early years of his adult life Lucan enjoyed the favour of the emperor Nero (who, aged 18, succeeded to the principate in AD 54). At the extravagant Neronian Games of, probably, 60, well-born Lucan won a prize for a poem praising Nero. The ensuing notoriety had him recalled from Athens where he had been studying. The emperor honoured him with the post of quaestor (making him Senator with access to a public career) before the legal age of 25. It seems likely that books 1–3 of his epic were composed in these few years of favour. But within four years Lucan had fallen out of favour. By 64, Nero, in a fit of what may have been professional jealousy (Nero also wrote poetry), suppressed any future publication or recitation of Lucan's poetry (Tacitus, *Annals* 15.49). The Pisonian conspiracy and the end followed within a year. Lucan died, aged 26, on 30 April, AD 65.

THE *CIVIL WAR* AND EPIC

The glamour of Lucan's life ought not to blind us to the fact that this is an epic poem written in the same genre as those of Homer and Virgil. The vision of the *Civil War* may reflect the poet's compromised life. Its timbre may be attributed in part to Lucan's intellectual vision and in part to the preferred schooling of his era. But there is a crucial third, the genre itself.

The Alexandrian epic, as the *Ciris* demonstrates, had been worked to a standstill. Mythological epic, on the grand scale, could hardly hope to rival Virgil. Ovid's ironic *tour de force* is too eccentric to provide an imitable model. As for the annalistic epic, its essentially eulogistic nature can hardly have appealed to a Republican malcontent. Lucan's solution, as my paraphrase of the first three books may have demonstrated, was to adapt the tradition of the historical epic by concentrating on a more limited time-span, by removing the divine apparatus, and by avoiding 'nationalistic' foundation myths. Lucan's *Civil War* represents for epic a new level of naturalism: history is now driven by human agents; national destiny and divine plan have become irrelevant.

THE BANNED BOOKS (*CIVIL WAR* 4–10)

Let us go back to the poem and look at the books produced during Lucan's years in the wilderness. Not unexpectedly the Republicanism seems to become more pronounced. Yet, when viewed as a whole, the vision of books 4–10 remains that of 1–3: themes such as those of degeneration, irreligiosity, and powerlessness recur, and that pervasive, compelling ethos of bad faith and of compromise remains constant.

Caesar's forces in Spain, Illyria, and North Africa (book 4)

Caesar fighting Afranius and Petreius near Ilerda (4.1–47) initiates the first of the four sections of this book. Lucan pictures Caesar's troops surrounded by floods and suffering from famine (4.48–120). When the floods subside, Caesar crosses the Sicoris causing the Pompeians to retreat (4.121–56). He pursues them and, later, both armies camp near one another. The soldiers of the two armies fraternize (4.157–205), until Petreius puts an end to this by ordering the massacre of those of Caesar's soldiers found in his camp (4.205–52). Petreius may be on the right side, but his actions are typical of the treachery and irreligiosity of those who have precipitated Rome's Civil War and loss of freedom. (The theme of irreligiosity is initiated at 4.110–20 by a prayer for an end to civil war.) Petreius' treachery receives its nemesis. He and his forces meet a dire end at 4.253–336. Petreius dies but his co-commander Afranius survives: forced by Caesar to surrender, he and his forces are released to safety (4.337–401). Evil Caesar's *clementia* provides an ironic contrast to the cruel irreligiosity of Pompeian Petreius.

Vulteius dominates the second section. Here Antonius, besieged by the Pompeians in Illyria, tries to escape with his soldiers on board three rafts (4.402–52). When one of these is checked, the soldiers on board kill themselves (4.452–581), at their commander Vulteius' urging. The suicide of Vulteius and his followers may foreshadow the death of Cato at Utica in 46 BC (recounted possibly in the prospective book 12 of the poem). Cato, defeated by the Caesarean forces, took his own life rather than surrender to his enemies. His death was consistent with a no-nonsense Stoicism which so valued the controlled death. Vulteius and his followers display the same Stoic resolve (4.573–81). But in this instance the suicide, though admirable, is wasteful, even futile (Saylor 1990). It has been enacted by forces prolonging civil war and hostile to the survival of Rome.

A death also concludes the third section. This is Curio's. It looks to the death of Pompey ending book 8 and, we may guess, to those never written, of Caesar in book 16, and of Cato in book 12. Curio crosses to Africa (4.581–660 – this narrative contains the legend of Antaeus) and, after defeating the Pompeian commander Varus (4.661–714), is surprised and defeated by Juba (4.715–98); like Rome itself Curio began well but in time suffered corruption (4.799–824). His death (and perhaps that of Juba) vindicates the claims of righteousness over evil (recall the prayer of 4.110–20). The claims of righteousness are also vindicated in the 'Alexandrian' digression describing the destruction by Hercules of the evil Antaeus (4.593–660). The digression recalls Hercules and Cacus in *Aeneid* 8 (Ahl 1976: 91ff.). Does this make Curio an Aeneas figure? If so, here is another death which points to the deformation of tradition. Lucan shows little sympathy in this book for the Caesarean or Pompeian cause. Perhaps the ban placed on his work had bred a bipartisan cynicism.

The armies marshal in Greece (book 5)

The countdown for the battle of Pharsalia begins in book 5. The centre of the action now is in Greece where the battle will take place. The narrative pace is heightened. This is most evident in the number of different scenes with which the book is composed: the extraordinary Roman Senate meeting in Epirus (5.1–64); Appius Claudius' bizarre consultation of the Delphic oracle (5.64–236); the mutiny of Caesar's forces (5.237–373); Caesar's passage to Rome and return to Epirus (5.374–503); his braving an Adriatic storm in a small boat (5.504–702); Antonius' eventual crossing from Brundisium (5.703–21); and, finally, the pathetic scene in which Pompey sends his wife Cornelia away to Lesbos for safety (5.722–815).

Appius Claudius Pulcher, one of Pompey's lieutenants, is the subject of one of the two outstanding sequences of this book. Appius, driven by fear, consulted the Delphic oracle to find out what the outcome of the campaign would be. The comparison with Aeneas' consultation of the Sibyl in *Aeneid* 6 is implicit (Ahl 1976: 127). Despite the Stoic tenor of this poem (Cato's objections to oracles are emphasized in book 9), Lucan interprets the closing of the Delphic oracle as another symptom of the inverted nature of the times. (The priestess' unwillingness to help gives further intim-

176

ation.) Appius is forced to compel the priestess to make her prediction. This is anticlimactic: rather than pointing out the imminent
defeat of Pompey and the collapse of the Republic, the oracle presents a riddling prophecy concerning Appius' own death. Appius,
misinterpreting the prediction, deserted his position as governor of
Greece and turned tail, hoping to save his own life. So much for
divination and the Roman aristocracy.

From the doleful tale of Appius Claudius Pulcher the narrative
moves sharply to the mutiny of Caesar's troops (5.237–373). This
scene makes the prospect of Pompey's downfall inevitable. Caesar
easily withstands the challenge. He seems to welcome it (5.300–16).
After quelling the mutiny Caesar collects a fleet and returns to Rome
to assume the dictatorship (5.374–402). Then, after crossing from
Brundisium to Epirus (5.403–60), he sets up camp opposite Pompey
(5.461–75). There follows one of the strangest scenes in ancient
literature. Because Mark Antony was proving slow in following
(5.476–503), Caesar determined to cross the Adriatic to Italy alone,
in a small boat, and during a storm (5.504–702). His purpose was to
force Antony to follow. That Caesar survived the voyage comes as
no surprise. Fortune and the gods support his enterprise. He is their
instrument of punishment for the Roman people. Caesar's self-
confidence in the face of this tempest (further evidence of his mega-
lomania) forces a comparison with Aeneas in his storm near the
beginning of *Aeneid* 1 (Morford 1967: 37ff.). Caesar becomes a type
of anti-Aeneas (compare Ahl 1976: 208).

Skirmishes in Epirus; Erichtho's *catabasis* (book 6)

Caesar's attempt to capture Dyrrachium begins the action. Pompey
anticipates Caesar's move and foils his advance (6.1–28). The cir-
cumvallation of Pompey's camp is equally unsuccessful: pestilence
breaks out in both camps (6.29–117) – and is given typically macabre
emphasis. Pompey almost turns the tables on Caesar when he attacks
one of Caesar's outworks. He is repulsed by the centurion Scaeva
(6.118–262). Subsequent sallies prove more successful: Pompey
attacks again and escapes from the blockade (6.263–313). His break-
out deserves special emphasis. Had he taken advantage of his position he could have defeated Caesar then and there (6.299–313). That
he did not is indicative of his fatal weakness. Scaeva's function
within this section of the poem also deserves special note; it has often
been discussed (Ahl 1976: 117ff.; Marti 1966). Scaeva's heroism is

admirable as far as it goes (and parallels Vulteius'). Yet, as Ahl points out, it 'is negative and counterproductive (*infelix*) because his virtue established a tyrant (6.257–62)'.

The march into Thessaly by Caesar, followed by Pompey (6.314–32), leads into a description of the region (6.333–412), the backdrop for the second half of the book. Pompey's son, Sextus Pompeius, anxious to determine the outcome of the battle (rather like Appius Claudius Pulcher), decides to consult the local witches (6.413ff.). After a macabre description of their diabolical practices (6.438–506), he consults Erichtho (6.507–68). He asks her of the future (6.569–623): Erichtho brings life to a corpse, who answers her questions before collapsing again to death (6.624–830). There is a clear but depressing equation to be made between this *catabasis* and that of Aeneas in *Aeneid* 6. In *Aeneid* 6 Aeneas met his father Anchises who predicted Rome's great future. In *Civil War* 6 there is a sordid young man with a disgusting witch predicting Roman calamity. The predictions of the corpse confirm Lucan's political views: the Pompeians will triumph in Elysium (6.803–5), Caesar will not (implied by 6.791–2).

The battle of Pharsalia (book 7)

On the eve of Pharsalia Pompey dreams that he is back in Rome in his own theatre, basking in the enthusiasm and applause of the Republican city just as he did when he was young (7.1–44). This acts as a commentary on the age and the powerlessness of the man. Lucan's editorializing makes quite evident the outcome of the battle. It is impossible not to sympathize with the doomed general. Yet Lucan has made it clear that we should not. So often in the *Civil War* we find ourselves, with major and minor characters, with major and minor events, unable to determine a correct response. The ambiguity with which we view Pompey acts as a real indication of his success as a literary creation.

Next morning, at sunrise, Pompey's troops clamour for battle and Cicero urges them on (7.45–85). Against his better judgement Pompey answers. Giving way to Cicero and to his troops he signals for battle (7.85–150). That Pompey is forced to fight in this manner is a real hint of his and the Republic's moral debility: little wonder that there follows a sequence of unfavourable prodigies (7.151–213), finishing with an outline of Pompey's battle array (7.214–34). Its magnitude further ratifies the improbability of his defeat. That this will happen underscores Pompey's debility. The dream, the decision to begin battle, the prodigies, the array of the army itself all partake of the theme of Republican degeneration.

Now Caesar: the contrast could not be greater. After momentary hesitation (7.235–49) he becomes completely confident. He is jubilant that the day of battle has come. When he addresses his soldiers (7.250–329) there is no mention of defeat. He foresees victory and urges a variety of violent acts, above all fratricide, a theme characteristic of the Caesareans since Laelius pressed this expedient at 1.359–86.

And back to Pompey: there is a rousing pre-battle speech (7.342–82) which is undercut at once by long, gloomy moralizing on the outcome of the battle (7.385–459). The battle of Pharsalia is described briefly at 7.460–616. It is a cataclysmic disaster from which Rome has to this day not recovered (7.617–46). But Lucan is more interested in the aftermath of the battle than he is in the battle itself. He devotes as much space to the contrasting portraits of Pompey in flight (7.647–727) and Caesar's battlefield breakfast (7.728–824) as he does to the whole clash. In defeat Pompey gains nobility. He flees not from fear, but to avoid throwing his troops into panic. Lucan, in his apostrophe of Pompey, openly demonstrates (7.680–711) a paradoxical admiration for Pompey and the Republic – a paradox captured by Cato's strange proclamation of loyalty to the Republic in book 2.

Lucan, in the lines following, goes out of his way to stress the wickedness of Pompey's opponents. He underscores the greed of Caesar's troops after the battle (7.728–63), their uneasy sleep (7.764–86), and the fact that the bodies of Pompey's troops lie unburied (7.789–92, compare 7.825–46). Perhaps the most bizarre indication of Lucan's hatred of Caesareanism is provided by his remarkable description of Caesar breakfasting *al fresco* on the morning after the battle (7.792–6). He arranged to take his food in full view of the battlefield so that he could, while eating, properly study the faces and features of the slain.

Pompey's death (book 8)

Book 8 is a minor tragic masterpiece. It begins with Pompey's flight from Thessaly to Lesbos where he had left his wife (8.1–49). Lucan stresses the affection between the pair. And for once it is not over-done (8.50–71). Their exchange (Pompey 8.72–85, Cornelia 8.88–105), though conditioned by rhetoric, is no less moving. The sympathy Cornelia evokes (8.146–58: the only sympathetically drawn female of the poem) is a reflection of the sympathy and affection we feel for the defeated Pompey. We follow Pompey's desperate progress first across the Aegean (8.159–201), then the Mediterranean – alone to start, then with his son, the necromancer Sextus, and King Deiotarus (8.202–43), as he courts the assistance of former allies. In Cilicia, at Phaselis, on the advice of his ally Lentulus (whose advice Lucan praises), he abandons a plan to seek the assist-ance of the Parthians (8.243–328: who were responsible for the death of Crassus, Cornelia's first husband), and is persuaded to seek refuge in Egypt (8.328–455), whither they sail (8.456–71). In Egypt a plot to murder Pompey is hatched by Pothinus and King Ptolemaeus (8.472–542). Pothinus manages to gain the acquiescence of the fickle young king (almost a mirror image of Nero – Quinn 1979: 84) by appealing to his sense of greed. The plan was simple. A certain Achillas was chosen for the job. Pompey was induced to enter a small boat where Achillas and his henchman Septimius carried out the murder (8.561–636). (They cut off his head and embalmed it – 8.663–91). Pompey's death is that of the Stoic: he faces it squarely and allows no sign of fear to show. At his end he gains the dignity lacking through most of this last phase of his life (Feeney 1986b). He almost becomes a tragic hero. The pattern of his life comes to resemble that of a hero like Achilles. Initially he is at one with his society, but age brings disjunction. It is only in the moving heroism of his death that he achieves a final reconciliation.

What do we make of his bizarre burial scene? Pompey's body is buried in a humble grave, only half cremated. Cordus' bravery in carrying out the burial is admirable (8.712–93). But Lucan cannot restrain his anger. So great a man should not be constrained by so petty a place (8.793–822) – he deserved the whole world. Quinn (1979: 91) sums up the indeterminacy:

> Has Lucan taken a passage . . . from Sophocles' . . . *Antigone* . . . does he challenge the reader to reflect that, when Antigone acted in open defiance without thought of the consequences, Cordus acts in abject terror and thus demeans the piety which has prompted his action?

Cato in North Africa (book 9)

In book 9 Cato finally reappears. We have not seen him since book 2. Given his prominence here, he would have continued to play an important role. This might have climaxed in book 16 with his Stoic suicide at the battle of Utica. The poem may have, in the planning stage, fallen into tetrads: Curio's death ending book 4, Pompey's at the end of 8, Cato's at 12, and Caesar's at 16.

Pompey's post-mortem fate begins book 9. Like Ovid's Julius Caesar (and as Lucan hoped for Nero), he was turned into a star (9.1–18). Pompey, therefore, avoids the Tartarean punishments described to Sextus Pompeius in book 6. Thence the narrative turns to Cato in retreat to Corcyra and Africa (9.19–50). In Africa, after Cato meets Cornelia (9.51–116) and the sons of Pompey (9.117–66), there takes place general mourning for Pompey (9.167–214). Cato adds his portion in the form of a panegyric to the murdered general (9.190–214).

Mutiny faces Cato – just as it did Caesar in Epirus (book 5). Caesar responded with violence, Cato with words. The speech proved inspirational (9.256–83) and Cato is able to set his followers to work on the capture of Cyrene. Thereafter, proposing to join Juba, he departs for Libya. The description of the Syrtes (9.303–18), of Lake Tritonis (9.319–47), and the mention of the garden of the Hesperides (9.348–67) inevitably recall the trials of Apollonius' Argonauts (*Argonautica* 4.1225–536) and, more generally, Alexandria. (It is as if the proximity of the burial place of Callimachus had inspired Lucan.) A second Alexandrian digression follows: this time it is a geographical excursus on Libya itself (9.411–44). Once Lucan has set the scene (in both the geographical and literary senses) he outlines the effects of the desert on Cato and his men. The troops suffer dreadfully from sandstorms and thirst (9.445–510). Cato, however, will have none of this weakness and refuses to drink (9.498–510) or drinks from unusual places (9.587–618). Lucan thus provides us with a striking, if over-pious, instance of Cato's Stoic credentials. When the march arrives at the temple of Hammon (9.511–43) he demonstrates a different type of Stoic virtue (9.544–63): he rejects the urging of Labienus to consult the oracles (9.564–86). Besides being good Stoicism, Cato's refusal places him firmly at odds with that other disreputable pair of oracle-mongers, the superstitious Appius Claudius Pulcher and Sextus Pompeius.

Further instance of Lucan's Alexandrianism is to be seen in the mythological *aition* of the Libyan serpents at 9.619–99 and in the description of the abilities of the local natives, the Psylli, who come to the aid of Cato's snake-ravaged soldiers (9.890–941). When Lucan turns to describe the human effects of the Libyan serpents, however, he outdoes anything produced by Apollonius (9.700–838). In Apollonius there are only two deaths, in Lucan the dead are legion and their manner of death macabre.

Why this intertextuality? One answer is that it provides Lucan with a means of demonstrating poetic allegiance (on Neronian Alexandrianism, see Sullivan 1985: 74–114). A second is that part of Lucan's experiment was to blend the traditions of the historical and the Alexandrian epics. A third answer is that the oblique references to Apollonius and Alexandria add an element of play to the texture of this part of the poem. This offsets the dour atmosphere engendered by the antics of Cato.

Once Cato has reached Leptis (9.942–9), the narrative is back to his adversary, Caesar. Lagging far behind in his pursuit, Caesar visits the Troad (9.950–99). There is, in the description of this visit, an unmistakable identification of Caesar with Aeneas, and of Rome with Troy (Ahl 1976: 219ff.). What does Lucan mean? Once there was Aeneas and Troy, one might paraphrase, now there is only Caesar and Rome (or Curio, book 4, or Appius Claudius Pulcher, book 5, or Sextus Pompeius, book 6) subverting Trojan tradition. The extent of the degradation is underscored when Caesar reaches Egypt to be presented with the head of Pompey, the embodiment of Rome as it once had or might have been (9.1000–34). Caesar's tears (9.1035–108) are salt for the Roman wounds.

Caesar in Egypt (book 10)

Caesar enters Alexandria and, as a first act, visits the tomb of Alexander the Great (10.1–19). Lucan launches a long diatribe against the life and exploits of this regent (10.20–52) – an oblique condemnation of Caesar's imperial ambitions. (It is difficult not to read Nero into Alexander.) Cleopatra is soon drawn into the tale. She requests protection for her brother and herself against Pothinus (10.53–103). For Lucan, the queen is the embodiment of lust and luxurious depravity (her *luxus* is made especially prominent at 10.107–71; compare 1.158–82 and 4.373–81). Caesar, true to character, has an affair with her. Thus, for the first time in the poem, the theme of the erotic assumes an important place. Once again, it is as if

Alexandria had inspired Lucan. Caesar's dalliance with Cleopatra and neglect of the military mission also evoke a clear parallel not only with Jason and Hypsipyle in *Argonautica* 1, but also and more recently Virgil's Aeneas and Dido.

Alexandrian influence persists. During the banquet which Cleopatra celebrated for Caesar – at which her fondness for luxury is again emphasized – he questions Acoreus concerning the source of the Nile (10.172–92). There is a long explanation (10.193–331). Acoreus' reply is often criticized: it is intrusive, unrelated to the narrative thrust, and over-long. This type of digressive geographical and scientific material was a particularly important part of the Alexandrian epic programme. There are other Alexandrian elements in the book, notably the generic variety. Book 10 began with a long, rhetorical diatribe, continued with a coloured description of Caesar and Cleopatra's love affair, moved then to a long digression of a scientific nature, and now is concentrated on another murder plot. In this instance that practised conspirator Pothinus urges Achillas to murder Caesar (10.332–98). The account is swiftly paced, even exciting, as Achillas and Pothinus collect troops (10.398–433) and besiege Caesar in the palace (10.434–509). The downfall of Pothinus (10.509–19) is especially satisfying. This man was the instigator of the murder of Pompey. The Alexandrian parallel between this and Apollonius' description of Jason and Medea's plot against Apsyrtus is made plain by Lucan (10.464–7 and 4.556).

And there, abruptly, with Caesar trapped on the mole of Pharos, and with the redoubtable Scaeva just spotted, the narrative ends. Presumably Lucan's own life ended soon after.

INDETERMINACY, BAD FAITH, AND LUCAN'S REPUTATION

Hallowed and mighty labour of poets! You snatch everything from oblivion and endow mortals with immortality. Caesar, do not be piqued by envy at this hallowed renown! If the Latin Muse may promise anything – as long as Homer's renown will last, that long will future generations read of me and you. Our Pharsalia will live on, and we will not be condemned by the forgetfulness of any generation.

That is *Civil War* 9.980–6. Lucan is responding to Caesar's visit to the ruins of Troy. The ruins of Troy stand as an example of the destruction time can inflict upon the famous: as Troy has crumbled, so will the renown of Caesar's victory over Pompey. It is at this point that the poet steps in with his poetic prophecy. The vaunt is of course ironic: Lucan's Pharsalia (his depiction of the battle – the poem) will provide Caesar's Pharsalia (the destructive victory) with immortality. But it will not be of the type Caesar imagined. The victory will provide future generations with an example of how not to behave.

And yet these lines have a curiously ambiguous ring. Lucan's fame has indeed become intertwined with that of Caesar and with his victory at Pharsalia – though not perhaps in the way these lines may have intended. This ironic conflation of the poet and his most loathed creation points again to the fractured, compromised vision which permeates the poem. The compromise, as we have seen, runs deep. It instances not merely bad faith, but seems often to generate a curiously indeterminate manner of viewing things. By indeterminate I mean not just ambiguous, but even unjudgemental and, sometimes, baffled. It forces us to question ostensible intention and to pose a sceptical second interpretation which undercuts Lucan's sincerity. This indeterminacy is, in my opinion, one of the most admirable and challenging features of Lucan's narrative. It slices to the very heart of Lucan's purported Republicanism. If Caesar can claim such loyalty, where does that leave *libertas*?

Let us look at a few other examples of this indeterminacy. Pompey's burial is one of the best. What do we make of Cordus and his hasty, half-hearted cremation (8.712–93)? As I noted before, Cordus' piety is to be admired. Yet his presumption in burying such a general, his inability to complete the task properly, and his offering such a humble grave to such a great man elicits Lucan's ire. Should it? I am not sure that Lucan knew quite what to make of Pompey's interment. There are many other examples. Recall Pompey on the eve of Pharsalia. He dreamt he was in Rome in his own theatre enjoying the applause of Republican Rome (7.1–44). What happens next? Lucan's editorializing makes quite evident the outcome of the battle. He seems unclear whether to direct our sympathies towards the general or whether they should be withdrawn. When Brutus consults Cato at 2.234–84 he receives the most indeterminate of replies (2.284–325): Cato disapproves of participation in that worst of all evils, civil war. Yet who could sit idle when Rome is in danger? Cato, therefore, will compromise himself. The heroism of Vulteius is similarly compromised: when his escape on a raft is prevented by the opposing Pompeians he and his soldiers bravely commit suicide (4.453–581). Lucan appears to admire their controlled, indomitable deaths. Yet, do not such deaths unnecessarily prolong the Civil War? Compare Scaeva. Caesar's forces, encamped at Dyrrachium, are almost overrun by the Pompeians. The attack was thwarted primarily by the heroism of this centurion (6.118–262). Yet Lucan seems to begrudge admiration for the hero, for such bravery does nothing to vindicate the claims of *libertas*.

There are other ways by which this indeterminacy becomes pronounced. To cite just one aspect: there is the destabilizing effect of Lucan's black humour. How seriously can we take the moral *exemplum* of a Cato when he will remarry in such a bizarre manner (2.326–91)? Can we take his heroism seriously when it is best conveyed by an ability to withstand the assault of unusual snakes? Can we really take Caesar's villainy seriously when he is depicted breakfasting *al fresco* on the morning after Pharsalia with a vista of the lifeless visages of his opponents (7.787–91)? That image encapsulates the ambiguity of Lucan's enterprise.

To dismiss Lucan's poem as an excessively perfervid and excessively rhetorical exercise is too easy. When read with an eye for the tradition from which it grew, the epic stands out. Lucan has attempted a variety of reformations. He has limited the scope of the historical epic and, in so doing, has invested it with a force that, if we compare Silius Italicus' recidivist poem, the long historical epic easily missed. Further, in turning his back on the Virgilian tradition and opting for the historical, Lucan has not, as we have seen, abandoned the Alexandrian innovations which Catullus, Virgil, and Ovid brought into the Roman genre. But, above all, Lucan has written a poem about ideas. Whatever Lucan's personal intention, the message which is purveyed by the poem is of passionate concern for freedom and virulent hatred of tyrants. That this message has been conveyed in the most macabre, even Gothic of fashions is no vice – how else could he have so accurately conveyed his fractured, self-loathing vision?

10

ROMAN EPIC AND THE EMPEROR DOMITIAN

EPIC AND TYRANNY

The emperor Domitian (ruled AD 81–96) was a monster. That is what Suetonius believed (not so Jones 1972, 1973, 1974; or Waters 1964). But whatever else Domitian may have been responsible for, he did preside over a literary renaissance (Coleman 1986). Of the writers active in the 90s (amongst others Tacitus, Quintilian, Pliny, and Martial) there survive the epics of three important writers. Statius wrote in twelve books a *Thebaid* (composed between *c.* 79 and 91), a mythological epic dramatizing the conflict between Oedipus' sons, Eteocles and Polynices. Silius Italicus wrote a long historical epic, the *Punica* (composed during the 90s), on the second Punic war. Valerius Flaccus took up the subject of Apollonius of Rhodes' epic. Of this incomplete mythological epic (composed between *c.* 80 and 92/3) eight books survive.

The three epics trade on nostalgia for a better, more heroic era. Their uncontroversial subjects may match uncontroversial lives. None suffered like Naevius, Ovid, or Lucan. It would, however, be over-simple to say that Statius, Silius, and Valerius lived lives that were closely attuned to imperial politics and that they made themselves safe by choosing imperially acceptable themes (compare Ahl 1984). The major preoccupation of Statius, Silius, and Valerius is to comment on the exercise of power and the maintenance of empire. Statius takes things even further. He deliberately undercuts a mythological appeal to nostalgia. Perhaps recent history helped shape his bleak vision. The Civil War after Nero's death – on which his father may have written, *Silvae* 5.3.195–204 – offers a real correlate for the strife between the two brothers in the *Thebaid* (Burck 1979: 308).

186

Statius' final plea for *clementia* offers a heartfelt, if banal solution to the impasse of his poem and of the late 60s.

Virgil's *Aeneid* may be felt everywhere. Yet it is Lucan's experimental epic which exerts the formative influence. Statius' admiration is patent. His awful picture of the effects of civil war, of the capriciousness and brutality of tyrannical and monarchal power, of the horrors of war, echoes the disgust made so plain by Lucan. Statius transfers Lucan from history into mythology. Silius responds in a much more pedestrian manner. His long poem suggests that the ironic criticisms against Lucan of Petronius' *Civil War* (see Appendix) were to be taken seriously (compare Martin 1975). Valerius Flaccus also rejects Lucan. Not only does he show epic with Virgilian trappings, but he evinces little concern either with the capriciousness of imperial power or with the violence of war. War, conquest, and expansion, for sanguine Valerius, represent the solidification of the *imperium Romanum*.

Lucan exerts another influence. Statius, Silius, and Valerius have written poems which, if not quite 'epics of ideas', have clear ideological postures. Different heroes embody different ideological aspects: the single hero ceases to hold the spotlight (Feeney 1986a). Silius may illustrate the point. In the broad historical process of the *Punica* (covering the years 218–201 BC) ideas supervene on history. Silius seeks to exemplify a battle between Roman *pietas* and Punic perfidy. He chose therefore to embody different aspects of the heroic impulse through two contrasting heroes: Hannibal, representing a figure of demonic and treacherous evil, dominates the narrative in books 1–12 of his epic; Scipio, his moral antipode, representing the incarnation of honesty, respect for the gods and human law, dominates books 13–17.

A final aspect of Lucan's influence relates to performance. The classicizing Valerius and the often pallid Silius are better read at the desk: in this sense they are true heirs to Virgil. Lucan, as was suggested in the last chapter, was meant for the podium. So too was Statius. But there is a difference. Lucan aims for the remarkable line, Statius for the remarkable sequence. The large number of digressions or tableaux within the narrative of the *Thebaid* points to this tendency (listed by Lesueur 1990: xxviiiff.). Such relatively brief passages especially suit the discontinuity of the public performance and its demands for immediacy.

A PROFESSIONAL WRITER: STATIUS

Publius Papinius Statius (*c.* AD 45–96) was born in Greek-speaking Naples, where his father, also a successful poet, was a teacher (see *Silvae* 5.3). Statius made a career at Rome of poetry (biography: Coleman 1988: xv–xx). His works seem to have received considerable popular acclaim. This led to intimate acquaintance with the high-up, eventually with the emperor Domitian. Much of his poetic output seems designed to flatter that audience: his *Silvae* ('impromptu pieces' published from 92 onwards) comprise, in five books, thirty-two occasional poems for this type of friend. Such was the esteem in which Statius was held that, probably in 89, he won an important literary prize in the annual festival at Alba instituted by the emperor Domitian (but was unsuccessful at the quinquennial Capitoline contest, probably in 94). Epic seems to have been in his blood. His cultured father composed one. Statius has left us the twelve books of the *Thebaid* and the fragments of the *Achilleid*.

My main concern is the *Thebaid*. But first let us briefly glance at Statius' *Achilleid*. The poem aims to tell the story of Achilles (synopsis: Dilke 1954: 8–10). In the one and a half surviving books there is Thetis, anxious to keep her son Achilles out of the Trojan war (1.20–282). So anxious was she that she disguised him as a girl and left him in the court of King Lycomedes (1.283–396) at Scyrus. While the Greek army at Troy clamoured for Achilles (1.397–559), he enjoyed an affair with Deidamia (1.560–674). It did not last. Ulysses and Diomedes unmasked him (1.675–926) and took him to Troy (1.927–60). *Achilleid* 2 is incomplete, presumably cut off after line 167 by Statius' death. Here Achilles sails for Troy (2.1–22). But there are also a number of interludes – Achilles distracted from Deidamia by Ulysses (2.23–48), Ulysses on the origin of the Trojan war (2.49–85), and Achilles' education as a youth (2.86–167). The timbre of the *Achilleid* is insistently light, episodic, and romantic (compare Aricò 1986). It recalls Ovid's *Metamorphoses* at its most playful (so Fantham 1979). King (1987: 130–3) has described the poem as an example of 'an advanced romantic tradition' and as 'essentially lighthearted'. It is as if Statius, ever the professional, felt that he had mastered tragic epic in the *Thebaid*. This time he was attempting its opposite generic pole, the comic epic.

The *Thebaid* is relentlessly serious. Was this in the nature of the myth tradition, or was this evidence of the influence of Statius' father? The tale was ancient and, to judge from Homer's scant references (in *Iliad* 5–6), was grim from its inception. Statius' more recent sources were unequivocally dour (so Aeschylus' *Seven against Thebes*, Sophocles' *Oedipus Tyrannus*, *Oedipus at Colonus*, and *Antigone*, Euripides' *Phoenician Women* and *Suppliant Women*, and Seneca's *Phoenician Women* and *Oedipus* – compare Dilke 1954: 8). Antimachus of Colophon, who wrote in the late fifth century BC, was another important model. His *Thebaid* no longer survives, but, according to ancient tradition, it was long and severe (Vessey 1971). The timbre may also reflect the influence of Statius' near contemporary, Seneca. In such startling plays as the *Phoenician Women*, the *Oedipus*, or even the *Thyestes*, Seneca's obsession with civil war, fratricide, corruption, and power may offer a basis for the ideas of the *Thebaid*.

What is Statius' version of the Theban myth trying to tell us (compare Gossage 1972)? The bloody feud between the brothers Eteocles and Polynices stands as an emblem for civil war and the corrupting nature of power. That the Theban myth acts as a commentary on Roman history is undoubted. There is, however, no simple historical analogy made between this feud and the civil wars of 69 or, more precisely, between personages of the *Thebaid* and real life: Eteocles and Polynices need no more represent Domitian and his brother Titus (whom he may have poisoned) than Romulus and Remus. Civil conflict was a persistent theme of Roman literature.

CIVIL WAR AND THE CORRUPTIONS OF POWER: THE *THEBAID*

Books 1–6: the 'Odyssean' *Thebaid*

Book 1 highlights many of the attributes of the *Thebaid*. The poem is firmly based on the narrative of earlier epic. It adapts a pattern evident in the first book of Virgil's *Aeneid*. After the by now obligatory invocation and praise of the emperor (1.1–45) there is the description of a confrontation between two heroes and, from one of these, a prayer to the gods for assistance. In Virgil the confrontation is between Juno and the Aeneadae. It is followed by a voyage, a storm, and a divine assembly. In Statius the divine assembly follows the confrontation (which is brought on by Oedipus who, cast aside by his sons, Eteocles and Polynices, prays for their punishment, 1.46–87; this curse sets them on the path to war, 1.123–96). In the divine scene of the *Aeneid* Jupiter settles the future of Rome. Here he determines to set Thebes and Argos against one another as punishment for their previous malefactions (1.197–302). Then follows the storm scene. It is a storm on land rather than on sea as in the *Aeneid*, and, instead of a single hero, there are two, Polynices and Tydeus (1.336–407). In the *Aeneid* the storm brought the hero to a haven, a strange city in which his resolve was tested (sexually). In the *Thebaid* the testing and the amatory elements have been separated. Polynices and Tydeus struggle through the night to Argos, to Adrastus' court where, on the threshold, they meet, fight (1.401–46), and, eventually, are reconciled (1.447–525). The amatory theme is enacted within Adrastus' court: at the banquet in their honour (compare Dido's banquet in final sections of *Aeneid* 1) Polynices and Tydeus are offered by Adrastus his daughters, Argia and Deipyle, in marriage (1.525–720).

Book 1 also makes clear the ideas of the *Thebaid*. When Oedipus curses his sons (compare especially 1.238–9: Eteocles and Polynices literally trample on their father's gouged-out eyeballs), their total lack of *pietas* (1.74–8) is made evident: they do not guide their blind father, they mock his blindness and ignore his groans. An absence of *pietas* (which, at 1.126ff., entails *furor*, *invidia*, *metus*, and a *saevus amor regendi*) becomes the motor force for catastrophe. An absence of *pietas* is linked to related Roman obsessions: civil war and bloody conflict between brothers. A clear portrait of the evils of tyranny is also a feature of this book. Eteocles and Polynices show all of its worst attributes. But these ideas are linked with no national vision. This is made most obvious in the speech of Jupiter at the council of the gods, a traditional place for outlining national and moral visions. Jupiter merely sets two wicked cities one against the other. There is no correlate made, in a positive or negative way, between either of the two heroes or the impending war and Roman destiny.

Book 1 has no central hero. Eteocles and Polynices, as I indicated above, are denounced early (1.238–9). Oedipus is a horror (1.46ff.: when he prays it is not to Jupiter, but to the gods of the underworld, 1.56–7). Tydeus is no better. He is a fratricide (1.402–3) whose anger and violence are demonstrated in the battle with Polynices. Adrastus is almost a sympathetic character: his rule and court are peaceful, prosperous, and, it seems, god-fearing (1.390–2). But he is powerless: he is old (1.390–1), lacks male children (1.393–4), and is unable to interpret the prediction of Phoebus (1.395–400).

Thebaid 1 is stylistically typical. The mood of the poem is remarkable in its concentration on the macabre (but not perhaps on the sentimental), and in its persistent evocation of ominous foreboding. These characteristics have representative illustrations in the descriptions of the appearance of Oedipus (1.46–87) and, soon afterwards, Tisiphone (1.89–113). In Oedipus' case it is not enough to say that he is blind. Statius stresses that he lives in eternal night, in the innermost part of his home, in a secret room hidden from the sun's rays; his eyes are empty and his hands are bloodstained, presumably from thrashing at the earth as he makes his imprecation. Tisiphone is no less impressive: she is described as sitting beside the sulphurous, gloomy Cocytus. Her presence amongst the shadows of night (it is always night in Statius) causes the earth itself to shake. As for her appearance, there are one hundred horned snakes in her hair, her eyes glow with an iron-coloured hue, her skin is swollen with poison and corruption, and from her mouth is emitted a fiery vapour.

Williams (1972: xvii) characterizes Statius' concentration on mood as the product of a desire to be striking not so much 'by intellectual wit or conceit or paradox, as by colour, exaggeration, brilliance'. This is most notable in the way he manipulates 'atmosphere and mood, colour and emotion'. This manipulation is especially evident in Statius' many tableaux (note the tale of Coroebus at 1.557–668): their seeming detachability allows and encourages a varied range of moods and emotions, above all created by that most communicable technique, hyperbole. The effect is instantaneous, rather intangible, and frequently localized within the text. It is at the same time baroque, mannerist, and luxuriant. These are all the qualities of a writer who aims at immediate, above all theatrical, communication with his audience.

Statius also enjoys polarities. Book 2 alternates at first between Thebes (2.65–133 and 2.389–495) and Argos (2.134–374), then shifts to the ambush carried out by Eteocles' retainers on Tydeus as he returns from Thebes (2.496–743). Geographical oscillation is matched emotionally. The ominous, macabre opening scenes (the calling up of the bloody shade of Laius, 2.1–31, the graphic description of Taenarum, 2.32–54) contrast with worn-out, festive Thebes. The subsequent visitation of Laius on the sleeping Eteocles (2.89–133) contrasts dramatically with the long narrative describing the betrothal of Polynices to Argia, and Tydeus to Deipyle (2.134–212), and the wedding day (2.212–43). This book provides the first clear characterization of Eteocles (Ahl 1986: 2873ff.). It is not flattering (Vessey 1986: 2981ff.). Eteocles is shown as a victim of the same monarchal designs as Polynices (Domink 1989).

Narrative skill, however, is not matched in Statius by a commitment to ideas. This is also evident in the third book which, like the second, alternates between Thebes and Argos. Book 3 explains the outbreak of war. We see that above all in the Argive anger of the third section of the book (3.324–721). But Jupiter's moralizing at 3.218–323 is something of a missed chance. Rather than outlining national destiny, he merely encourages war between the two cities. Perhaps the most important section for ideas is 3.59–113. Here Maeon, the sole survivor of the ambush on Tydeus, gives his reaction to the designs of Eteocles. Eteocles has begun an unholy, fratricidal war: thus is recapitulated the theme of civil war. Maeon caps his denunciation by doing the proper Stoic thing: he takes his own life (on suicide, see McGuire 1989). Maeon's monologue helps in three ways. It allows us to understand Eteocles as a greater villain than Polynices. It restresses the rights and wrongs of what is taking place within the poem. It provides us with a moral alternative (a very Stoic one, it seems) to the moral bankruptcy which permeates the poem.

In *Thebaid* 4 Statius is once again stitching together well-established epic elements. The catalogue of 4.1–344 looks to *Aeneid* 7 and *Iliad* 2, the necromantic episode (4.345–645) has its origins in *Aeneid* 6 and *Odyssey* 11, Hypsipyle derives in part from Apollonius (compare Valerius Flaccus' *Argonautica* 2) and, of course, from the legend itself. Statius seems, once again, more concerned with tradition than with ideas. Take the necromantic episode: unlike *Aeneid* 6 or *Civil War* 6, it offers no ideas. Statius, ever intent on atmosphere, seems content, in his narrative, to delay as far as possible the climax of the scene, which is Laius' prediction of victory but misfortune for Thebes. But this is a transitional book. It seems designed above all to clear the way for the *tour de force* of Hypsipyle's narrative.

'Alexandrian' is the best description for *Thebaid* 5. Its sheer episodic variety – containing amongst other things a murder plot, sexual infidelity, miraculous escape, abduction by pirates, a dragon, death threats, infant death, and the sudden appearance of long-lost children – is reminiscent of Callimachus (the Hecale legend may be referred to at 5.431–2) and Apollonius. There is also the love theme (Hypsipyle's romance with Jason is described at 5.453–85) which evokes the erotic world of the Alexandrian miniature epic. Is the Alexandrian timbre to be interpreted as a challenge to the classicizing Valerius (Williams 1978: 206 mentions another example)? Hypsipyle appears in both authors. So does Jason. It is significant that Jason is condemned at 5.472–4 (like Eteocles he is *periurus*, 5.473–4, and *efferus*). Valerius' Jason, on the other hand, is a blemishless young aristocrat.

How do the themes of this book tie in with the rest of the poem? The story offers an exemplary account of *pietas* and *clementia*. The earliest of the events on Lemnos show Hypsipyle taking pity on and protecting her aged father, Thoas; the final ones show her pitied, then saved from Lycurgus' angry subjects by Thoas and Euneus, her two sons by Jason (twins to be contrasted with Eteocles and Polynices). The Hypsipyle digression provides an alternative to the impious violence acted out by the male cast of the *Thebaid*.

Statius closes the 'Odyssean' sequence of the *Thebaid* with the relative calm of the funeral rites (6.25–248), then funeral games (6.296–946) for the unfortunate Opheltes. The sense of closure is strong. The funeral games of *Aeneid* 5 and *Iliad* 23 mark the end of narrative phases within their poem. So do they in *Thebaid* 6.

Books 7–12: the 'Iliadic' *Thebaid*

Trojans begin to battle against the Italians in *Aeneid* 7. *Thebaid* 7 is the beginning of the combat between the Thebans and the Argives. The remaining books detail the fate of the 'seven against Thebes' and Thebes' post-war peace.

War fever, a divine 'assembly', a teichoscopy, outbreak of war, and the death of the first of the 'seven against Thebes' form the basis of the first part of the Iliadic *Thebaid*. Mars begins the war fever in Argos (7.1–144); but not without rousing the pro-Theban feelings of Bacchus. Bacchus pleads for his city with his father, Jupiter (7.145–92 – the 'assembly'). Jupiter's pronouncements (7.193–221) match those of the first book: the sons of Oedipus and the Argives deserve to die for their lack of *fides* and *pietas* (7.217). Then follows the teichoscopy of Antigone and Phorbas (7.243–373) and events leading to the outbreak of war (7.398–627: note especially the pair of frenzied tigers who precipitate the conflict, 7.564–607). Following the outbreak of hostilities (7.628–87) there is the *aristeia* and the remarkable death of the blameless seer Amphiaraus (7.688–823): he is taken down to Hades unharmed.

The descent into Hades of the pious Amphiaraus is grimly humorous and implies a bizarre comparison with Aeneas' passage through the underworld in *Aeneid* 6. Amphiaraus descends at 8.1–20, much to the consternation of its denizens (8.14–16). Pluto, unaccustomed to such daylight (8.33) and thinking Hades has been invaded (8.34–6), sends Tisiphone to encourage the conflict in the upper world. Amphiaraus explains his presence to an irritated Pluto (8.84–122, stressing the treachery of his wife at 8.104–5 and 120–2). Meanwhile in the upper world Amphiaraus' death is taken more seriously (8.127–217).

Tydeus' death provides a climax for the book. He is Amphiaraus' moral antipode. We come to him via a Bacchic festival at Thebes (8.218–58), Thiodamas' selection as Amphiaraus' replacement (8.259–341), and the beginning of hostilities (8.342–455). The *aristeia* of Tydeus begins at 8.456. It climaxes with a description of Tydeus, mortally wounded, demanding and receiving the head of his slayer, Melanippus (8.716–50), then gnawing into the still warm brains (8.751–66). If we were unsure of Tydeus' moral standing, this section makes it clear.

The third and fourth of the 'seven' perish in *Thebaid* 9: the vile Hippomedon at 9.86–569, and the upright Parthenopaeus at 9.570–907. The *aristeia* of Hippomedon depends for its depiction on *Iliad* 20 and the account there of Achilles' brutal slaughter of the Trojans in the River Scamander. Hippomedon sets about slaughtering the Thebans in the River Ismenus (9.225–314). Killing the river's relative Crenaeus turns the god against him (9.315–445). Achilles escaped the Scamander, Hippomedon does not escape the Ismenus (9.446–539). The excesses of the *aristeia* of Hippomedon place him within the same moral ambit as characters such as Tydeus and Eteocles.

The *aristeia* and death of Parthenopaeus offer a contrast. His doom is apparent from the outset (9.570–669). Our sympathy is manipulated by his being introduced through a portrait of his mother, Atalanta (9.570–669), by his acting as a type of doublet for Crenaeus in the previous section (compare 9.683–711 to 9.319–33), by his closeness to the goddess Diana (9.821–40), and by the final portrait of Parthenopaeus uttering a dying message concerning his mother (he had given way too readily to the heroic impulse). But his death, heroic in the same way as that of Lucan's Vulteius, is rendered futile by the ignoble cause for which he fights.

In the first of the four exceptionally dramatic narratives of *Thebaid* 10, Juno has the victorious Thebans drugged to sleep to make way for an Argive attack (10.1–155). This section is Statius at his most audience-conscious: the descriptions, for example, of the cave of sleep (10.84–117) or of the prophetic frenzy of Thiodamas (10.156–75) assume a life of their own, almost separate from the narrative thrust. Then there is the night raid of the Argives upon the sleeping Thebans and the deaths of Hopleus and Dymas (10.176–448, blending *Iliad* 10, the night raid of Odysseus and Diomedes, and *Aeneid* 9, the night raid of Nisus and Euryalus). But more is involved than mere allusion. If the butchery of 10.262–346 repels, the depiction of the devotion of Hopleus and Dymas (10.347–448) is an ideal. In their attempt to rescue the corpse of Tydeus they show a type of loyalty which the main protagonists of this poem lack – even if, like Parthenopaeus, their loyalty is misplaced.

Hopleus and Dymas initiate the beginnings of a climax within the *Thebaid*. Dymas' Stoic suicide looks to the death of Menoeceus (10.627–826). The Argives, capitalizing on the success of the attack on the sleeping Thebans, storm one of the gates of Thebes. Their attack is repelled by Creon's son, Menoeceus – a sacrificial victim (10.610–15). Linked with *Virtus* (disguised as Manto – 10.632–49 – and with *pietas* at 10.780; compare also his interview with Creon at 10.690–734 and contrast the relations of Oedipus with his children), Menoeceus acts as a paradigm for proper moral behaviour. Not so his foil, Capaneus, the fifth of the seven against Thebes (10.827–939 narrate his death). Capaneus advances as far as the parapets of Thebes. Divine disapproval stops him there. He is blasted by a thunderbolt, the sign of Jupiter's sulphurous wrath (10.907–39).

Polynices and Eteocles finally meet in book 11. Jupiter's assent (11.122–35) to Tisiphone's plan (11.57–112) to begin the conflict between the brothers indicates that this duel represents the acting out of his will (outlined at 1.197–302 and 7.193–221). *Pietas* embodied shows how we ought to react to the duel 11.457–81). Incorporating the very ethical marrow of the epic, this allegorical figure is driven off by Tisiphone. Notice also the apostrophe of 11.574–9 which stresses again the horror of the fraternal conflict. The relevance for Rome with its history of civil war will be obvious. And the message for contemporary Rome is broadened in the fourth section when Creon takes power. He is a petty but ruthless autocrat who capitalizes on the death of the two combatants, 11.648–72.

Unexpectedly this climactic book offers no solution to the cycle of fraternal conflict and *furor*. That is provided by the next book. Creon has forbidden the burial of the Argive dead (12.94–103). Unaware of this the Argive women, led by Argia and Deipyle, set out to reclaim their dead (12.105–40). Despite learning of Creon's opposition (12.141–72), Argia determines to go ahead alone to tend her husband's corpse (12.173–227). Here she meets Theban Antigone, come to perform the same duty (12.349–408). They are discovered by Creon's guards (12.409–63). Events have reached an impasse: 12.481–781 provide a solution. As Argia and Antigone take refuge on the altar of clemency (12.481–518) Theseus arrives (12.519–39). After learning of Creon's arrogant behaviour he rallies his own and local followers (12.587–655). They attack Thebes and Theseus kills Creon (12.752–81). Both Thebans and Argives rejoice in Creon's death (12.782–96).

The central symbol for the book is the image of the altar of clemency (12.481–518, Ahl 1986: 2890ff.). Clemency (the Latin is *clementia*) or mercy is the very quality which has been so lacking throughout the poem. Oedipus lacked it; Eteocles, Polynices, and Tydeus lack it. The few characters who seem to possess it perish (Maeon, Amphiaraus, and Menoeceus). Clemency, we are meant to assume, would countervail against the unceasing round of fraternal and civil slaughter. *Clementia*, however, must be balanced against Creon's death. Creon's edict, which ought to represent a positive action, is the very antithesis of clemency – it prolongs the bloody misery of the first eleven books. In a sense Creon deserves death. But would *clementia* not have spared him? Statius uses a very light touch. We are relieved to see the villainous Creon destroyed. Yet doubts linger. Creon's death is no long-term solution to the round of fraternal and civil strife. The lightness of touch is crucial, for an identification of Theseus with the emperor Domitian is inevitable (Vessey 1973: 314ff.; Dominik 1989: 91–2).

WHO WAS VALERIUS FLACCUS?

Very little is known of the life of Gaius Valerius Flaccus. The poem suggests that he may have been of aristocratic birth. This may be supported by the characterization of Jason, the ideological conservatism of the poem, and by indications at 1.5 and 8.239–41 that he was a *quindecimvir sacris faciundis*. (This group of usually well-born individuals originally looked after the Sibylline Books, but, by Valerius' time, supervised those foreign cults which were deemed acceptable in Rome.) It is unclear whether Valerius began the poem under Vespasian (ruled AD 69–79), Titus (ruled 79–81), or Domitian (ruled 81–96) (D'Espèrey 1986: 3072–5). There are references to Titus and his *Templum Divi Vespasiani* (temple of the deified Vespasian) at 1.13–16, and to the eruption in 79 of Vesuvius, at 3.208–9, 4.507–9.

Quintilian's brief but favourable reference to Valerius at *Instituta* 10.1.90 may indicate that he completed *Argonautica* during the reign of Domitian in AD 92 or 93.

The *Argonautica* represents a further reaction against Lucan's model of epic. Silius, we will see, reverts to the traditional historical model of Ennius, albeit one made modern through the medium of the text of Virgil. Valerius Flaccus' correction involved little originality. He adopted the ideological solution of Statius: a reversion to the mythological model. Valerius avoids, more is the pity, the mannerism (and Alexandrianism) of Lucan and Statius. His narrative does not move in small, episodic, epyllion-like chunks. Rather Valerius prefers to produce a reasonably linear (and easier to follow) narrative.

As for choice of story, the legend of the Argonauts was one of the most popular in antiquity. We have already discussed its history in connection with Apollonius (see Chapter 4). There were several Roman versions. Late in the first century BC Terentius Varro Atacinus produced a Latin translation of Apollonius. And Ovid, in *Metamorphoses* 7, reproduced aspects of the tale. Such versions, of course, usually exclude treatment of the later married life of Jason and Medea. Accounts of that survive from Euripides, Seneca, and, in a more stylized manner, from Ovid.

Valerius' generic preferences may be unoriginal. His adaptation of divine causation is, however, quite sophisticated and utterly unlike the version of Apollonius. Apollonius' hero seemed to represent Alexandrian man and looked to the compromised hero of the epyllion. Valerius' hero represents the best of Roman Republican youth: he is driven on by a desire for *gloria* (1.77) and by a sense of *religio* (1.80: 'trust in heaven'). Jason's mission represents the fulfilment of the will of Jupiter. The speech of Jupiter at 1.531–60 indicates that the Argonauts are the harbingers of the Roman empire. Jason becomes a kind of a proto-Aeneas, even a proto-emperor (especially evident in the assimilation of Jason to Hercules, 5.130, 5.487–8). Though original, this is a fatally compromised reading of myth. Despite Valerius' best efforts Jason is twice compromised. First, Jason was no admirable figure in traditional versions of the story (Hadas 1936). To attempt to make him so represents an almost wholesale rewriting of tradition. Second, Jason was compromised by history itself. To parallel Roman youth or the Roman emperor with such a morally ambiguous hero may easily result in the most unflattering of equations.

ROMAN ARGONAUTS IN PURSUIT OF AN ELUSIVE EMPIRE: THE *ARGONAUTICA*

Books 1–4: to Colchis: launching the *Argo*

The backbone of books 1 and 2 is provided by the Virgilian sequence of invocation (and proem), confrontation, divine assembly, voyage by sea, storm, followed by arrival in a strange land where amatory complications may arise. Let us begin with the invocation and proem (1.1–21). This portion (seeming to praise in turn Vespasian, Titus, and Domitian (D'Espèrey 1986: 3072–5)) makes clear the most basic parallel of the poem, that between Jason and the emperor. Just as Jason superintended the first sea voyage, so did Vespasian participate in Claudius' voyage to England (1.8–9) which extended the Roman empire beyond the ocean. Narrative proper begins with 1.22–63 where the confrontation between Pelias and Jason is outlined. Pelias (another Eteocles) is a wicked tyrant. He is worried about future rivalry from young Jason. To solve the problem he sends him on a probably fatal mission (1.44–57). Jason's reaction is telling (1.64–90). Unlike Apollonius' depressive hero, Valerius' Jason, after momentary doubt (1.79), is fired by a desire for *gloria* (1.77) and by a sense of *religio* (1.80: 'trust in heaven'). The task, he soon learns, is one sent by Jupiter (compare 1.241 and 2.5) and is to be accepted gratefully.

Preparations for the voyage (1.91–183), the launching of the *Argo* (1.184–254), the reactions of those to be left behind (1.294–349), and a catalogue of the heroes (1.350–497) follow. It is easily forgotten that we are witnessing the re-creation of the very first sea voyage (not at issue in Apollonius' account.) The daring and dangers are persistently emphasized by Valerius. The novelty of this voyage is vital, for it signals a shift in the global balance of power (1.531–60). This will eventually climax in the dominance of Rome.

The divine assembly occurs at 1.498–573: Jupiter's speech at 1.531–60 (coming, unlike the Virgilian speech, before the set-piece storm) implies that the Argonauts are harbingers of the Roman empire. The voyage, Jupiter explains, will shift the balance away from the east to Greece, and from Greece eventually to the west, presumably to Hesperia. Jason becomes, therefore, a proto-Roman (a proto-Aeneas or emperor). Thence the marked difference between the Apollonian and the Valerian Jason.

Following the storm (1.574–692) there is a variation on the Virgi-

198

lian pattern. At 1.693–851 are Jason's parents who decide to end their own lives rather than fall into the hands of Pelias. The scene echoes that at the beginning of the book between Pelias and Jason. There with Pelias we had a perfect Stoic villain. Here with Jason's father, Aeson, (1.767–70) we have a perfect Stoic hero.

Hypsipyle and Hesione

Jason arrives at a strange city in book 2. This is Lemnos where women rule. Valerius' version (2.82–427) is unlike that of Apollonius. His Lemnians, driven to a frenzy by Venus, are intentionally repulsive (2.184–7, for example). The *pietas* demonstrated by Hypsipyle when she spares her aged father, Thoas, is all the more remarkable, and stands in stark contrast to that of her compatriots. Valerius' focus is the crime of the Lemnian women (they slaughtered all bar one of the men on the island) and Hypsipyle's *pietas*. This version of the myth functions largely in blacks and whites. Jason and Hypsipyle (near doublets) are both upright, heroic figures who believe in *pietas* and Jupiter. They exhibit none of the ambiguities of Achilles, Odysseus, Apollonius' Jason, or even Virgil's Aeneas.

Hercules' rescue of Hesione (2.451–578 – omitted in Apollonius, but a traditional part of the saga) provides an ethical reenactment of the Jason and Hypsipyle story. Hesione has been exposed on a sea cliff as an offering to the sea monster which has persistently molested the Phrygian people. Hercules, taking pity on Hesione and the Phrygians, kills the monster and frees the girl and her people. Hercules rids the world of another evil and allows a triumph of civilization and *pietas* over barbarity and *furor*. Elsewhere in the poem (5.130, 5.487–8) Hercules is identified with Jason. In Roman epic Hercules is often identified with the emperor (compare 2.572–3.) Hercules provides us with another instance of the moral worth of Jason and, by extension, of the Roman empire.

Cyzicus and Hylas

Valerius is keen on causation. In Valerius' epic Cyzicus does not perish by accident. In a hunt he had accidentally slain a lion sacred to the goddess Cybele (3.15–31); his death pays the penalty for that crime. Valerius, unlike Apollonius, plays down the irrational aspect of Cyzicus' death. After the slaughter Mopsus the seer delivers a short discourse aiming to explain the listlessness into which the Argonauts have sunk: it is the result of blood-guilt. He tells how this may be expiated. After death, he continues, there is punishment for the wicked and, it is implied (3.377–416), a type of reward for the good. Here we seem to return to Cyzicus. He will doubtless be rewarded. Valerius also minimizes the space allotted to a description of Cyzicus' death: the vigorous, mildly macabre battle stretches over 3.95–248, while Cyzicus' death is limited to 3.220–48. Nor does Cyzicus' wife, Clite, commit suicide (3.314–31).

Stoic resolve and Stoic heroism allow the Argonauts to surmount the Cyzicean trials. So do they when Hylas is lost. In Apollonius' version Hylas is lost to Hercules by accident. In Valerius he is lost because of the malign hostility of Juno (3.48–546). The loss of Hylas (Hercules' lover – 3.736) provides the setting for Hercules eventually to exhibit a type of virtue (*virtus*) based not on simple physical ability, but on a *virtus* of the spirit. Hercules, through his various trials, assimilates a spirit of perseverance and, with this, a type of internal Stoic heroism and fortitude. So does Jason, Hercules' doublet.

Amycus and Phineus

Burck (1979: 225) stresses that three things are made sure by the fourth book of Valerius' *Argonautica*. First, once the Clashing Rocks have been passed, the Minyae have passed the worst and their progress to Colchis is now guaranteed. Second, they have been tested as a crew and have exhibited themselves as capable of mastering the dangers of the voyage. Third, Jason, especially in his role as guide of the Argo through the Symplegades, demonstrates that he has now become the real leader of the voyage.

Testing remains the key thematic element of this book. The first episode, the combat of Pollux with the vicious Amycus (4.99–343: a villain who usually boxes to death the visitors to his shores), represents a clear-cut instance of good tested, then triumphing over evil. Pollux, the son of a god, takes on and kills Amycus. It is Hercules and Hesione over again. The epyllion-like interlude to follow (told by Orpheus and describing the wanderings of Io, 4.344–421) provides a release from the tension of the exciting contest with Amycus. The subsequent tale – of Phineus, his misfortunes (4.422–64), his rescue from the Harpies by Calais and Zetes (4.465–528), and Phineus' prediction (4.553–624) – recreates the heightened ambience of the previous episode. Despite Phineus' checkered background and the deservedness of his punishment, the conflict with the Harpies reenacts that between Pollux and Amycus, and that between Hercules and the sea monster. The final episode of the book describes the passage between the Clashing Rocks (4.637–710) and on into the Black Sea. Heroic and Stoic resolve is once again tested and, once again, is found to be equal to the task.

Books 5–8: Colchis and escape; Arrival at Colchis and war

Argonautica 5.1–176 narrates the final stages of the voyage to Colchis. Here occur the deaths of Idmon and Tiphys (5.1–62). These fatalities were of considerable moment in Apollonius' version. Here they are described with the minimum of emotion. In Apollonius they represented further instances of the theme of chance and powerlessness. In Valerius they are further tests.

Book 5 marks a new turn for the narrative. We see Colchis for the first time (beginning at 5.177), meet the dire Aietes, and Medea (5.278–95 and 329–99). There is an account of the civil strife between Aietes and his brother Perses (5.259–77). After Jason reaches Aea and meets Aietes and his retinue (5.399–557) there takes place a display not just of the Argonauts before Aietes, but also of a selection of Colchian heroes (including Absyrtus) before the Argonauts (5.558–617). The book also makes clear the characterization of Aietes and Medea. Aietes is *perfidus* (5.289) and takes little heed of his people (5.264). (Jason, by contrast, is made parallel to the estimable Hercules at 5.487–8 and 5.130, and is impelled to Colchis and to Aietes by *fides* and *iustitia*, 5.498). Medea is not brought sympathetically into the poem (5.219–20 and 5.329–99). In Valerius' epic she is an utter villain (the murderer of Absyrtus who displays no *pietas* towards her father – 4.13–14). This makes it all the easier for him to idealize Jason.

The Argonauts came to Colchis at a bad time. Aietes is at war with his brother, Perses. Book 6 recounts the battle between the Colchians, aided by Jason and the Argonauts, and Perses and the Scythians. This interlude, a traditional part of the legend, does not appear in Apollonius' epic. The book provides what seems to be for Silver epic the near obligatory civil war. It also parades Jason's *virtus*. A brief survey of the contents of the book bears this out. After an invocation (6.32–41), a catalogue of Perses' forces (6.42–170), and a brief survey of the Colchian and Argonautic forces (6.171–81), there follows a long battle interlude (6.182–426). The Iliadic flavouring ought to be apparent. Medea briefly occupies the limelight (6.427–

506; note that at 6.470ff. Valerius is at pains to stress the wickedness of Medea's love). Then follows more fighting (6.507–74) with Medea pointing Jason out to her father from the battlements (a teichoscopy, 6.575ff.). After momentarily pausing to stress Medea's increasing infatuation (6.657–89) Valerius returns to the slaughter (6.690–751). Jason, like the emperor, resolves civil war.

Medea's lovesickness and escape

She does not come off well. Medea was already smitten in book 6. But her sense of shame enabled her to resist desire (7.1–25). Two events turn the tables. Aietes reneges on his agreement with Jason (7.32–100). Juno has Venus (7.153–92), disguised as Circe (7.193–291), trick her into giving way. Now we are at the nub. Medea, in her agonizing at 7.300–22, is compared to a reluctant Bacchante. She knows she is shamelessly abandoning her father (7.309) and that she will become infamous (7.310). She cannot decide whether to follow her sense of *pudor* or the *furor* occasioned by her love. But, drawn to her magic, she gives way to passion (7.323–70). That she opts for evil, in Valerius' telling, is in no way mitigated. Once she has made her decision Valerius is content to denounce her: at 7.461–2 he states that she is guilty (*nocens*) and that her sense of shame (*pudor*) is irrevocably lost. Why does Valerius treat Medea so unsympathetically? The answer resides in his ideology. The Argonauts and Jason in particular are primeval Romans. They embody the best of the nation: civilizers, scourges of evil, warriors, statesmen. Medea's evil emphasizes their worthiness.

The final book begins (8.1–23) with Medea still torn between desire and duty: she longs to stay with her father and in her homeland, but the attractions of Jason are too great. The stress on betrayal of family (picked up also at 8.134–74) represents one of Valerius' contributions to the telling of the legend. It is, as Catullus 64 and the *Ciris* demonstrate, a peculiarly Roman view. At 8.24–133 Medea with her magic (8.83–91) assists Jason to gain the fleece. Apollonius avoided over-stressing Medea's magical nature until he had the relationship with Jason well established. Valerius, bound to denigrate Medea, has it constantly before our eyes.

Jason does not come off well either. He is too reliant on women. Medea almost coaches him in his attempt on the fleece (8.68–133). This is hardly what one would expect of a hero (made plain also by Medea's brother, Absyrtus, 8.353–5). He is faithless too. When

Medea begs him in future to stay faithful to her (8.45–53) the irony is unavoidable: we know that he will not. The disastrous consequences of the marriage are almost impossible to avoid and Valerius stresses them at several places (8.206, 224, and 248–51). When Absyrtus and the Colchians are near, the crew press Jason to hand Medea back to her brother (8.385–99). Medea has already contemplated suicide through fear of her brother (8.306–17). When Jason decides to abandon her (8.400–7), she threatens, cajoles, and begs for his loyalty (8.408–62).

Valerius' epic breaks off abruptly at 8.467. This is a most awkward moment. Medea, in Jason's eyes, may be evil. But how could the upright young man of books 1–7 butcher Medea's brother? If he does, he runs the risk of undermining all of the ideological substructure Valerius has so far been at pains to establish. It can never be known why Valerius was unable to complete his poem. (It would, however, have ended with this book.) I suspect that he was blocked by the logical impasse into which he had written himself. The portrait of Jason is becoming increasingly unflattering. Had Jason murdered Absyrtus it would have been worse. Valerius' problem is this. His equation of Jason with the emperor, with Aeneas, with Hercules, and with Rome requires a hero who acts as the very model of *pietas* and *fides*. So far so good. But if he murders Absyrtus, this will cease. Jason will, therefore, place emperor and Rome and the whole ideological underpinning of the epic in a most unfavourable light. It is just as well the poem concludes where it does.

GOING THROUGH THE MOTIONS: SILIUS ITALICUS

Silius (AD 26–101) was not a literary person. Most of his long life was spent in the Roman civil service. Pliny the Younger (*Letters*. 3.7) provides an overview of his career. Although viewed by his contemporaries with suspicion because of his conduct under the emperor Nero, Silius managed to become consul in 68 and, through connection with Vitellius (briefly emperor in 69), gained a proconsulship in Asia minor, maybe in 77. Understandably he was wealthy. Silius composed his long epic on the second Punic war (entitled the *Punica* or *Punic Wars*) between the ages of 56 and 70 (Burck 1979: 256). Book 3 was written perhaps in 84, book 14 somewhere between 93 and 96 (Burck 1979: 256ff.). Silius met a bookish end. Aged 75 and suffering from an incurable ulcer, he determined to follow the teachings of his Stoic instructor, Epictetus. He starved himself to death.

Silius' *Punica* takes up Ennius' subject, the war between Rome and Carthage of 218–201 BC (the second Punic war – see Chapter 5). Silius, however, abridges Ennius' time-span, contenting himself with the events of 218–201. Silius seems to have relied less on Ennius than on later sources. His language is Virgilian and his historical sources are legion (Burck 1979: 259). The antiquarian nature of Silius' project requires emphasis: Ennius had lived through the second Punic war. Silius wrote of it almost 300 years later.

What did Silius intend by producing an epic on the second Punic war? Burck (1979: 257) suggests that Silius was deliberately turning his back on the era in which he lived. The dangerous era of the Julio-Claudians, then the civil wars following the death of Nero, may have driven him to valorize an earlier, somehow more heroic era. The *Punica*, that is, recommends a Rome that reflects and respects traditional values. But it seems equally likely that Silius' choice of his topic may reflect a current of cultural optimism, even national revival under Domitian (Waters 1964). Admiration for Republican and Augustan literary and social activities is a marked characteristic of contemporary writers such as Tacitus and Quintilian. Domitian's own Augustan leanings are apparent.

Burck (1979: 258) rightly stresses the relationship of the *Punica* to Virgil's *Aeneid*. It is as if Silius were attempting to produce a poem that was a continuation of Virgil's epic. The Virgilian flavour has two important corollaries. First, by choosing an Ennian theme but deploying it in a Virgilian manner Silius may be attempting to rewrite, even correct, what he may have seen as the inaccuracies and barbarities of the Ennian version. The second corollary concerns Lucan. We have already observed that the *Punica* seems deliberately unlike Lucan's *Civil War* (see Chapter 9). The Virgilian posture of the *Punica* acts as a kind of antidote to the heresies of Lucan's epic.

Are there ideas within the *Punica* which provide it with meaning and with unity? These are best comprehended in the scene towards the beginning of book 15 where Virtue (*Virtus*) and Pleasure (*Voluptas*) compete for Scipio's allegiance. Scipio's conflict and his decision is one first dramatized by the Sophistic philosopher, Prodicus. The player in Prodicus' philosophical drama is usually Hercules (whose importance for the *Punica* is stressed by Bassett 1966). In the *Punica* it is Scipio (Burck 1979: 282–3; Bassett 1966). Scipio's decision to pursue the war against the Carthaginians is represented by Silius as an acceptance of a life devoted to the pursuit of *Virtus*. (It is not unlikely that Domitian, who also claimed a link with Hercules, should be connected with Scipio – compare McGuire 1985: 189. Domitian is addressed at 3.607ff., cf. 14.684–8.) Thus the Rome of the second Punic war and its leaders, Scipio, Marcellus, Fabius, and Aemilius Paulus, embody that moral attribute (contrast McGuire 1985). There is a second, related notion: a desire for *gloria* or *nomen* ('renown'), when blended with *furor* (violence matched with moral irresponsibility), is disastrous: Hannibal incarnates such corruption. Contemporary Rome, wracked recently by civil war and corrupt leadership (modern-day Hannibals), ought to take warning from the Scipios, the Marcelli, and the Fabii.

MORAL LESSONS FROM ANCIENT HISTORY: THE *PUNIC WARS*

Books 1–6: the ascendance of Hannibal

Concerned with the lead-up to the siege of Saguntum, books 1 and 2 form an approximate narrative unit; they link logically with book 3 describing Hannibal's progress from Saguntum, across the Alps and on into Italy. Books 4 and 5 outline the first of the great clashes between the Romans and the Carthaginians in the battles of Ticinus (218 BC), Trebia (218 BC), and Lake Trasimene (217 BC). Then book 6 shows the aftermath of Trasimene. Hannibal appears invincible in these books.

Silius makes the importance of his divine machinery obvious from the outset. Juno's hatred of Rome (1.42–54 and 125–37) is the cause of the war. It was the enmity of Juno which caused so much grief for the Aeneadae in Virgil's *Aeneid* and for the Trojans in Homer's *Iliad* (Feeney 1990 discusses Juno's lasting hostility to Rome). Burck (1979: 264–5) points out that Juno's speeches balance Jupiter's speech at 17.344–84 which determines the final outcome of the conflict, and Proteus' prediction (7.435–93) of everlasting power for Rome which begins the second hexad.

The characterizations of Hannibal and of his father, Hasdrubal, are given considerable attention. Hasdrubal is awful (1.144–81). He enjoys power because it affords him the opportunity for cruelty. His son Hannibal is scarcely better: as a boy he swore an oath to take vengeance on the Romans; and even at that age he proved faithless to his pledges, cunning, unjust, godless, evil, and a hater of peace who lusted after human blood (1.56–119). As a man he became impervious to physical discomfort and danger (1.239–67). Physically Hannibal and Hasdrubal were well equipped for the pursuit of *gloria*; spiritually their pursuit was vitiated by the presence of such vices.

The bloody siege of the Spanish city of Saguntum (founded, significantly, by Hercules, Scipio's doublet, 1.273), which absorbs the remainder of book 1 and all of book 2 (McGuire 1985 is stimulating here), provides the first opportunity to view Hannibal in action. Hannibal is a brave, if bloody (2.233–63), leader. But his initial attack is treacherous, performed in defiance of the treaty sworn before the gods (1.692–4) that bound Carthage and Rome (1.268, 1.296). The point is of some importance. The siege of Saguntum initiates the second Punic war. That Hannibal instigates the war by treaty breaking is in keeping with his schematized characterization.

Book 3 offers some predictable elements: a long catalogue of Hannibal's forces (3.214–405) recapitulating the catalogues of Homer, Apollonius, and Virgil; a narrative of his crossing the Pyrenees from Spain into France, then the Alps into Italy (3.406–556), which, according to Burck, matches Aeneas' storm at sea. Just as Jupiter and Venus converse after Aeneas storm in *Aeneid* 1, so they do here: Jupiter outlines Rome's destiny (3.571–629). One less predictable element is the image of Hercules (who sent the goddess Loyalty to encourage resistance at Saguntum, 2.475–525). The hero turned god becomes a leitmotif of the poem: he seems to embody the moral destiny of Rome (Bassett 1966). Hannibal is on the loose in Italy in books 4 and 5. Here there are key battles leading up to the disaster at Cannae (216 BC): the Roman defeats of Ticinus (4.135–479), Trebia (4.525–704), and Lake Trasimene (5.186–687). The battle scenes are dreary. Perhaps the most interesting aspect of these two books is the schematized characterization of Flaminius, consul for 217. By making light of bad omens and of the warnings of the seer Corvinus, he was responsible for the Roman disaster at Trasimene. Flaminius, on a spiritual level, might be likened to Hannibal (but more especially to the baleful Varro who precipitates the disaster at Cannae). Flaminius illustrates the simple proposition that a pursuit of *gloria* which is hampered spiritually by *dementia* and *furor* (5.106) provides a potent recipe for disaster.

Book 6 is one of the most successful within the *Punica*. The three most important sections of this book concern the Roman hero of the first Punic war, Regulus (6.101–551), the selection of the Roman nero Q. Fabius as general (6.590–618), and Hannibal's viewing of the temple wall paintings at Liternum of the first Punic war (6.641–716). Regulus stands out. The flashback to his invasion and imprisonment in North Africa is done with real sympathy. His return to Rome, the pressures placed upon him by the Roman Senate, the Carthaginians, and his wife, and his horrendous death in Carthage are vivid. Regulus offers a peerless example of *virtus*. A brave but honest and god-fearing man, he stands as a polar opposite to the cruel, dishonest Hannibal, or the foolish and precipitate Flaminius. The general Quintus Fabius ought to be compared (6.589–618). He may be directly contrasted with the rash and foolish Flaminius. Fabius' chief virtues, apart from his courage and endurance, were caution and desire to spare the lives of his fellow Romans (6.619–40). Fabius cuts less of a dash than Regulus or Scipio, but his Roman sense of honour is no less great.

Books 7–12: before and after Cannae

The *Punica* likes to begin books by extolling a Roman or Rome. In book 7 it is Fabius (7.20–73). This is provided dramatically by Cilnius, a Roman captive, who stresses to Hannibal that Fabius, descended from Hercules (7.35: here he is again), is from a clan whose bravery, loyalty to Rome, and piety are outstanding; Fabius, though old, is gifted with foresight, shrewdness, and calm and caution. Silius highlights the qualities of Fabius' character not just through Cilnius, or by description of his martial tactics (7.90–161 and 7.212–59), but also by contrasting him with the *furor*-driven Minucius who takes on the Carthaginians only to require rescue by Fabius (7.523–79).

The piety of not just Fabius but also the Roman people is demonstrated elsewhere in this book. Hannibal's impious ravaging of the Apulian countryside (7.212–59) is contrasted with the piety of the traditional Apulians, one of whose number was rewarded by a visit from the god Bacchus (7.162–211). The impiety of the Carthaginians is clear when their fleet arrives at Caieta. The divine local nymphs are terrified. It is only Proteus' prophecy (matching Jupiter's in book 1) of final Roman triumph that provides them solace (7.409–593).

The narrative of the terrible Roman defeat at Cannae (books 9 and 10) is very selective and does not really capture its magnitude. Silius does not provide a background against which the actors fight (compare Livy's more successful description of these events). In *Punica* 9 we view a series of duels between isolated individuals. Silius' most successful touch is to allow the easily swayed consul Aemilius Paulus to become the narrative mainstay. He becomes a symbol for the Roman fighting man at Cannae and with his fortunes swing those of Rome. Aemilius Paulus conforms to a type of epic hero whom we have often seen: initially at odds with his society, through crisis he regains his courage and becomes an outstanding *exemplum* of the moral fortitude of his people (10.1–325).

Description of the aftermath of Cannae focuses on conditions at the Campanian city of Capua. Too wealthy, too luxurious (11.28–54), and too effete (11.288–302), it was easily led astray by the likes of a Pacuvius (11.55ff.) Little wonder that the Capuans, with only small resistance (11.190–258 and 11.303–68), go over to the Carthaginians (11.130–89). (Capua was not forgiven its treachery until 90 BC.) Even Hannibal, after a winter in the town, is enfeebled by its pleasures (11.377–482). Capua marks a turn in Hannibal's fortunes. Subsequent attacks upon Neapolis, Cumae, and Puteoli (12.1–103) are unsuccessful. Silius goes to great lengths to demonstrate the severity of Hannibal's rebuff by Marcellus in his attempted siege of Nola (12.158–294). Henceforth Roman victory becomes more possible: their confidence is immediately raised by a favourable oracle from Delphi (12.295–341). By now the Romans have Capua blockaded and are able to resist an attack by Hannibal's roaming forces (12.479–506). Hannibal's subsequent advance on Rome (his advance to the walls of Rome has been a motif from the first book) is the high point of his success (12.507–40). But if the advance of 211 BC marks the culmination of Hannibal's efforts, it also marks the end, for on his first attack he is driven back by Fulvius Flaccus (12.558–73).

Books 13–17: Scipio

Burck (1979: 268) notes that book 13, like 1 and 6, begins with a contrast between the religious Romans and *impius* Hannibal. The comparison is made by contrasting the invincibility of Rome and its Palladium with Hannibal who, on learning from the Roman deserter Dasius that the city is invincible (13.30–81), sacks the temple of Feronia (13.82–91). Scipio enters the narrative after the retaking of Capua (13.94–380) and after the report of the annihilation in Spain of his father, uncle, and their army (13.381–4). He is an Aeneas figure (hence the pilgrimage to Hades, 13.400–895, where he learns of Rome's future and the fate of Hannibal).

Marcellus' successes in Sicily provide the first concrete instance of the tide turning in Rome's favour. After an excursus on the dynastic chaos of the island (14.79–109), there are descriptions of Marcellus' storming of Leontini (14.125–77), of his blockade of Syracuse (14.178–91), of Archimedes' efforts against the Roman forces (14.292–352), of a sea fight (14.353–579), a plague (14.580–617), and of the final capture of the city (14.618–84). Marcellus is Scipio's doublet. His military preeminence has already been emphasized (at 1.133 and 3.587 there is the winning of *spolia opima* – these were the spoils offered when a Roman general killed an enemy leader in single combat; in book 12 the confrontation with Hannibal at Nola). At Syracuse Marcellus is not just a good general; he wages war in accordance with the will of the gods (14.292–8) and exhibits mercy (14.665–75).

In book 15 Scipio is centre-stage. Near the outset of the book Scipio is visited by Virtue and Pleasure who compete for his allegiance. Scipio follows the advice of Virtue, opting to accept the command in Spain (15.18–151). Secure in his leadership and in the advice of the ghost of his father, he lands in Spain and captures New Carthage (15.152–250). It is only for Rome's sake we welcome Scipio's choice. Ethical decisions do not make compelling reading: unethical Hannibal or wavering Aemilius Paulus interest more than the man who restores a Spanish maiden to her lover (15.251–85). Having assured us of the moral worth of Scipio, Silius briefly deals with the war against Philip of Macedon (15.286–319), Fabius' capture of Tarentum (15.334–98), and, briefly, the baleful news of the defeat by Hannibal of Marcellus and Crispinus – and the death of the former (15.334–98). Scipio's putting Hasdrubal to flight across the Alps (15.399–514) does not quite avenge Marcellus, but it does force the battle of Metaurus (15.601–807 – 207 BC), Roman revenge for Cannae.

Scipio is again likened to Aeneas. Having driven the Carthaginians from Spain (16.23–167), he crosses to North Africa to the Numidian court of King Syphax (16.168–274). Ill omens force return to Spain. Here the parallel between Aeneas and Scipio becomes apparent: Scipio celebrates funeral games in honour of his father (16.275–591; compare *Aeneid* 5), whose death was reported in book 12. After the games Scipio returns to Italy to seek permission to cross to Africa. Against the wishes of Fabius (16.592–700) he does so

(17.46–58) and forces the retreat to Carthage of Hasdrubal and the recall of Hannibal from Italy (17.146–337) – to which Hannibal reacts indecisively (17.218–91). The scene is now set for the climactic battle of Zama (17.385–617 – 202 BC).

Before the battle is fought Silius sets up a number of simple equations to enable a proper estimation of Roman moral worth. The first is the conveying of the image of the goddess Cybele from Phrygia to Italy. It is received at Ostia by Scipio Nasica, the most virtuous Roman then living. The episode, though based in historical fact, illustrates the piety of the Romans (17.1–32). When Claudia – a woman whose chastity had been impugned – hauled the ship ashore she vindicated her purity (17.33–45). Only the chaste could touch the rope with impunity. Impiety is North African. We can see that in the next episode. When Scipio again meets *infidus* Syphax he warns him not to break faith with the Romans. This he does. But his camp is burnt and he is taken prisoner (17.59–145). Just before the final battle Jupiter and Juno converse about the fate of Hannibal (17.338–84). The interlude picks up Juno's statement at the beginning of book 1 and signals the conclusion of the poem. Once again the moral battle-lines are drawn. These receive their final playing out in the almost exciting description of the battle of Zama (17.385–617). The poem concludes, thereafter, with the return in triumph to Rome of its dull moral hero, Scipio (17.618–54), and the triumph of a righteous empire. If we can read the emperor Domitian into the portrait of Scipio, we can read the triumphant conclusion of the *Punica* as a vindication of his bloodthirsty regime. Silius perceived a moral message in Zama. So should we.

11

ENDS AND BEGINNINGS: LATE ANCIENT EPIC

LATE EPIC

Rigor mortis is not a characteristic of late classical epic. If the health of the genre is at its strongest when it is most open to thematic and generic variety, then late epic is sound. The major forms survive. They evolve, however, to produce a bewildering tangle of related, but superficially dissimilar subgenres. The long mythological epic survives (Vian 1963: xxiii cites some lost examples), as does the long ecomiastic epic. Particularly popular was the shorter epic. The miniature epic (limited to approximately 1,400 lines) was not like the Alexandrian product: it varies from simple myth narrative, from the encomiastic, via the adventurous application of allegory, to the romantic work of Vandal Africa. There also developed a strong metaphrastic tradition (Herzog 1975) which, in the manner of Hellenistic writers such as Philo the Elder or Theodotus (see Chapter 4), turned biblical narrative into epic verse. Two of the most striking examples of late epic are the long, often ribald mythological hybrid, the *Dionysiaca* of Nonnus, and the long 'biographic' epic, Venantius Fortunatus' life of St Martin of Tours.

It is too easy to dismiss the remarkable diversity of this epic jungle as evidence of a species not wholly of the first rank. A lack of central characters and issues, and a striving to be compendious, are said to be weaknesses in most of the poems. (How often have we heard these first two objections brought against Hellenistic or Silver Latin epic?) This loss of intensity is frequently blamed upon the eclipse of Rome itself and, with it, the loss in prestige of Latin and of the artificial Greek still composed in the east. Above all, it is sometimes asserted, the Dark Ages extinguished the eminence of the written word. In this period the torch passed to the barbaric vernacular cultures of the

211

north – to the oral epic traditions evident in German poetry, in the poetry of the old English, and in the Norse literature of Scandinavia. These are but textbook truisms: the epic literature of late antiquity is a vibrant and rewarding species. That it is little read is more the result of the exigencies of university curricula than of any intrinsic lack of value.

Paraphrase, for such a large and varied collection, is out of the question. Instead I will limit myself simply to pointing out what exists and how some of this material may be categorized and approached. Perhaps this brief compilation may sharpen the curiosity of a few readers. Much of this material exists in translation. And, if you are bold enough to try the Latin or the Greek, you will find the language in most cases less daunting than that of the 'classical' periods.

POETIC AUTONOMY? THE REVIVAL OF THE MINIATURE EPIC

The bewildering variety of forms taken by epic during the fourth, fifth, and sixth centuries is nowhere more evident than in the sub-genre of the miniature epic. This extremely popular type embraces concerns as diverse as praise, history, travel, allegory, and myth. A clue to the rationale of the 'epyllion' in late antiquity may be offered by that most specialized of forms, the ecphrasis (a description within a poem of a work of art (Kurman 1974; Race 1988: 56ff.; Hunter 1989: 112)). We have seen this before – it was a standard element of the narrative epic. In the fourth, fifth, and sixth centuries it could become free-standing (generally on the ecphrasis see Friedländer 1912 and Downey 1959).

Ausonius (c. 310–93) offers a representative example. *Cupido cruciatur* or 'Cupid crucified' (text and translation: Evelyn White 1951) is his poem. It contains a purported description of a painting of Zoïlus which he had seen at Trèves. Cupid is being nailed to a cross. He is being punished by a number of famous mythological heroines who had perished because of love. The theme of the poem (frustrated love) is typical of the Alexandrian epyllion. Indeed, its arrangement – into blocks each representing the different heroines – is not unlike the epyllion practice of narrative juxtaposition. (Perhaps he absorbed the technique from Ovid.) Whatever Ausonius' thematic concerns – and they are far from obvious – it seems clear that the *Cupido cruciatur* is designed as a literary *tour de force*. The ingenuity, the humour, the learning all point to a text designed to test reader and writer, to produce the type of aesthetic pleasure associated with visual art. Could we best describe the *Cupido cruciatur*, and perhaps the free-standing ecphrasis, as an 'autonomous' poetic art whose *raison d'être* is primarily aesthetic?

Poetic autonomy may offer the simplest means of understanding the several other fragmentary examples of this type. Christodorus of Coptus, writing at the end of the fifth century, has left 416 ecphrastic hexameters (the second book of the *Palatine Anthology* (Lesky 1966: 818–19)). His epic describes some of the statues in the gymnasium of Zeuxippus. Three poems survive which were written by followers of Nonnus. The first (Friedländer 1912) is by Paulus Silentiarius (a description of the Constantinople cathedral, the Hagia Sophia, and of its singers' pulpit). The second (Friedländer 1912), in two books, is by Johannes of Gaza (it is a description of a rendering of the cosmos in a Gaza conservatory). The third may be found in a Viennese manuscript. Lesky (1966: 818) describes it as follows: 'after a brief iambic prologue, a very successful ecphrasis of the times of the day and man's activities during them. The battle of light with dark, of the warmth of the sun with damp cold, imparts movement to the whole poem.'

Mythology provided a grammar of human experience for the ancient poet. It also provided a particularly entertaining body of literature for stories. The 'grammatical' function of myth seems to have become less pronounced in some of the poems of late antiquity. Rather, myth seems to have provided another means by which the poet could display ingenuity, irony, humour, and metrical facility. Like the ecphrasis, mythological epic, especially the miniature epic, seems to demonstrate these qualities. The interface between ecphrasis and mythological narrative is neatly captured in a straightforward fifth-century miniature epic (Bright 1987: viii) written by Reposianus (text and translation: Wight Duff 1961). This poem, in 182 lines, describes the uncovering of the affair between Venus, the goddess of love, and her lover, Mars, the god of war. (The inspiration may have been *Odyssey* 8.266–366.) The poem, an intensely visual, if saccharine, creation, seems almost to mirror a painting in its detail. Ecphrasis and myth blend to leave us in a world of 'poetic autonomy'.

And how else should we understand Claudian's *De raptu Proserpinae* ('On the Rape of Proserpina')? This poem (written possibly during the first two years of Claudian's stay at the court at Milan, it is dedicated to Florentinus, city prefect from August 395 to the end of 397 – after which date he fell out of favour with Stilicho) narrates the tale of the abduction by Pluto of Proserpina, the daughter of the goddess of corn, Ceres (text and translation: Platnauer 1963). The narrative is straightforward, but the subject matter and erotic timbre owe much to Alexandria. The first book describes the lead-up to the abduction, the second (at times reminiscent of Moschus' *Europa*) details the abduction to Hades, the incomplete third describes Ceres' doleful but angered reaction. The poem blends panegyric with the more traditional elements of narrative epic (chastised by Cameron 1970: 265) and revels in set speech and long, ecphrastic-like description. The treatment is ingenious and unlike that to which we have become used (Roberts 1989: 24–8 posits a context). Displaying few moral concerns, this poem is best described as a *tour de force*.

The miniaturizing of what had been large scale narrative offers a challenge to the poet's skill as adapter. Claudian attempted this in his *De raptu*. So do the little-known poems of Tryphiodorus and Colluthus. Take Tryphiodorus (who may have written in either the 3rd or 4th centuries AD – compare Cameron 1970: 478ff.): his challenge was to create short narrative from material elsewhere treated at great length (in Homer, in Virgil, or in Quintus Smyrnaeus). He composed in Greek a poem (of 691 hexameters) entitled the *Sack of Troy* (text and translation: Mair 1958). The narrative flows easily. There is no Alexandrian interweaving of stories. It begins (after a brief prologue) by describing the situation at Troy in the tenth year of the war and Athena's plan to have the Trojan horse constructed. We watch the horse constructed, manned, and led by Sinon's trickery into Troy. Despite Cassandra's predictions, and despite Helen's suspicions, the horse is welcomed and the city sacked – the climax of the epic. The story is well known – even too well known – but it has not always been told with such brevity.

Colluthus (perhaps writing as late as the fifth century) managed to go one step further. He compressed his Greek *Rape of Helen* into 394 verses (text and translation: Mair 1958). His tale was derived from the long cyclic epics (in this case the *Cypria* – see Chapter 3) and it focuses on a series of events rather than on a single character. There are three acts in the poem: in the first section (1–192) there is the beauty contest at the wedding of Peleus and Thetis which awarded Helen to Paris; in the second (193–327) there is the abduction; in the third (328–94: the emotional apogee of the epic) there is described the reaction of Helen's daughter Hermione to her mother's departure.

Much the same point could be made of the anonymous *Orphic Argonautica* (text and translation: Vian 1987). The poem has elements suggesting that it was serious about religion (Orphism – most evident in the theogonies and cosmogonies of lines 12–32 and 421–31). Yet it reads as an exercise in poetic ingenuity. Learned borrowings (Vian 1987: 18ff.: from Apollonius, from the *Homeric Hymns*, from Valerius' *Argonautica*, and even from Timaeus) buttress a creative impulse set on miniaturism. This is indicated both by size and by the choice of narrator. Narrated by the legendary poet Orpheus for his pupil Musaeus (a common fiction in Orphic poetry), the tale of the voyage of the *Argo* is compressed into 1,376 hexameters. Apollonius and Valerius needed five times as many lines (see Chapters 4 and 10).

The demands of a poetry designed above all to create the literary *tour de force* also seem best to explain the thrust of the recently discovered Alcestis poem (text and translation: Marcovich 1988). This *Alcestis*, perhaps to be dated to the second half of the fourth century (Marcovich 1988: 99ff.), is based on Euripides' *Alcestis*. Its theme (like that of the *Ciris*) is *pietas* (Marcovich 1988: 6): it dramatically narrates the sacrifice Alcestis made of her own life for her husband, Admetus. The ideas are hardly novel. The *Alcestis* poet seems more interested in turning Euripides into a Latin miniature epic. Marcovich (1988: 4) argues that the poem is an instance of *ethopoeia* – a type of ancient character study. Even on those grounds the poem does not quite work – character study has been done better elsewhere. I suspect that the author of this interesting discovery was more interested in displaying his own cleverness. This is art for art's sake.

PUTTING GOD BEFORE ART: MINIATURE EPIC AND RELIGION

Mythology and religion do mix easily. The *Orphic Argonautica* offers some indication. Musaeus' brilliant miniature epic, *Hero and Leander*, offers another. In this poem the impulse flies above any simple claims to poetic autonomy. *Hero and Leander* seems to be designed to demonstrate the ethical claims of Christian Neoplatonism.

Musaeus, who was possibly a teacher (of rhetoric, poetics, and philosophy, 'and expert in the scholarly interpretation of the classical prose- and verse-authors' – see Gelzer in Trypanis *et al.* 1975: 297 – may have been a follower of Nonnus and may have written in the second half of the sixth century. Gelzer (Trypanis *et al.* 1975: 300) believes that he was a Christian Neoplatonist. *Hero and Leander* tells the tale of two lovers separated not just by social status, but also by the Hellespont: Hero lives in a lighthouse in Abydus with her servant, Leander on the opposite shore in Sestus. Nationality renders a proper liaison impossible. They meet secretly and at night in the lighthouse. Leander bravely swims the Hellespont guided by a lamp held by his beloved. Until winter: a storm blows out Hero's lamp and overwhelms Leander. Next morning his ravaged body is washed up on the rocks beneath Hero's lighthouse. In grief she throws herself from the lighthouse to join Leander. The story was much imitated in later literature (Donno 1963; Alexander 1967).

What does it mean? Gelzer (Trypanis *et al.* 1975: 316) suggests that there is 'a "higher" meaning which Musaeus concealed allegorically beneath the surface of the love-story he narrated'. The love story acts as a 'symbolic representation of transcendental truths'. Contemporary allegorical interpretation reads texts on three levels. The superficial is represented by the story itself. The second or 'moral' level 'is interpreted as the love found in marriage'. The third level is the 'theoretical' or 'theological'. On this level the poem 'represents the life of the philosophical soul'. The first section of *Hero and Leander* (28–231) represents the life of the soul 'in heaven before birth'. Here, by selecting a god to be followed, it begins its 'heavenly procession' which will ultimately lead to union with God. The selection of the personal god here has its parallel in the 'selection' and beginning of love between Hero and Leander. The second part (232–88) represents the soul's life on earth. The ecstasy of the love between Hero and Leander is a reenactment and recollection, albeit on a carnal level, of the mystical union of the soul with God. The third part (289–343) represents the release of the soul from the shackles of mortal flesh. It looks forward, through the union in death of the two lovers, to the union of the soul with God.

Blossius Aemilius Dracontius, a Christian and a lawyer who lived in Vandal Carthage during the late fifth century, also applies a blend of mythology and miniaturized epic to religious ends. Dracontius has left three miniature epics (discussed by Bright 1987). These are gathered into a collection of short hexameter poems entitled *Romulaea* – this includes rhetorical exercises, marriage hymns, and mythological miniature epics, the *Hylas*, the *Rape of Helen*, and the *Medea*.

Bright (1987), the most recent commentator on these poems, has argued that they are Christian tracts dressed up in mythological garb. For example, in the *Rape of Helen* (was this poem written in response to Colluthus?) the poet not surprisingly assigns the disaster of Troy to the marriage of Helen and Paris (1987: 135). Bright (1987: 135) argues that the *Rape of Helen* highlights such issues as 'the sanctity of marriage, the heroine who violates that sanctity (assisted but not really driven by the hero) and the disaster which follows'. The *Medea*, which offers a notable example of miniaturizing, in its combination of the Apollonian and Euripidean narratives (did Dracontius have his sights on the *Orphic Argonautica* here?) is also Christian. Bright (1987: 83) argues that Medea is depicted as 'the source of passion and the source of evil', Jason is an innocent. This simplistic characterization of Medea owes something to Seneca, Valerius, and perhaps the *Orphic Argonautica*. The *Hylas* (based, as we have seen, upon an episode from the *Argonautica*) represents a type of love which is diametrically opposed to that of the Christian: this is especially evident in the sexual emotions felt by Hylas and Hercules (Bright 1987: 43).

The most exciting of these religious epics was composed by Prudentius (a Spaniard who lived 348–*c*. 410). It is the *Psychomachia* ('The Battle for the Soul'). Like Musaeus' epic, the *Psychomachia* (text and translation: Thomson 1969) is allegorical, but its 915 verses make the extraordinary intellectual leap of abandoning mythological narrative in favour of Christian allegory. This is an epic account of the single combats not between mythological heroes, but between the personifications of the Christian Virtues and Vices: rather than Achilles fighting Hector, or Aeneas fighting Turnus, here there is Faith fighting Worship-of-the-old-gods, or Chastity in conflict with Lust. Despite the fact that the *Psychomachia* was in the Middle Ages a most popular poem and, it is claimed (Thomson 1969: xiii), the 'ultimate inspiration of much moral allegory and of much religious and ecclesiastical art', the poem is nowadays not often recognized for the remarkably innovative piece that it is. This is no fault of Prudentius. Since the *Psychomachia* too much allegorical water has flowed beneath the prosodical bridge.

THE HISTORICALLY CIRCUMSTANTIATED EPIC: POEMS ABOUT REAL LIFE

There are a few poems which resist the blandishments of poetic autonomy, of religion, and of the universal. Here we witness a type of poetry which commits itself to 'the untidy and perhaps obscure specificity of transient historical situations'. Emrys Jones, speaking of sixteenth-century English verse, has aptly described this type of poetry as 'historically circumstantiated'. Much of the attraction of such poetry – and it can evoke a real imaginative sympathy – results from its being so historically specific.

One of the most fascinating examples (properly autobiographical) of the 'historically circumstantiated' is the *Eucharisticus* of Paulinus of Pella. (At 616 hexameters it is also a miniature epic. Here we seem to witness a biographical subspecies of epic.) The poem (text and translation: Evelyn White 1951), in a rough, not always sympathetic manner, describes the life of Paulinus, a wealthy Roman citizen resident in Bordeaux, who, due to the barbarian incursions of the period, fell on hard times and eventually discovered Christ. What this poem lacks in finesse it gains in archaeological force. The strength of this old man's witness to an extraordinary life (he may have been 83 when he composed the poem; the year was AD 459) renders this poem one of the most compelling of its or any era. Compare the life of Saint Martin by the itinerant Venantius Honorius Clementianus Fortunatus (*c.* 540–600). This poem was composed in fulfilment of a vow made once to the saint. The biography (in four books of hexameters) was undertaken at the urging of his friend, Gregory of Tours, and composed perhaps between 573 and 576. If this epic is not as compelling as that of Paulinus, perhaps we can blame the twin demons of eulogy (is there too much of it in this poem?) and its being based on a prose narrative by Sulpicius Severus. The historically circumstantiated is often displaced by mere hagiography.

Travel literature seems also to have had an audience in late antiquity. Ausonius composed the best-known example in his *Mosella* (text and translation: Evelyn White 1951). This praise poem depicts the River Moselle in 483 hexameters: there are pictures not only of the physical environs of the river, but also of the buildings that line it and the fish that swim in it. There is also his less compelling *Order of Famous Cities*. Composed towards the end of the fourth century, it is a poetic celebration of twenty important cities of the Roman world. Ausonius was not alone in this enthusiasm. Lesky (1966: 818) mentions a pair of Greek 'travel' poems, composed in the sixth century. The first, by Paulus Silentiarius, limns the hot springs in Bithynia. The second, by Christodorus of Coptus, provides histories of various cities.

Much of the poetic output of Claudian is built on specific historical situations. Surviving amongst his poetry is a considerable body of eulogistic and vituperative verse (text and translation: Platnauer 1963). Much of the eulogistic poetry is addressed directly to the remarkable general, Stilicho, or to his regent, Honorius. Understandably the vituperative poetry is directed towards their opponents.

Claudian wrote for his living. Thus we find him moving in 395 to the Roman court at Milan whence he sends laudatory letters (in hexametric verse) to his friends Probinus and Olybrius. He remained in Milan, perhaps on the staff of the general Stilicho, for the next five years. Stilicho seems to have been the most remarkable Roman general of that troubled period. He was one of the few commanders who was capable of containing the barbarian incursions which eventually led to the sacking of Rome in 410. Much of Claudian's honorific verse was directed towards this man: narratives of his successful military campaigns (*The War against Gildo* – Gildo who, in North Africa, had revolted and blocked the corn supply to Rome – and *The Gothic War* – celebrating Stilicho's defeat of the Gothic general Alaric at the battle of Pollentia in 402), honorific verse on his consulship (*On Stilicho's Consulship* in three books) and vituperative poems directed against his enemies (*Against Rufinus* in two books, and *Against Eutropius* also in two books). Throughout the period Stilicho was responsible to the emperor Honorius (who, four years after the death of Claudian, had the general put to death). There is, therefore, honorific verse directed towards Honorius: a pangeyric on his marriage with Maria, and panegyrics on his fourth and sixth consulships.

There is also Corippus. His *Johannis* (otherwise know as *The Libyan Wars*) is sometimes described as the last epic of late antiquity. It was written in eight books and describes the conquest of the Moors between AD 546–8 by John Troglitha (Johannes), a general of the Byzantine regent, Justinian (ruled 527–65). Little is known of Corippus' life. He was, it seems, a teacher in the Byzantine province of North Africa (Cameron 1976: 1ff.) and composed his historical epic soon after 548.

Unfortunately the *Johannis* has no readily available translation (Latin text: Diggle and Goodyear 1970). It might be as well, therefore, briefly to summarize the story. It begins with the summoning of Johannes by Justinian and his being conveyed (through a storm) to North Africa. After receiving the envoys of the Moorish leader, Antalas, Johannes explains to his soldiers the military duplicity of their opponents. The second book shows us what the Moors are really like. We are meant to contrast them with just Johannes who has tried to settle things through diplomacy. A long 'digression' occupies book 3. The tribune, Caecilides Liberatus, details what Africa was like before their coming. He narrates the events of AD 525–46: the early life of the Moorish leader, Antalas, the eclipse of the Vandal empire, the success of the Byzantine commander, Belisarius, the peace that followed, and the rise of Antalas. Half way through book 4 we are back to the present. Johannes prays that he may be able to help benighted Africa. Then news comes that Antalas has rejected his overtures. The religious theme becomes more pronounced in the fifth book. The battle between the Romans and the Moors (in which the Moors are routed) is a Christian triumph. In book 6 there is a reverse: Johannes' forces are defeated and the general only just manages to escape. Now a lull before the final climax: in book 7 the troops recuperate over the winter, new forces arrive, preparations are made for the decisive battle, and Caecilides mounts a night operation. The final book has Christian Johannes routing the Moorish forces.

The *Johannis* stands on its immediacy. A major characteristic is a lack of elaboration. Corippus' poem lacks the variety of earlier epic: there is no divine machinery, little mythology, there are virtually no women, and, above all, there is little appeal to the past. Contemporary relevance and an uncomplicated desire to praise Johannes and, by contagion, Justinian seem also to explain the lack of ideas in the poem: there is no complex hero, nor could the religious theme (the Romans exemplify Christian *virtus*) be said to dominate the poem. For modern readers the lack of variety and complexity may seem a drawback. But that is to ignore the obvious aims of this simple, readable poem. Historically circumstantiated, it provides a window into an almost lost era.

TRYING TO BE UNIVERSAL: THE COMPENDIOUS EPIC

Some epics try to fit in everything. It is as if they were attempting to provide a universal register of human experience. Perhaps that was the aim of Quintus Smyrnaeus. This learned poet laboured over his fourteen books on the Trojan legends during the fourth century (Lesky 1966: 815). The *Posthomerica* ('What happened after Homer') may be designed to fill the gap created by the lost cyclic epics, the

Aethiopis and the *Sack of Troy* by Arctinus and the *Little Iliad* by Lesches (Vian 1963: xxiiiff.; see also Chapter 3). The learned Quintus tells what happened after the ending of the *Iliad*: he begins with the death of the Amazon queen, Penthesilea, and concludes with the departure of the Achaeans. This compendious poem is held together by two things: the anticipated sack of Troy, and, according to Vian (1963: xiv–xviii), a religious ideal which aims to explain the place of humans within the order of things. Vian explains this universalizing philosophy as follows: the capriciousness and levity of the Homeric gods are replaced in the *Posthomerica* by less individuated gods who act seriously and are subservient to the authority of Zeus. Zeus himself is above all the executive of a form of Stoic Fate with which all cosmic forces are seen to be in accord. Humans function within the parameters laid down by this Stoic Fate.

Pagans like Quintus were not the only writers compelled by a concern with universal registers. The Christians were too. 'If the Gospels did not lend themselves so admirably to epic treatment', observes Raby (1953: 76), 'the story of the Old Testament was rich in scenes of romantic and dramatic possibility, which could be made to minister, in the highest degree, to the cause of Christian edification.' The tradition, as we have seen, began in Alexandria with Greek versions of the Old Testament by metaphrasts such as Philo the Elder or Theodotus. The Old Testament largely remained the focus of the flourishing tradition of biblical hexametric paraphrase (Herzog 1975; Kartschoke 1975; Roberts 1985). A fragmentary fifth-century paraphrase apparently narrating events from Genesis to Judges provides one example. This is the *Heptateuchus* of Cyprian (Raby 1953: 76). There are versions of Genesis by Hilary of Arles and by Claudius Marius Victor (Raby 1953: 77). Alcimus Ecdicius Avitus (*c.* 450–*c.* 525), who succeeded his father as Bishop of Vienne in South Gaul, provides another example of this tradition. His poem, in five books narrating selectively the story from Genesis to the crossing of the Red Sea, has been praised highly by Raby (1953: 78).

But the New Testament had its devotees. One of the earliest, if not the earliest, Latin practitioners of this form was the Spanish priest Gaius Vettius Aquilinus Juvencus who, in approximately 330, composed an epic paraphrase of the Gospel stories in over 3,000 verses. Doubtless Juvencus' purpose was to entice educated readers from pagan literature, by offering a Christian text that provided heroic themes untainted by the mendacities of paganism. Caelius Sedulius, born early in the fifth century, continued this tradition with his

Carmen Paschale (Raby 1953: 108ff.; Springer 1988). This begins with a hexametric account of the miracles of the Old Testament which prefigure Christ's coming, then continues in the remaining books to narrate miracles of Christ; the poem concludes with the Ascension. Two centuries after Juvencus the Italian poet Arator (Raby 1953: 117ff.) attempted the same themes: in two books he produced a versifed account of the Acts of the Apostles from the Ascension to the visit of St Paul to Rome.

It was not all biblical paraphrase. The greatest of all these writers – and my own favourite – is the redoubtable Nonnus. Composing in the second half of the fifth century, he is the Rabelais of ancient epic.

Who has read Nonnus? His *Dionysiaca*, in forty-eight books, does not sound promising: it purports to narrate the god Dionysus' conquest of India. (Nonnus, I should also mention, is believed to be the author of a hexameter paraphrase of the Gospel of St John.) More than any other epic writer of this period he sums up the tradition but, at the same time, points one way forward. Nonnus' sources were Alexandrian. And through such writers he looks back to Homer. Yet the vast sprawl of his narrative, with its variegated and inter-twined strands, looks sideways (or is it forward?) to the novel.

The forty-eight books of the *Dionysiaca* (the length of the *Thebaid* of Antimachus of Colophon; it is also the combined length of the *Iliad* and the *Odyssey*) tell the story of the god Dionysus' Indian expedition and his battles against the king Deriades. The epic, almost in passing, details a universal history of Dionysus. The *Dionysiaca* is, in the broadest sense, an encomium of the god. Vian (1976: xxf.) points out that many of the traditional elements of this type are to be seen in the *Dionysiaca*: description and praise of the addressee's fatherland and ancestors (books 1–6), of his birth (books 7–8), of his education (books 9–12), of his military accomplishments (books 13–40) and his accomplishments in peacetime (books 40–8), and finally of his death and the honours gained thereby (here symbolized by Dionysus' admission to Olympus towards the end of book 48).

The *Dionysiaca* is compendious. It is also a determinedly prolix work: there are digressions on mythological, astronomical, and scientific manners, there are descriptions and ecphraseis, epigrams, hymns, and chunks of rhetoric (Vian 1976: xlviiiff.). But Nonnus' obvious enthusiasm for digression does not mean that the poem as a whole is without organizing principles. Vian (1976: xviiiff.) points out that the structure of the poem is based on two groups of twenty-four books (each of which is begun by a prelude). The profusion of Nonnus' narrative, furthermore, is directed towards a goal. This is given to us in a speech by Zeus at 7.73–105: Zeus intends to provide the human race with wine, to allow them to forget their sorrows. (Wine is almost a metaphor for the *Dionysiaca* itself.) To this end he will bring to birth his son, Dionysus, who will provide this boon. Of Dionysus, Zeus says that, after his struggles with the Giants and with the Indians, he will be received as a god into Olympus.

Nonnus' narrative deserves to be read more. It fulfils most of the criteria which, in the first chapter of this book, I suggested were present in a satisfying epic poem. The poem evokes a self-contained and appealing world in the mythical past when things were somehow better than they are now. There is, furthermore, a high degree of aesthetic play, indicated by the bewildering variety of sources used to weave the poem and by its satisfying, if strict, metrics. The poem, what is more, can speak directly. There is no Virgilian 'private' voice. But, if we cannot identify directly with the travails of Dionysus, we can easily with the constant sexual imbroglios woven into the fabric of the *Dionysiaca*. And, finally, the poem does have its ideas, even if these are parodic, deflationary ones. The *Dionysiaca*, perhaps only after Apollonius' *Argonautica* and Ovid's *Metamorphoses*, is closest in spirit to modern literary preoccupations. It provides a remarkable place to conclude a survey of the ancient epic. But it also provides a remarkable place from which to begin exploration of the modern generic inheritants.

APPENDIX:

THE EPIC AND THE NOVEL

The generic link between epic and the ancient novel has been mentioned more than once. To clarify this matter further I will briefly outline some of the less contested similarities between epic and the ancient novel. Although the genres were separate there was considerable overlap. Perry (1967: 46) described the ancient novel as 'latter-day epic'. Reardon (1969) adds 'in a non-heroic world'.

THE IDEAL GREEK NOVEL

The chief characteristics of the conventional Greek romantic novel may be deduced from the extant works of Chariton, Xenophon of Ephesus, Longus, Heliodorus, and Achilles Tatius (Perry 1967: 122ff.). A pair of highly moral young lovers will form the focus of this ideal Greek novel, but their erotic experience will be detailed in a context of travel and adventure. The basic pattern of such stories is constant. Sudden love between hero and heroine is thwarted by 'bizarre obstacles set up by malevolent fortune' (Walsh 1970: 8). The lovers – abducted by pirates, carried off by bystanders, concerned or lewd – must overcome a series of trials and temptations in their search for one another. (The theme of the search is what enables the writer to include a variety of adventures, varied travel lore, and a liberal lacing of 'wonders'.) The honour from the favouring gods for their love and loyalty is a final, happy reunion, rewarded by 'perennial bliss'.

THE *ODYSSEY* AND THE GREEK NOVEL

The affinities of the Greek novel with Homer's *Odyssey* are often mentioned (Perry 1967: 50–3; Hägg 1983: 110). If Homer's lovers,

Penelope and Odysseus, are not quite young, they are remarkably, if incidentally, faithful. Their separation and reunion form the core of the poem. Both must overcome a series of trials and obstacles. Odysseus is assisted and delayed by a variety of individuals whose motives vary from the concerned to the lewd. Odysseus and Penelope are assisted by the favour of the gods and their loyalty and love are rewarded finally by a happy reunion. Anderson (1982: 2) adds other similarities. There are Odysseus' amorous trials with Calypso, Nausicaa, and Circe. He also stresses that 'a long action of travel and separation has plenty of scope for entertaining falsehood'.

THE *ARGONAUTICA* AND THE GREEK NOVEL

Heiserman (1977) stressed the relatedness of the *Argonautica* to the Greek novel. I have already indicated the manner by which Jason resembles the hero of the Greek novel. Anderson (1982: 3, 1984: 38) also notes the resemblances between *Argonautica* 3–4 and the ancient romantic novel. There are two young lovers in these books who, at least in Medea's case, exhibit faithfulness and affection. Both must overcome a series of trials and obstacles before they can be together (Jason's gaining the fleece, the pursuit of Apsyrtus, the threats of Alcinous and Arete). And their love, aided by Hera and Athena, is rewarded, perhaps not perennially, by the veneer of a happy reunion. Anderson (1982: 3) stresses other similarities: that 'love is presented in a significant partnership with themes of religion and sorcery'; he notes the wonders that confront the hero (such as the *Argo* riding in mid-air); that the resolution of the love theme is dependent on a chastity test: 'Arete warns Jason to marry Medea before he is forced to hand her back to her father as a virgin.'

THE *SATYRICON* AND THE EPIC

Klebs (1889) maintained that Petronius' *Satyricon*, the earlier of the two extant ancient Roman novels, was 'a sort of a parody of the *Odyssey* and epics like it' (Sullivan 1968: 92). On the most general level the *Satyricon* details, like the *Odyssey*, the picaresque wanderings of a persecuted hero. The links, however, are more precise. Encolpius, the protagonist of the *Satyricon*, is hounded across land and sea by the wrath of a god, Priapus rather than Odysseus' Poseidon (see *Satyricon* 139.2, Ernout). Giton, hidden beneath the bed to escape Ascyltus, is compared to Odysseus hidden under a sheep to escape from the cave of the Cyclops. Encolpius' tortured liaison with Giton parodies that of Odysseus with Calypso and Circe. The whole of the Circe episode is reminiscent of events in *Odyssey* 10 where the real Circe dominates the narrative. The storm and shipwreck passage mirrors *Odyssey* 5 (perhaps more readily than *Aeneid* 1 (Walsh 1970: 37)) and Croton, therefore, with its *femme fatale* must match and parody Nausicaa. The *cena Trimalcionis* may be intended to recall the banquets on Phaeacia of *Odyssey* 7–8. More general epic parody may be contained in the picture-gallery episode which has 'its epic parallels in the Shield of Achilles and Virgil's description of the scenes decorating Dido's temple' (Sullivan 1968: 96). Perhaps the lower-class ambience of the poem (a series of decaying coastal towns) is intended to play off against the aristocratic, heroic world of Homeric epic.

THE EPIC INSERT OF THE *SATYRICON*, THE *BELLUM CIVILE*

The overall epic ambience of the *Satyricon* renders less unexpected the peculiar epic insert, the *Bellum civile* ('Civil War'). (The insert at *Satyricon* 89, usually entitled the *Troiae halosis* or 'Sack of Troy' – compare *Aeneid* 2 and Tryphiodorus' poem of the same name – is not strictly epic. It is composed in a tragic metre, the iambic trimeter, and seems more directed against such Senecan tragedies as the *Agamemnon* and the *Trojan Women* than against traditional epic (Sullivan 1968: 186ff.).) The *Bellum civile*, a work delivered by the poetaster Eumolpus and occupying *Satyricon* 118–24, details Julius Caesar's invasion of Italy in 49 BC. This is the subject of the published books 1–3, of Lucan's *Bellum civile*, which epic poem, as we have seen, also dealt with the invasion of Italy by Julius Caesar. The contents of Petronius' *Bellum civile*, however, differ in emphasis from Lucan's narrative. The poetic insert begins with an outline of the corruption ('affluence, decadence, and greed') to which Rome has sunk and which is responsible for the war (1–44). (My paraphrase is based on Sullivan 1968: 171.) Electoral corruption defeats Cato – the corruption does no good for the lower classes and forces the issue of war (45–60). Next the leaders, Crassus, Pompey, and Caesar, are introduced (61–6). Divine machinery is brought in: Dis, lord of the underworld, pleads with Fortune to cause war for Rome (67–99). Fortune agrees (100–21), as does Jupiter (122–40). There follows a description of Caesar's determining to embark on the Civil War

(141–76) and his crossing the Alps (177–209). The account now shifts to Rome and to Pompey's desertion of the capital (210–44). Finally follows a further depiction of divine machinery: the gods supporting each side are enumerated while Discord appears to urge the world towards civil war (244–94).

It is difficult not to read Eumolpus' poem (whether ironic, parodic, critical, or even affectionately meant) as a correction, most probably, of the characteristics of Lucan's poem (Sullivan 1985: 162–72, 1982) or of the characteristics of modernist poets like Lucan (Burck 1979: 203–7). The coincidences are too great. Both poems treat the same event; one is remarkable for its absence of divine machinery, the other pointed in its inclusion of the divine; one vehement in its criticism of tyrannical whimsy, the other indifferent; one novel in its contemporary treatment of epic theme, the other tediously traditional. Anderson (1982: 99–102) and Walsh (1970: 49) are surely over-dismissive in rejecting Lucan as Eumolpus' target.

THE EPIC HERO OF APULEIUS'
METAMORPHOSES

Apuleius' *Metamorphoses*, the second of the two Roman novels, does not readily conform to the pattern of the ideal Greek novel. It is seldom compared with epic (Finkelpearl 1990). What I would like to suggest are two simple points. The first is that the moral evolution of Lucius mirrors that which I have suggested is basic to the depiction of the traditional epic hero. We have seen, in connection with the Gilgamesh epic, Homer's *Iliad* and *Odyssey*, and Virgil's *Aeneid*, the importance for the epic hero of some form of a crisis, and how the hero's response to this crisis is at the heart of the epic. The crisis, I have argued, usually causes the hero to become alienated from his human and divine communities. Personal tragedy, brought on by moral failure, and subsequently accompanied by long physical or spiritual wandering, allows him to gain a deeper understanding of his own nature. Having become the possessor of such virtues as loyalty, patience, endurance, empathy, and a proper sense of shame before his community and his gods, the hero returns to his people where he occupies his rightful place. There is associated with the hero in many epics a simple pattern of sin, alienation, and final reconciliation (compare Reardon 1991: 169ff.). Lucius' transformation (I am following Walsh's (1970) illuminating reading of the novel) is precipitated by moral failure. His metamorphosis into an ass may be viewed as a reflection of his moral turpitude in much the same way Odysseus' wanderings or Achilles' 'exile' are reflections of moral reprehensibility. Lucius' final transformation back into human form (like Achilles' reconciliation with Priam or Odysseus' with his home and family) is indicative of his moral evolution. There is of course no dissection of the 'heroic impulse' in Apuleius. This is 'bourgeois', not 'heroic', literature.

Related to this first point is my second. Perhaps Lucius' 'sin', which is compelled above all by curiosity and lust, may be compared to that of Odysseus in Polyphemus' cave. Odysseus here is driven by curiosity and by lust, if not sexual at least for material gain. The result for both heroes is comparable. There is an enforced separation from home, both are 'disguised' (Odysseus as a beggar, Lucius as an ass), and both are hounded by the wrath of a god (Poseidon for Odysseus, Isis for Lucius).

THE MODERN NOVEL AND THE EPIC

The ancient Greek novel is highly stylized. It may be this as much as Christianity which accounts for its eclipse. Its stylization renders it unlike the modern novel. Definitions of the modern novel are not easily formulated. Some aspects, as I stated in the first chapter, are clear: its capaciousness, its readiness to adapt and to adopt other generic types, its resultant ability to evolve, and its near formlessness do not cause us to deny its generic reality. The modern novel, that is, may be 'defined' by its lack of generic parameters. The modern novel is, therefore, indefinitely adaptable because of its capacity to absorb and modify the characteristics of other genres. This is not a point that could be made of the Greek novel – with the exception perhaps of Petronius' 'novel'. The same point has been made of ancient epic, at least in its most experimental periods. Apollonius, for example, under the influence perhaps of Callimachus, blends a variety of non-epic characteristics into his epic: romance, the sentimental, the erotic, travel, scientific and didactic lore, humour, a sharp juxtaposition of the heroic and the 'bourgeois'. So does the sprawling and picaresque epic of Nonnus. The *Dionysiaca* breaks all of the rules: it is at once compendious and specific, it blends romance, sexual innuendo, and religion, the heroic with the non-heroic, the humorous with the serious. Like the modern novel, its generic affiliations are promiscuous. Epic works such as the *Argonautica* of Apollonius, the *Dionysiaca* of Nonnus, and, to add a third, the *Metamorphoses* of Ovid, seem to exist on the interface between traditional epic and what we consider as the modern novel. The influence or the 'devolution' of the epic is not confined to these works. The epic characteristics of the various novels mentioned above is further evidence of this trend. They may emphasize the simple point that, in terms of generic evolution, the modern and the ancient novel are descendants of the ancient epic (Heiserman 1977; Bakhtin 1981).

BIBLIOGRAPHY

Ahl, Frederick (1976) *Lucan: An Introduction*, Ithaca: Cornell University Press.

—— (1984) 'The Rider and the Horse: Politics and Power in Roman Poetry from Horace to Statius', *Aufstieg und Niedergang der römischen Welt* 32.1: 40–124.

—— (1986) 'Statius' "Thebaid": A Reconsideration', *Aufstieg und Niedergang der römischen Welt* 32.5: 2803–912.

Alexander, Nigel (ed.) (1967) *Elizabethan Narrative Verse*, London: Edward Arnold.

Allen, W., Jr (1940) 'The Epyllion: A Chapter in the History of Literary Criticism', *Transactions of the American Philological Association* 71: 1–26.

Anderson, A. R. (1928) 'Heracles and his Successors: A Study of a Heroic Ideal and the Recurrence of a Heroic Type', *Harvard Studies in Classical Philology* 39: 7–58.

Anderson, Graham (1982) *Eros Sophistes: Ancient Novelists at Play*, Chico, California: Scholars Press.

—— (1984) *Ancient Fiction: The Novel in the Greco-Roman World*, London: Croom Helm.

Aricò, Giuseppe (1986) 'L' "Achilleide" di Stazio: tradizione letteraria e invenzione narrativa', *Aufstieg und Niedergang der römischen Welt* 32.5: 2925–64.

Auerbach, Erich (1973) *Mimesis: The Representation of Reality in Western Literature*, trans. Willard R. Trask, Princeton: Princeton University Press.

Austin, Norman (1975) *Archery at the Dark of the Moon: Poetic Problems in Homer's 'Odyssey'*, Berkeley: University of California Press.

Bakhtin, M. M. (1981) 'Epic and Novel', *The Dialogic Imagination*, ed. M. Holquist, Austin: University of Texas Press.

Barkhuizen, J. H. (1979) 'The Psychological Characterization of Medea in Apollonius of Rhodes, *Argonautica* 3.744–824', *Acta Classica* 22: 33–48.

Barsby, John (1978) *Ovid, Greece and Rome*, New Surveys in the Classics 12, Oxford: Clarendon Press.

Bassett, E. L. (1966) 'Hercules and the Hero of the *Punica*', *The Classical Tradition: Literary and Historical Studies in Honour of Harry Caplan*, ed. Luitpold Wallach, Ithaca: Cornell University Press.

Beye, Charles Rowan (1982) *Epic and Romance in the 'Argonautica' of Apollonius*, Carbondale and Edwardsville: Southern Illinois University Press.

Bishop, J. H. (1951) 'The Debt of the *Silvae* to the Epyllia', *La Parola del Passato* 21: 427–32.

—— (1988) *The Cost of Power: Studies in the 'Aeneid' of Virgil*, Armidale: University of New England Publishing Unit.

Bowra, C. M. (1952) *Heroic Poetry*, London: Macmillan.

—— (1972) *From Virgil to Milton*, London: Macmillan.

Boyle, A. J. (1986) *The Chaonian Dove: Studies in the 'Eclogues', 'Georgics', and 'Aeneid' of Virgil*, Mnemosyne Supplement 94, Leiden: E. J. Brill.

Bremer, J. M. (1987) 'Full Moon and Marriage in Apollonius' *Argonautica*', *Classical Quarterly* ns 37: 423–6.

Bright, David F. (1987) *The Miniature Epic in Vandal Africa*, Norman: University of Oklahoma Press.

Büchner, Karl (1967) 'Das Naeviusproblem: Mythos und Geschichte', *Studien zur römischen Literatur*, vol. VI, Wiesbaden: Franz Steiner.

Bulloch, A. W. (1985) 'Hellenistic Poetry', *The Cambridge History of Classical Literature: I: Greek Literature*, eds. P. E. Easterling and B. M. W. Knox, Cambridge: Cambridge University Press.

Burck, Erich (ed.) (1979) *Das römische Epos*, Darmstadt: Wissenschaftliche Buchgesellschaft.

Cairns, Francis (1989) *Virgil's Augustan Epic*, Cambridge: Cambridge University Press.

Cameron, Alan (1970) *Claudian: Poetry and Propaganda at the Court of Honorius*, Oxford: Clarendon Press.

Cameron, Averil (ed. and trans.) (1976) *Flavius Cresconius Corippus: In laudem Iustini Augusti minoris libri IV*, London: Athlone Press.

Camps, W. A. (1969) *An Introduction to Virgil's 'Aeneid'*, Oxford: Oxford University Press.

—— (1980) *An Introduction to Homer*, Oxford: Clarendon Press.

Canfora, Luciano (1988) *The Vanished Library: A Wonder of the Ancient World*, trans. Martin Ryle, Berkeley: University of California Press.

Carpenter, Rhys (1962) *Folk Tale, Fiction, and Saga in the Homeric Epics*, Berkeley: University of California Press.

Cary, M. (1962) *A History of Rome down to the Reign of Constantine*, 2nd edn, London: Macmillan.

Chadwick, H. M. (1912) *The Heroic Age*, Cambridge: Cambridge University Press.

Chadwick, H. M. and N. K. (1932–40) *The Growth of Literature*, 3 vols, Cambridge: Cambridge University Press.

Chadwick, John (1990) 'The Descent of the Greek Epic', *Journal of Hellenic Studies* 109: 174–7.

Clarke, Howard (1981) *Homer's Readers: A Historical Introduction to the 'Iliad' and the 'Odyssey'*, Newark: University of Delaware Press.

Clausen, W. V. (1964) 'Callimachus and Latin Poetry', *Greek, Roman and Byzantine Studies* 5: 181–96.

—— (1987) *Virgil's 'Aeneid' and the Tradition of Hellenistic Poetry*, Berkeley: University of California Press.

Clay, Jenny Strauss (1983) *The Wrath of Athena: Gods and Men in the 'Odyssey'*, Princeton: Princeton University Press.

Cole, Thomas (1969) 'The Saturnian Verse', *Yale Classical Studies* 21: 3–73.

Coleman, K. M. (1986) 'The Emperor Domitian and Literature', *Aufstieg und Niedergang der römischen Welt* 32.5: 3087–115.

—— (ed.) (1988) *Statius: 'Silvae' IV*, Oxford: Clarendon Press.

Coleman, R. G. (1971) 'Structure and Intention in the *Metamorphoses*', *Classical Quarterly* ns 21: 461–77.

Conte, Gian Biagio (1986) *The Rhetoric of Imitation: Genre and Poetic Memory in Virgil and Other Latin Poets*, ed. Charles Segal, Ithaca: Cornell University Press.

Cox, Alister (1969) 'Didactic Poetry', *Greek and Latin Literature: A Comparative Study*, ed. John Higginbotham, London: Methuen.

Crowther, N. B. (1970) 'ΟΙ ΝΕΩΤΕΡΟΙ, Poetae Novi and Cantores Euphorionis', *Classical Quarterly* ns 20: 322–7.

Crump, M. M. (1931) *The Epyllion from Theocritus to Ovid*, Oxford: Basil Blackwell.

D'Espèrey, Sylvie Franchet (1986) 'Vespasien, Titus et la littérature', *Aufstieg und Niedergang der römischen Welt* 32.5: 3048–86.

Davies, Malcolm (1989) *The Epic Cycle*, Bristol: Bristol Classical Press.

Dickson, T. W. (1932) 'Lost and Unwritten Epics of the Augustan Poets', *Transactions of the American Philological Association* 63: lii–liii.

Diggle, J. and Goodyear, F.R.D. (eds) (1970) *Flavii Cresconii Corippi Iohannidos seu de bellis Libycis libri VIII*, Cambridge: Cambridge University Press.

Dilke, O. A. W. (1972) 'Lucan's Political Views and the Caesars', *Neronians and Flavians: Silver Latin I*, ed. D. R. Dudley, London: Routledge & Kegan Paul.

—— (ed.) (1954) *Statius: 'Achilleid'*, Cambridge: Cambridge University Press.

Dodds, E. R. (1968) *The Greeks and the Irrational*, Berkeley: University of California Press.

Dominik, William J. (1989) 'Monarchal Power and Imperial Politics in Statius' *Thebaid*', *Ramus* 18: 74–97.

Donno, Elizabeth Story (1963) *Elizabethan Minor Epics*, London: Routledge & Kegan Paul.

Downey, G. (1959) 'Ekphrasis', *Reallexikon für Antike und Christentum* 4: 922–43.

Duckworth, G. (1962) *Structural Patterns and Proportions in Vergil's 'Aeneid'*, Ann Arbor: University of Michigan Press.

Dudley, D. R. (ed.) (1972) *Neronians and Flavians: Silver Latin I*, London: Routledge & Kegan Paul.

Dyck, Andrew R. (1989) 'On the Way from Colchis to Corinth: Medea in Book 4 of the *Argonautica*', *Hermes* 112: 455–70.

Edmonds, J. M. (ed. and trans.) (1950) *The Greek Bucolic Poets*, London: William Heinemann.

Edwards, Mark W. (1987) *Homer: Poet of the 'Iliad'*, Baltimore: Johns Hopkins University Press.

BIBLIOGRAPHY

Evelyn White, Hugh G. (ed. and trans.) (1951) *Ausonius*, 2 vols, London: William Heinemann.

Fantham, Elaine (1979) 'Statius' Achilles and his Trojan Model', *Classical Quarterly* ns 29: 457–62.

Feeney, D. C. (1986a) 'Epic Hero and Epic Fable', *Comparative Literature* 38: 137–58.

—— (1986b) '"Stat magni nominis umbra." Lucan on the Greatness of Pompeius Magnus', *Classical Quarterly* ns 36: 239–43.

—— (1990) 'The Reconciliations of Juno', *Oxford Readings in Vergil's 'Aeneid'*, ed. S. J. Harrison, Oxford: Oxford University Press.

—— (1991) *The Gods in Epic: Poets and Critics of the Classical Tradition*, Oxford: Clarendon Press.

Fenik, Bernard (1968) *Typical Battle Scenes in the 'Iliad': Studies in the Narrative Techniques of Homeric Battle Descriptions*, Hermes Einzelschriften 21, Wiesbaden: Franz Steiner.

—— (1974) *Studies in the 'Odyssey'*, Hermes Einzelschriften 30, Wiesbaden: Franz Steiner.

Ferguson, J. (1973) *The Heritage of Hellenism*, New York: Science History Publications.

Finkelpearl, Ellen (1990) 'Psyche, Aeneas, and an Ass: Apuleius *Metamorphoses* 6.10–6.21', *Transactions of the American Philological Association* 120: 333–47.

Finley, John H., Jr (1978) *Homer's 'Odyssey'*, Cambridge, Mass.: Harvard University Press.

Finley, M. I. (1962) *The World of Odysseus*, Harmondsworth: Penguin Books.

Finnegan, Ruth (1977) *Oral Poetry: Its Nature, Significance, and Social Context*, Cambridge: Cambridge University Press.

Fowler, A. (1982) *Kinds of Literature: An Introduction to the Theory of Genres and Modes*, Oxford: Clarendon Press.

Fraenkel, Eduard (1935) 'Naevius', *Paulys Real-Encyclopädie der classischen Alterumswissenschaft* Suppl. 6: 622–40.

Frame, Douglas (1978) *The Myth of Return in Early Greek Epic*, New Haven: Yale University Press.

Fränkel, Hermann (1945) *Ovid: A Poet between Two Worlds*, Berkeley: University of California Press.

—— (1952) 'Apollonius Rhodius as a Narrator in *Argonautica* 2.1–140', *Transactions of the American Philological Association* 83: 144–55.

—— (1960) 'Ein Don Quijote unter den Argonauten des Apollonios', *Museum Helveticum* 17: 1–20.

—— (1975) *Early Greek Poetry and Philosophy*, trans. Moses Hadas and James Willis, Oxford: Basil Blackwell.

Fraser, P. M. (1972) *Ptolemaic Alexandria*, 2 vols, Oxford: Clarendon Press.

Friedländer, Paul (1912) *Johannes von Gaza und Paulus Silentiarius: Kunstbeschreibungen justinianischer Zeit*, Leipzig: Teubner.

Galinsky, G. Karl (1969) *Aeneas, Sicily, and Rome*, Princeton: Princeton University Press.

—— (1975) *Ovid's 'Metamorphoses': An Introduction to the Basic Aspects*, Oxford: Basil Blackwell.

233

—— (1990) 'Hercules in the *Aeneid*', *Oxford Readings in Vergil's 'Aeneid'*, ed. S. J. Harrison, Oxford: Oxford University Press.

Getty, R. J. (ed.) (1940) *M. Annaei Lucani De Bello Civili Liber I*, Cambridge: Cambridge University Press.

Glenn, Edgar M. (1986) *The 'Metamorphoses': Ovid's Roman Games*, Lanham: University Press of America.

Goldhill, Simon (1991) *The Poet's Voice: Essays on Poetics and Greek Literature*, Cambridge: Cambridge University Press.

Goold, G. P. (ed. and trans.) (1983) *Catullus*, London: Duckworth.

—— (1990) 'Servius and the Helen Episode', *Oxford Readings in Vergil's 'Aeneid'*, ed. S. J. Harrison, Oxford: Oxford University Press.

Gossage, A. J. (1972) 'Statius', *Neronians and Flavians: Silver Latin I*, ed. D. R. Dudley, London: Routledge & Kegan Paul.

Gransden, K. W. (1984) *Virgil's 'Iliad': An Essay on Epic Narrative*, Cambridge: Cambridge University Press.

Gratwick A. S. (1983) 'Ennius' *Annales*', *The Cambridge History of Classical Literature*, vol. 2, part 1, *The Early Republic*, eds E. J. Kenney and W. V. Clausen, Cambridge: Cambridge University Press.

Green, Peter (1990) *Alexander to Actium: The Historical Evolution of the Hellenistic Age*, Berkeley: University of California Press.

Griffin, Jasper (1977) 'The Epic Cycle and the Uniqueness of Homer', *Journal of Hellenic Studies* 97: 39–53.

—— (1979) 'The Fourth *Georgic*, Virgil, and Rome', *Greece and Rome* 26: 61–80.

Gruen, Erich S. (1986) *The Hellenistic World and the Coming of Rome*, Berkeley: University of California Press.

Gutzwiller, K. J. (1981) *Studies in the Hellenistic Epyllion*, Beiträge zur Klassisiche Philologie 114, Königstein: Hain.

Hadas, Moses (1936) 'The Tradition of a Feeble Jason', *Classical Philology* 31: 166–8.

Hägg, Tomas (1983) *The Novel in Antiquity*, Oxford: Basil Blackwell.

Hainsworth, J. B. (1991) *The Idea of Epic*, Berkeley: University of California Press.

Halliwell, Stephen (1986) *Aristotle's 'Poetics'*, London: Duckworth.

Hardie, P. R. (1986) *Virgil's 'Aeneid': 'Cosmos' and 'Imperium'*, Oxford: Clarendon Press.

Harrison, S. J. (ed.) (1990) *Oxford Readings in Vergil's 'Aeneid'*, Oxford: Oxford University Press.

—— (1990a) 'Some Views of the *Aeneid* in the Twentieth Century', *Oxford Readings in Vergil's 'Aeneid'*, ed. S. J. Harrison, Oxford: Oxford University Press.

Haskins, C. E. (ed.) (1887) *M. Annaei Lucani Pharsalia*, intro. by W. E. Heitland, London: George Bell & Sons.

Häußler, Reinhard (1976) *Das historische Epos der Griechen und Römer bis Vergil: Studien zum historischen Epos: I. Teil: Von Homer zu Vergil*, Heidelberg: Carl Winter.

Heath, M. (1989) *Unity in Greek Poetics*, Oxford: Clarendon Press.

Heinrichs, Katherine (1991) *The Myths of Love: Classical Lovers in Medieval Literature*, University Park: Pennsylvania State University Press.

Heiserman, A. (1977) *The Novel before the Novel*, Chicago: Chicago University Press.

Herzog, R. (1975) *Die Bibelepik der lateinischen Spätantike: Formgeschichte einer erbaulichen Gattung*, Theorie und Geschichte der Literatur und der schönen Künste, Bd 37, Munich: Fink.

Higginbotham, John (ed.) (1969) *Greek and Latin Literature: A Comparative Study*, London: Methuen.

Hollis, A. S. (ed.) (1990) *Callimachus: 'Hecale'*, Oxford: Clarendon Press.

Hope Simpson, R. and Lazenby, J. F. (1970) *The Catalogue of Ships in Homer's 'Iliad'*, Oxford: Clarendon Press.

Hopkinson, Neil (ed.) (1988) *A Hellenistic Anthology*, Cambridge: Cambridge University Press.

Horrocks, Geoffrey C. (1987) 'The Ionian Epic Tradition; Was There an Aeolic Phase in its Development?', *Minos* 20–2: 269–94.

Horsfall, N. M. (1990) 'Dido in the Light of History', *Oxford Readings in Vergil's 'Aeneid'*, ed. S. J. Harrison, Oxford: Oxford University Press.

Hunter, R. L. (1988) '"Short on Heroics": Jason in the *Argonautica*', *Classical Quarterly* ns 38: 436–53.

—— (1989) *Apollonius of Rhodes: 'Argonautica' Book III*, Cambridge: Cambridge University Press.

Hutchinson, G. O. (1988) *Hellenistic Poetry*, Oxford: Clarendon Press.

Huxley, G. L. (1969) *Greek Epic Poetry, from Eumelos to Panyassis*, Cambridge, Mass.: Harvard University Press.

Jacobson, H. (1983) (ed. and trans.) *The 'Exagoge' of Ezekiel*, Cambridge: Cambridge University Press.

Jenkyns, Richard (1982) *Three Classical Poets: Sappho, Catullus, and Juvenal*, London: Duckworth.

Jocelyn, H. D. (1972) 'The Poems of Quintus Ennius', *Aufstieg und Niedergang der römischen Welt* I.2: 987–1026.

—— (1984) 'Servius and the "Second Edition" of the *Georgics*', *Atti del Convegno mondiale scientifico di studi su Virgilio*, Rome: Arnaldo Mondadori Editore.

Johnson, W. R. (1987) *Momentary Monsters: Lucan and His Heroes*, Ithaca: Cornell University Press.

Jones, B. W. (1972) 'A Note on the Flavians' Attitude to the Censorship', *Historia* 21: 128.

—— (1973) 'Domitian's Attitude to the Senate', *American Journal of Philology* 94: 79–91.

—— (1974) 'Senatorial Influence in the Revolt of Saturninus', *Latomus* 33: 529–35.

Jones, Peter V. (1988) *Homer's 'Odyssey': A Companion to the English Translation of Richmond Lattimore*, Bristol: Bristol Classical Press.

Kartschoke, Dieter (1975) *Bibeldichtung: Studien zur Geschichte der epischen Bibelparaphrase von Juvencus bis Otfrid von Weissenburg*, Munich: Fink.

Kearns, Emily (1982) 'The Return of Odysseus: A Homeric Theoxeny', *Classical Quarterly* ns 32: 2–8.

Kenney, E. J. (1977) *Lucretius, Greece and Rome*, New Surveys in the Classics 11, Oxford: Clarendon Press.

King, Katherine Callen (1987) *Achilles: Paradigms of the War Hero from Homer to the Middle Ages*, Berkeley: University of California Press.

Kirk, G. S. (1965) *Homer and the Epic*, Cambridge: Cambridge University Press.

Klebs, E. (1889) 'Zur Komposition von Petronius' Satirae', *Philologus* 47: 623–35.

Klein, Theodore M. (1983) 'Apollonius' Jason: Hero and Scoundrel', *Quaderni Urbinati di Cultura Classica* ns 13: 115–26.

Knauer, G. (1964) *Die 'Aeneis' und Homer*, Göttingen: Vandenhoeck & Ruprecht.

Knox, Peter E. (1986) *Ovid's 'Metamorphoses' and the Traditions of Augustan Poetry*, Cambridge Philological Society Supplementary Volume No. 11, Cambridge: Cambridge Philological Society.

—— (1990) 'In Pursuit of Daphne', *Transactions of the American Philological Association* 120: 183–202.

Koster, Severin (1970) *Antike Epostheorien*, Wiesbaden: Franz Steiner.

Kurman, George (1974) 'Ecphrasis in Epic Poetry', *Comparative Literature* 26: 1–13.

Langerbeck, H. (1958) 'Margites', *Harvard Studies in Classical Philology*, 63: 33–63.

Lapidge, M. (1979) 'Lucan's Imagery of Cosmic Dissolution', *Hermes* 107: 344–70.

Lawall, Gilbert (1966) 'Apollonius' *Argonautica*: Jason as Anti-Hero', *Yale Classical Studies* 19: 121–69.

Leach, Eleanor Windsor (1974) 'Ekphrasis and the Theme of Artistic Failure in Ovid's *Metamorphoses*', *Ramus* 3: 102–42.

Lefkowitz, Mary R. (1981) *The Lives of the Greek Poets*, Baltimore: Johns Hopkins University Press.

Lennox, P. (1980) 'Apollonius, *Argonautica* 3,1ff. and Homer, *Hermes* 108: 45–73.

Lesky, Albin (1966) *A History of Greek Literature*, trans. James Willis and Cornelis de Heer, London: Methuen.

Lesueur, Roger (1990) *Stace: Thébaïde: livres I–IV*, Paris: Société d' édition 'Les belles lettres'.

Levi, Peter (1985) *A History of Greek Literature*, Harmondsworth: Viking.

Lloyd-Jones, Hugh (1971) *The Justice of Zeus*, Berkeley: University of California Press.

Lloyd-Jones, Hugh and Parsons, Peter (eds) (1983) *Supplementum Hellenisticum*, Berlin: Walter de Gruyter.

Lord, Albert B. (1960) *The Singer of Tales*, Cambridge, Mass.: Harvard University Press.

Lyne, R. O. A. M. (1978a) *'Ciris': A Poem Attributed to Vergil*, Cambridge: Cambridge University Press.

—— (1978b) 'The Neoteric Poets', *Classical Quarterly* ns 28: 167–87.

—— (1987) *Further Voices in Vergil's 'Aeneid'*, Oxford: Clarendon Press.

McGuire, Donald T., Jr (1985) 'History as Epic: Silius Italicus and the Second Punic War', Ph.D. thesis, Cornell University.

—— (1989) 'Textual Strategies and Political Suicide in Flavian Epic', *Ramus* 18: 21–45.

Mackie, C. J. (1991a) 'Nox erat . . . : Sleep and Visions in the *Aeneid*', *Greece and Rome* 38: 59–61.

—— (1991b) 'Turnus and his Ancestors', *Classical Quarterly* ns 41: 261–5.

MacL. Currie, H. (1985) *Silver Latin Epic*, Bristol: Bristol Classical Press.

Mair, A. W. (ed. and trans.) (1958) *Oppian, Colluthus, Tryphiodorus*, London: William Heinemann.

Marcovich, Miroslav (ed. and trans.) (1988) *Alcestis Barcinonensis: Text and Commentary*, *Mnemosyne* Supplement 103, Leiden: E. J. Brill.

Mariotti, Scevola (1986) *Livio Andronico e la traduzione artistica*, Urbino: Università degli studi di Urbino.

Marmorale, Enzo V. (ed.) (1953) *Naevius Poeta*, Florence: La Nuova Italia Editrice.

Marti, B. (1966) 'Cassius Scaeva and Lucan's *Inventio*', *The Classical Tradition: Literary and Historical Studies in Honour of Harry Caplan*, ed. Luitpold Wallach, Ithaca: Cornell University Press.

Martin, René (1975) 'Quelques remarques concernant la date du *Satiricon*', *Revue des Etudes Latines* 53: 182–224.

Martindale, Charles (1986) *Charles Milton and the Transformation of Ancient Epic*, London: Croom Helm.

Mayer, R. (ed.) (1981) *Lucan: 'Civil War' VIII*, Warminster: Aris & Phillips.

Merchant, P. (1971) *The Epic*, London: Methuen.

Morel, Willy (1975) *Fragmenta poetarum Latinorum epicorum et lyricorum praeter Ennium et Lucilium*, Stuttgart: Teubner.

Morford, M. P. O. (1967) *The Poet Lucan: Studies in Rhetorical Epic*, Oxford: Basil Blackwell.

Mueller, Martin (1986) *The 'Iliad'*, London: Allen & Unwin.

Murray, Oswyn (1980) *Early Greece*, London: Fontana.

Nagler, M. N. (1974) *Spontaneity and Tradition: A Study in the Oral Art of Homer*, Berkeley: University of California Press.

Nagy, Gregory (1979) *The Best of the Achaeans: Concepts of the Hero in Archaic Greek Poetry*, Baltimore: Johns Hopkins University Press.

Nelis, Damien P. (1991) 'Iphias: Apollonius Rhodius, *Argonautica* 1.311–16', *Classical Quarterly* ns 41: 96–105.

Newman, J. K. (1967) *Augustus and the New Poetry*, Collection Latomus vol. 88, Brussels.

—— (1986) *The Classical Epic Tradition*, Madison, Wisconsin: University of Wisconsin Press.

Notopoulos, J. A. (1949) 'Parataxis in Homer', *Transactions of the American Philological Association* 80: 1–23.

Olson, S. Douglas (1990) 'The Stories of Agamemnon in Homer's *Odyssey*', *Transactions of the American Philological Association* 120: 57–71.

Otis, Brooks (1964) *Virgil: A Study in Civilized Poetry*, Oxford: Clarendon Press.

—— (1975) *Ovid as an Epic Poet*, 2nd edn, Cambridge: Cambridge University Press.

Owen, E. T. (1966) *The Story of the 'Iliad'*, Ann Arbor: University of Michigan Press.

Page, D. L. (1955) *The Homeric 'Odyssey'*, Oxford: Clarendon Press.

—— (1959) *History and the Homeric 'Iliad'*, Berkeley: University of California Press.

Parry, Adam (1963) 'The Two Voices of Virgil's *Aeneid*', *Arion* 2.4: 66–80.

Parry, Milman (1971) *The Making of Homeric Verse: The Collected Papers of Milman Parry*, ed. Adam Parry, Oxford: Clarendon Press.

Parsons, P. J. (1977) 'Callimachus: Victoria Berenices', *Zeitschrift für Papyrus und Epigraphie* 25: 1–50.

Perry, Ben Edwin (1967) *The Ancient Romances: A Literary-Historical Account of their Origins*, Berkeley: University of California Press.

Platnauer, Maurice (ed. and trans.) (1963) *Claudian*, 2 vols, London: William Heinemann.

Pöhlmann, Egert (1973) 'Charakteristika des römischen Lehrgedichts', *Aufstieg und Niedergang der römischen Welt* 1.3: 813–901.

Pöschl, V. (1962) *The Art of Vergil: Image and Symbol in the 'Aeneid'*, trans. G. Seligson, Ann Arbor: University of Michigan Press.

Powell, J. U. (1970) *Collectanea Alexandrina*, Oxford: Clarendon Press.

Putnam, M. C. J. (1961) 'The Art of Catullus 64', *Harvard Studies in Classical Philology* 65: 165–205.

—— (1965) *The Poetry of the 'Aeneid': Four Studies in Imaginative Unity and Design*, Cambridge, Mass.: Harvard University Press.

Quinn, Kenneth (1968) *Virgil's 'Aeneid': A Critical Description*, London: Routledge & Kegan Paul.

—— (1969) *The Catullan Revolution*, rev. edn, Cambridge: W. Heffer & Sons.

—— (1972) 'Did Virgil Fail?', *Cicero and Virgil: Studies in Honour of Harold Hunt*, ed. John R. C. Martyn, Amsterdam: Hakkert.

—— (1977) *Catullus: The Poems*, 2nd edn, London: St Martin's Press.

—— (1979) *Texts and Contexts: The Roman Writers and their Audience*, London: Routledge & Kegan Paul.

Raby, F. J. E. (1953) *A History of Christian-Latin Poetry from the Beginnings to the Close of the Middle Ages*, 2nd edn, Oxford: Clarendon Press.

Race, William H. (1988) *Classical Genres and English Poetry*, London: Croom Helm.

Reardon, B. P. (1969) 'The Greek Novel', *Phoenix* 23: 291–309.

—— (1991) *The Form of Greek Romance*, Princeton: Princeton University Press.

Redfield, James M. (1975) *Nature and Culture in the 'Iliad': The Tragedy of Hector*, Chicago: Chicago University Press.

Reinhardt, Karl (1960) 'Die Abenteuer der Odyssee', *Tradition und Geist*, ed. Carl Becker, Göttingen: Vandenhoeck & Ruprecht.

Richardson, L. (1944) *Poetical Theory in Republican Rome*, New Haven: Yale University Press.

Roberts, Michael (1985) *Biblical Epic and Rhetorical Paraphrase in Late Antiquity*, Liverpool: Francis Cairns.

—— (1989) *The Jeweled Style: Poetry and Poetics in Late Antiquity*, Ithaca: Cornell University Press.

Ross, D. O., Jr (1975) 'The *Culex* and *Moretum* as Post-Augustan Literary Parodies', *Harvard Studies in Classical Philology* 79: 235–63.

Rowell, Henry T. (1947) 'The Original Form of Naevius' *Bellum Poenicum*', *American Journal of Philology* 68: 21–46.

Rudd, Niall (1990) 'Dido's *Culpa*', *Oxford Readings in Vergil's 'Aeneid'*, ed. S. J. Harrison, Oxford: Oxford University Press.

Rutherford, R. B. (1982) 'Tragic Form and Feeling in the *Iliad*,' *Journal of Hellenic Studies* 102: 145–60.

—— (1985) 'At Home and Abroad: Aspects of the Structure of the *Odyssey*', *Publications of the Cambridge Philological Society* 31: 133–50.

—— (1986) 'The Philosophy of the *Odyssey*', *Journal of Hellenic Studies* 106: 145–62.

Saylor, Charles (1990) '*Lux Extrema*: Lucan, *Pharsalia* 4.402–581', *Transactions of the American Philological Association* 120: 291–300.

Schein, Seth L. (1984) *The Mortal Hero: An Introduction to Homer's 'Iliad'*, Berkeley: University of California Press.

Schmidt, K. (1953) *Vorstudien zu einer Geschichte des komischen Epos*, Halle: Niemeyer.

Segal, C. P. (1962) 'The Phaeacians and the Symbolism of Odysseus' Return', *Arion* 1.4: 17–64.

—— (1969) 'Myth and Philosophy in the *Metamorphoses*: Ovid's Augustanism and the Augustan conclusion of Book XV', *American Journal of Philology* 90: 257–92.

—— (1971) *The Theme of the Mutilation of the Corpse in the 'Iliad'*, Mnemosyne Supplement 17, Leiden: E. J. Brill.

—— (1989) *Orpheus: The Myth of the Poet*, Baltimore: Johns Hopkins University Press.

Shapiro, H. A. (1980) 'Jason's Cloak', *Transactions of the American Philological Association* 110: 263–86.

Silk, M. S. (1987) *The 'Iliad'*, Cambridge: Cambridge University Press.

Skutsch, O. (ed.) (1985) *The 'Annals' of Q. Ennius*, Oxford: Clarendon Press.

Solodow, Joseph B. (1988) *The World of Ovid's 'Metamorphoses'*, Chapel Hill: University of North Carolina Press.

Springer, Carl P. E. (1988) *The Gospel as Epic in Late Antiquity: The 'Paschale Carmen' of Sedulius*, Vigiliae Christianae Supplement 2, Leiden: E. J. Brill.

Strzelecki, L. (1964) *Cn. Naevii belli punici carmen*, Leipzig: Teubner.

Sullivan, J. P. (1968) *The Satyricon of Petronius: A Literary Study*, London: Faber & Faber.

—— (1982) 'Petronius' *Bellum Civile* and Lucan's *Pharsalia*: A Political Reconsideration', *Neronia 1977*, eds. J. M. Croisille and P. M. Fauchère, Clermont-Ferrand, 151–5.

—— (1985) *Literature and Politics in the Age of Nero*, Ithaca: Cornell University Press.

Suzuki, Mihoko (1989) *Metamorphoses of Helen: Authority, Difference, and the Epic*, Ithaca: Cornell University Press.

Syme, R. (1939) *The Roman Revolution*, Oxford: Clarendon Press.

Taplin, O. (1980) 'The Shield of Achilles within the *Iliad*', *Greece and Rome* 27: 1–21.

Thalmann, William G. (1984) *Conventions of Form and Thought in Early Greek Epic Poetry*, Baltimore: Johns Hopkins University Press.

Thomas, C. G. (ed.) (1970) *Homer's History: Mycenaean or Dark Age?*, New York: Holt, Rinehart, & Winston.

Thomson, H. J. (ed. and trans.) (1969) *Prudentius*, 2 vols, London: William Heinemann.

Thornley, George, Edmonds, J. M., and Gaselee, S. (eds and trans.) (1960) *'Daphnis and Chloe' by Longus. The Love Romances of Parthenius and Other Fragments*, London: William Heinemann.

Thraede, Klaus (1962) 'Epos', *Reallexicon für Antike und Christentum*, 5: 983–1042.

Tillyard, E. M. W. (1954) *The English Epic and its Background*, London: Chatto & Windus.

Toohey, Peter (1984) 'Politics, Prejudice, and Trojan Genealogies: Varro, Hyginus, and Horace', *Arethusa* 17: 5–28.

—— (1990a) 'Some Ancient Histories of Literary Melancholia', *Illinois Classical Studies* 15: 143–61.

—— (1990b) 'What Was an Epic Hero?', *Past, Present and Future: Ancient World Studies in Australia*, commemorative volume of *Antichthon*, ed. Robert Sinclair, 33–9.

Trypanis, C. A., Gelzer, T., and Whitman, C. (eds and trans.) (1975) *Callimachus. Musaeus: Hero and Leander*, London: William Heinemann.

Van Nortwick, Thomas (1991) *Somewhere I Have Never Travelled: The Second Self and the Hero's Journey in Ancient Epic*, New York: Oxford University Press.

Vessey, D. W. T. C. (1970) 'Thoughts on the Epyllion', *Classical Journal* 66: 38–43.

—— (1971) 'The Reputation of Antimachus of Colophon', *Hermes* 99: 1–10.

—— (1973) *Statius and the 'Thebaid'*, Cambridge: Cambridge University Press.

—— (1986) '*Pierius menti calor incidit*: Statius' Epic Style', *Aufstieg und Niedergang der römischen Welt* 32.5: 2965–3019.

Vian, Francis (ed. and trans.) (1963) *Quintus de Smyrne: La Suite d'Homère: Tome 1: livres I–IV*, Paris: Société d'édition 'Les belles lettres'.

—— (ed. and trans.) (1976) *Nonnos de Ponoplis: Les Dionysiaques: Tome I: chants I–II*, Paris: Société d'édition 'Les belles lettres'.

—— (ed. and trans.) (1987) *Les Argonautiques Orphiques*, Paris: Société d'édition 'Les belles lettres'.

Walsh, P. G. (1970) *The Roman Novel: The 'Satyricon' of Petronius and the 'Metamorphoses' of Apuleius*, Cambridge: Cambridge University Press.

Warmington, E. H. (ed. and trans.) (1935) *Remains of Old Latin I: Ennius and Caecilius*, London: William Heinemann.

—— (ed. and trans.) (1936) *The Remains of Old Latin II: Livius Andronicus, Naevius, Pacuvius, and Accius*, London: William Heinemann.

Waszink, Jan Hendrik (1972) 'Zum Anfangsstadium der römischen Literatur', *Aufstieg und Niedergang der römischen Welt* 1.2: 869–927.

Waters, K. (1964) 'The Character of Domitian', *Phoenix* 18: 49–77.

Wender, Dorothea (1978) *The Last Scenes of the 'Odyssey'*, Mnemosyne Supplement 52, Leiden: E. J. Brill.

West, M. L. (1988) 'The Rise of the Greek Epic', *Journal of Hellenic Studies* 108: 151–72.

Whitman, Cedric H. (1965) *Homer and the Heroic Tradition*, New York: W. W. Norton & Company Inc.

Wight Duff, J. and Duff, Arnold M. (eds and trans.) (1961) *Minor Latin Poets*, London: William Heinemann.

Wilkinson, L. P. (1955) *Ovid Recalled*, Cambridge: Cambridge University Press.

—— (1969) *The 'Georgics' of Virgil: A Critical Survey*, Cambridge: Cambridge University Press.

Willcock, Malcolm M. (1970) *A Commentary on Homer's 'Iliad': Books I–VI*, London: Macmillan.

—— (1976) *A Companion to the 'Iliad'*, Chicago: University of Chicago Press.

Williams, Gordon (1968) *Tradition and Originality in Roman Poetry*, Oxford: Clarendon Press.

—— (1978) *Change and Decline: Roman Literature in the Early Empire*, Berkeley: University of California Press.

—— (1983a) *Technique and Ideas in the 'Aeneid'*, New Haven: Yale University Press.

—— (1983b) 'The Genesis of Poetry in Rome', *The Cambridge History of Classical Literature*, vol. 2, part 1, *The Early Republic*, eds E. J. Kenney and W. V. Clausen, Cambridge: Cambridge University Press.

Williams, R. D. (ed.) (1972) *P. Papini Stati Thebaidos Liber Decimus*, Mnemosyne Supplement 22, Leiden: E. J. Brill.

—— (ed.) (1980a) *The 'Aeneid' of Virgil: Books 1–6*, New York: St Martin's Press.

—— (ed.) (1980b) *The 'Aeneid' of Virgil: Books 7–12*, London: Macmillan.

—— (1990) 'The Purpose of the *Aeneid*', *Oxford Readings in Vergil's 'Aeneid'*, ed. S. J. Harrison, Oxford: Oxford University Press.

Wiseman, T. P. (1974a) *Cinna the Poet and Other Roman Essays*, Leicester: Leicester University Press.

—— (1974b) 'Legendary Genealogies in late-Republican Rome', *Greece and Rome* 21: 153–64.

Wolf, F. A. (1985) *Prolegomena to Homer, 1795*, trans. with introduction and notes by A. Grafton, G. W. Most, and J. Zetzel, Princeton: Princeton University Press.

Zanker, G. (1977) 'Callimachus' Hecale: A New Kind of Epic Hero?', *Antichthon* 11: 68–77.

—— (1979) 'The Love Theme in Apollonius Rhodius' *Argonautica*', *Weiner Studien* nf 13: 52–75.

—— (1987) *Realism in Alexandrian Poetry: A Literature and its Audience*, London: Croom Helm.

Ziegler, Konrat (1934) *Das hellenistische Epos: Ein vergessenes Kapitel griechisher Dichtung*, Leipzig and Berlin: Teubner.

INDEX

(The Table of Contents will also provide help in locating authors, their epics, the parts of their epics, and some of their themes. Chapter subheadings will also offer some orientation.)